$ 3.00
8.00

CLARENDON GERMAN SERIES

General Editor: P. F. GANZ

GOTTFRIED BENN

SELECTED POEMS

AF875933

CLARENDON GERMAN SERIES

Under the general editorship of P. F. GANZ
Fellow of Hertford College
Reader in German in the University of Oxford

FRANZ KAFKA: SHORT STORIES
CARL ZUCKMAYER: THREE STORIES
WILHELM RAABE: UNRUHIGE GÄSTE
BERTOLT BRECHT: SELECTED POEMS
F. DÜRRENMATT: DIE PANNE AND DER TUNNEL
G. E. LESSING: LAOKOON
CH. M. WIELAND: DER PROZESS UM DES ESELS SCHATTEN
ANNETTE VON DROSTE-HÜLSHOFF: POEMS
GOETHE: THREE TALES
GERHART HAUPTMANN: VOR SONNENAUFGANG
GOTTFRIED KELLER: TWO STORIES
RAINER MARIA RILKE: SELECTED POEMS
HEINRICH HEINE: ATTA TROLL, EIN SOMMERNACHTSTRAUM
DEUTSCHLAND, EIN WINTERMÄRCHEN
SEVENTEEN MODERN GERMAN SHORT STORIES
JEAN PAUL: SCHMELZLES REISE NACH FLÄTZ
HERMANN BROCH: SHORT STORIES
FRIEDRICH HÖLDERLIN: DER TOD DES EMPEDOKLES
HUGO VON HOFMANNSTHAL: FOUR STORIES
CARL STERNHEIM: BÜRGER SCHIPPEL

Other volumes in preparation

GOTTFRIED BENN

SELECTED POEMS

EDITED BY

FRIEDRICH WILHELM WODTKE

Professor of German Language and Literature
University of Kiel, Germany

OXFORD UNIVERSITY PRESS

1970

Oxford University Press, Ely House, London W.1

GLASGOW NEW YORK TORONTO MELBOURNE WELLINGTON
CAPE TOWN SALISBURY IBADAN NAIROBI DAR ES SALAAM LUSAKA ADDIS ABABA
BOMBAY CALCUTTA MADRAS KARACHI LAHORE DACCA
KUALA LUMPUR SINGAPORE HONG KONG TOKYO

© *Selection, introduction, and notes*
OXFORD UNIVERSITY PRESS 1970

Permission to reproduce the text of the poems is gratefully acknowledged to the following publishers: Limes Verlag Max Niedermayer, Wiesbaden, *Gesammelte Werke* III, 2nd edition 1963—Nos. 1–31, 33, 34, 37, 41, 49, 51–7; Peter Schifferli, Verlags A.-G. 'Die Arche', Zürich, *Statische Gedichte*, 1948 — Nos. 32, 35, 36, 38–40, 42–8, 50

Introduction and notes translated by Ann Harding

PRINTED IN GREAT BRITAIN
AT THE UNIVERSITY PRESS, OXFORD
BY VIVIAN RIDLER
PRINTER TO THE UNIVERSITY

CONTENTS

TO MY WIFE

ILSE WODTKE

INTRODUCTION

Benn's Life

GOTTFRIED BENN was born on 2 May 1886 in the village of Mansfeld in West Priegnitz, 'in einem Dorf von dreihundert Einwohnern etwa in der Mitte zwischen Berlin und Hamburg',[1] the eldest son of a Protestant priest, Gustav Benn. He grew up in the village of Sellin in Neumark, where his parents had moved in the year of his birth, 'ein Dorf mit 700 Einwohnern in der norddeutschen Ebene, großes Pfarrhaus, großer Garten, drei Stunden östlich der Oder'.[2] His father was an orthodox Protestant, whose father and grandfather had been village priests in Mansfeld before him, a hard and severe man who was nevertheless advanced in his ideas and inclined towards Christian Socialism. Benn commented later:

> Da meine Väter über hundert Jahre zurück evangelische Geistliche waren, durchdrang das Religiöse meine Jugend ganz ausschließlich. Mein Vater, jetzt emeritiert, war ein ungewöhnlicher Mann: orthodox vielleicht nicht im Sinne der Kirche, aber als Persönlichkeit; heroisch in der Lehre, heroisch wie ein Prophet des Alten Testaments, von großer individueller Macht wie Pfarrer Sang aus dem Drama von Björnson, das man in meiner Jugend spielte: Über die Kraft.[3]

[1] *Epilog* (1922), *GW* IV, p. 7.
[2] *Lebensweg eines Intellektualisten* (1934), *GW* IV, p. 26.
[3] *Fanatismus zur Transzendenz* (1930), *GW* IV, p. 235.

In 1884 he had married the French-Swiss governess, Caroline Jaquier, who bore him eight children:

> Meine Mutter war französische Schweizerin, sprach nie richtig Deutsch, eine rein romanische Familie aus Fleurier, bei Yverdon, Kanton Neuchâtel, ich bin also nur 50% germanisch, daher meine Mischlingsmelancholie.[1]

> In der Ehe meine Eltern vereinigten sich also das Germanische und das Romanische, diese beiden maßgeblich gewordenen Komponenten der europäischen Bevölkerung; man kann auch sagen, das Deutsche und das Französische.[2]

Benn always attributed the intellectual tensions and conflicts in himself to this antithesis in the character of his parents; he attached great importance to the intellectual milieu of the Protestant parsonage, in which he grew up and whence such a large number of German intellectuals have originated since the Reformation.[3] Yet there prevailed in his parents' house only a 'ganz amusisches Gedankenleben', as Benn ironically put it in his late poem *Teils-teils*.[4] He himself was an imaginative child and entertained his brothers and sisters with poems and stories. We know very little about Benn's childhood, his school days, or what he read when he was young.[5] He went to the village school and received instruction, first from his father and later, together with the sons of the Count von Finkenstein, from a tutor, Herr Wehner, whom he still remembers in one of his late poems.

Benn was then sent as a boarder to the Friedrich Gymnasium in Frankfurt an der Oder where he made friends with the future poet Klabund (Alfred Henschke, 1890–1928),

[1] Letter (10 June 1946) to Johannes Weyl, *ABr.*, p. 101.
[2] *GW* IV, p. 24.
[3] *Der deutsche Mensch* (1933), *GW* I, p. 231.
[4] *GW* III, p. 339.
[5] The first years of his life were completely conditioned by his rural existence among the village children.

who was in the same house. Benn later stressed how fortunate he had been in receiving a classical education. For many years he had a careful grounding in Latin and Greek, which formed the basis of his deep attachment to classical culture; this he deepened throughout his life by his own reading, and it profoundly influenced the whole of his work. The only modern language he learnt there was French, with which he was already familiar because of his mother. English, on the other hand, remained foreign to him all his life; though he used such English words as 'nevermore' or 'Fifth Avenue' in his poems, he was not sure how to pronounce them. All his life he thus felt closer to French poetry, though in his later years he studied many modern English and American poets (T. S. Eliot, W. H. Auden, Stephen Spender, Ezra Pound, and others). Having successfully passed his leaving certificate, he left school at the age of seventeen.

As a country parson, his father had to support his many children on a very small income. Gottfried wanted to study medicine, but was forced, against his own wishes, to study theology and German philology for two years, first in Marburg, and finally for one term in Berlin. These two years had a profound effect on Benn's intellectual outlook and work, above all on his polemic against orthodox Christianity and the philosophy of Kant, whose epistemological approach was then being taught in Marburg by the neo-Kantians Herman Cohen and Paul Natorp. Benn remained silent about these experiences for a long time, and it was not until he lectured at the University of Marburg after the Second World War that he mentioned how, in the winter term 1903–4, he had attended a course of lectures on 'Poetics and Literary Methodology' by the well-known Heine expert Ernst Elster, which he had found very stimulating.

However, his desire to study medicine was stronger than his father's will, and in 1905 he was admitted to the Kaiser Wilhelm Academy of Army Medicine, the so-called 'Pépinière'. Here his studies were largely free of charge, but in return he was obliged to serve one year as a regular army doctor for every term of study. For the first time in his life the young Benn felt in his element, and he later recalled with gratitude these years as a student, when in addition to lectures and courses on medicine and science he was able to attend lectures on philosophy and art:

> Rückblickend scheint mir meine Existenz ohne diese Wendung zur Biologie völlig undenkbar . . . Und eines lehrte sie die Jugend, da sie noch ganz unbestritten herrschte: Kälte des Denkens, Nüchternheit, letzte Schärfe des Begriffs, Bereithalten von Belegen für jedes Urteil, unerbittliche Kritik, Selbstkritik, mit einem Wort die schöpferische Seite des Objektiven.[1]

While he was still a student he had to fulfil his first period of military service with the Second Regiment of Foot Guards, and after this he took his preliminary medical examination at Easter 1908. He then became a house physician at the Berlin Charité Hospital. During this period he experimented with his first poems and essays on the history and problems of psychiatry, a field which he soon abandoned, however, because of his hypersensitivity. His study of 'The Aetiology of Epilepsy in Puberty' won him a prize from Berlin University in 1911, and in 1912 his studies concluded with his final medical examinations and a thesis on *The Incidence of Diabetes Mellitus in the Army*, for which he received his doctorate.

Benn was then an army doctor for only a short while: he was found to have a congenital defect (floating kidneys),

[1] *GW* IV, p. 28.

which made him unfit for active service or for garrison duty. It was not until the outbreak of the First World War that he returned to active service as a military doctor. In the meantime he worked as a medical assistant in various hospitals in Berlin-Charlottenburg, and in the spring of 1914 he travelled to North America as a ship's doctor. Because of the violent seasickness from which he suffered, he turned down a job he was offered as a ship's doctor on a sailing ship travelling to Vladivostok—providentially, since the ship sank. Instead he became a locum for a short time in a T.B. sanatorium in the Fichtelgebirge, and it was these experiences and impressions which inspired him to write his first short story *Gehirne* in 1915.

Whilst he was still a student the young Benn had already produced a number of poems in the style of the early Rilke, and a prose dialogue, *Gespräch*, in which he praised the work of the Danish Impressionist Jens Peter Jacobsen (1847–85) and saw his artistic goal as a synthesis of scientifically exact description with modern expression. His cycle of poems *Morgue und andere Gedichte* marked a radical breakthrough to the new expressionist art which came into vogue from about 1910. This cycle was published by Alfred Richard Meyer in the series *Flugblätter* in March 1912, giving rise to both sensation and scandal, for in these poems Benn turned, in a gross and cynical language hitherto unknown in Germany, his gruesome impressions from anatomy, pathology, the women's hospital, and Berlin café society into provocative images and aggressive criticism of contemporary life. The young poet, who until then had been completely unknown, burst upon the scene with these poems and came to know members of the expressionist movement, then represented above all in such periodicals as Franz Pfemfert's *Die Aktion, Zeitschrift für freiheitliche Politik und Literatur*, *Der Sturm*, published by

Herwarth Walden, and René Schickele's *Die Weißen Blätter*, in which Benn's subsequent poems and prose writings appeared. During the last two years before the war, Benn read his own poems aloud at many literary evenings organized by *Aktion*, and in Berlin he met the then leading Expressionist writers—Carl Einstein, Alfred Lichtenstein, Alfred Wolkenstein, Paul Zech, and others.

Both his life and his early lyrical writings were greatly influenced by his love for the somewhat older poetess Else Lasker-Schüler (1876–1945), who had just separated from Herwarth Walden. Like Ina Seidel, she at once felt Benn's deep sensibility behind the cynicism of the *Morgue* poems and she offered him her enthusiasm and her love. To her Benn dedicated his second collection of poems *Söhne. Neue Gedichte* (1913), which, in its fantastic play of Jewish and oriental images, already revealed the influence of Lasker-Schüler's poetry. Throughout his life Benn praised her as a 'großes lyrisches Genie',[1] indeed 'die größte Lyrikerin, die Deutschland je hatte'.[2] She supported him with a prose piece *Doktor Benn*, which appeared in *Aktion* on 25 June 1913, and which sharply characterized the young poet and his Morgue poems:

. . . lang bevor ich ihn kannte, war ich seine Leserin, sein Gedichtbuch — Morgue — lag auf meiner Decke: grauenvolle Kunstwunder, Todesträumerei die Kontur annahm. Leiden reißen ihre Rachen auf und verstummen, Kirchhöfe wandeln in die Krankensäle und pflanzen sich vor die Betten der Schmerzensreichen an. Die kindtragenden Frauen hört man schreien aus den Kreißsälen bis ans Ende der Welt. Gottfried Benn ist der dichtende Kokoschka. Jeder seiner

[1] Dedication of the text *Das Unaufhörliche, Oratorium* (18 Nov. 1931).

[2] In his *In Memoriam — Rede auf Else Lasker-Schüler* (23 Feb. 1952) in which he reintroduced her to Germany.

Verse ein Leopardenbiß, ein Wildtiersprung. Der Knochen ist sein Griffel, mit dem er das Wort auferweckt.

This relationship with the poetess, who lived a very eccentric life, broke up when Benn met his first wife, the actress Edith Brosin (*née* Osterloh), on the Baltic island of Hiddensee in the summer of 1914. Her stage name was Eva Brandt and she was eight years older than him. In the course of the general mobilization at the outbreak of the First World War, Benn was called up as a medical officer on 1 August. He married Edith on the same day at Leoni on Lake Starnberg, and adopted her son Andreas. On 8 September 1915 Benn's only child, his daughter Nele, was born to Edith at Hellerau, near Dresden, where she lived during the war.

Benn was sent to Belgium, where he took an active part in the siege of Antwerp (8 October), for which he later received the Iron Cross 2nd Class. He was then appointed senior physician to the military government in Brussels, where he stayed for three years. Looking back, Benn portrayed this period as a particular climax in his life, a period when he was granted sufficient time to pursue his own poetry:

Ich war Arzt an einem Prostituiertenkrankenhaus, ein ganz isolierter Posten, lebte in einem konfiszierten Haus, elf Zimmer, allein mit meinem Burschen, hatte wenig Dienst, durfte in Zivil gehen, war mit nichts behaftet, hing an keinem, verstand die Sprache kaum; strich durch die Straßen, fremdes Volk; eigentümlicher Frühling, drei Monate ganz ohne Vergleich, was war die Kanonade von der Yser, ohne die kein Tag verging, das Leben schwang in einer Sphäre von Schweigen und Verlorenheit, ich lebte am Rande, wo das Dasein fällt und das Ich beginnt. Ich denke oft an diese Wochen zurück; sie waren das Leben, sie werden nicht wiederkommen, alles andere war Bruch.[1]

[1] *Epilog*, *GW* IV, pp. 7–8.

Late in the autumn of 1915 he took part in the court-martial of Miss Edith Cavell, the English nurse who was shot as a spy. Benn was obliged to witness the execution and to sign the death certificate. Later, in 1928, he wrote an account of this for a newspaper. In Brussels there was no lack of intellectual stimulus, since there he met the authors Carl Einstein, Wilhelm Hausenstein, Otto Flake, Rudolf Alexander Schröder, Alfred Flechtheim, and others, who were stationed there with the German army. He often visited a Berlin acquaintance, the dramatist Carl Sternheim, on his estate La Hulpe in Groenendal, near Brussels, and got to know Carl's wife, Thea, who remained his close friend for many years. His meetings with Sternheim inspired him to experiment with the dramatic form: he wrote a satirical one-act play *Etappe*, in which he bitterly criticized the corruption of the German military authorities, and also the short dramas *Der Vermessungsdirigent* and *Karandasch*, in which he anticipated the tendencies of the drama of the absurd. The twenty poems which comprise his lyrical production during these years in Brussels came out with the publishers of *Aktion* in 1917 under the collective title *Fleisch*. His most poetically significant work was his *Rönne-Novellen*, so called after the main character, the doctor Werff Rönne. These *Novellen* were published in 1916 by the Kurt Wolff-Verlag in Franz Werfel's *Der Jüngste Tag* series under the title *Gehirne-Novellen*.

In 1917 Benn was able to return to Berlin and, after a short period as medical assistant at the Charité hospital, he opened his practice as a specialist in skin and venereal diseases at 12, Belle-Alliance Straße in the south-west of Berlin (he continued to practise there until 1935). His wife moved with her children Andreas and Nele to a flat in 20, Passaner Straße in the west of Berlin. Benn gave up this flat after his wife's sudden death in Jena in 1922 after a gall-bladder operation. He sent his adopted son Andreas to a boarding-school, and entrusted the education of his daughter Nele to his Danish friend Ellen Overgaard, the 'Dänin' whom he met on the train from Jena to Berlin, towards the end of 1922. She was a singer and was often on tour, but she met Benn both in Berlin and also frequently in Copenhagen, where her husband was the manager of a shipyard. Although this relationship ended after about five years, Nele remained in Copenhagen, married a Dane, Preben Topsøe, and took Danish nationality. Benn's twin grandchildren, Tine and Vilhelm, were born to the couple in 1944.

During the twenties, Benn led a lonely widower's existence, making many short-lived friendships and suffering from deep depressions, to which he gave expression in the epilogue to the edition of his *Gesammelte Schriften*:

> Wie soll man da leben? Man soll ja auch nicht . . . siebenunddreißig Jahre und total erledigt, ich schreibe nichts mehr — man müßte mit Spulwürmern schreiben und Koprolalien; ich lese nichts mehr — wen denn? die alten ehrlichen Titaniden mit dem Ikaridenflügel in Stullenpapier? ich denke keinen Gedanken mehr zu Ende . . .[1]

The suicide of his friend Lili Breda, an actress who had urged him to marry her, moved him very deeply. Lili, who had been his close friend since 1928, and who was described by Tilly Wedekind as 'eine bildschöne Frau. Groß und blond, eine Sächsin',[2] killed herself in 1929 by jumping from the window of her fifth-floor flat. When Benn, whom she had told of her intentions shortly before,

[1] *GW* IV, p. 11.

[2] Tilly Wedekind, 'Meine Erinnerungen an Gottfried Benn' in *Den Traum alleine tragen. Neue Texte, Briefe, Dokumente* (Wiesbaden, 1966), pp. 80–114.

arrived, she was already dead.[1] Only his friendship with Tilly, the widow of the dramatist Franz Wedekind (1864–1918), who was the same age as Benn, brought any light into the gloom of these years. Around 1930 she was under contract to make guest appearances in Berlin theatres in plays by Wedekind and Sternheim. She spent three summers in Berlin with Gottfried Benn and remained in close contact with him until his second marriage in 1937; they then broke up, and it was not until after the Second World War that they started to write to each other and to enjoy a new friendship—on an intellectual plane.

Despite all his emotional sufferings and physical deprivations during the years of inflation, Benn's creative activity continued, and further poetry and prose appeared after the 1922 publication of his *Gesammelte Schriften* by his Jewish friend Erich Reiss. He also made many new friends, such as the art dealer Franz N. Zatzenstein, with whom he drove to Paris in 1924, and whom he accompanied on a further three journeys to France and Spain during the years that followed. These journeys resulted in an account of his impressions in the form of short essays, in which he strongly advocated Franco-German understanding. In the autumn of 1931 he took a holiday with Erich Reiss at Schwarzburg in Thuringia, where he visited the places where Goethe had lived. Here he conceived his important essay *Goethe und die Naturwissenschaften*, which appeared in the Goethejahr 1932 in the *Neue Rundschau*, together with essays on Goethe by Thomas Mann, Ortega y Gasset, and others. He became a member of the Berlin PEN club and was the subject of a number of literary scandals connected with his work and with himself. In 1928 the poet Max

[1] In 1928 his friend for many years, the poet Klabund, also died, and Benn gave the funeral oration. His stepson Andreas died from T.B. in 1930 at the age of 18.

Herrmann-Neisse wrote a favourable review of Benn's *Gesammelte Prosa* in the July number of the socialist periodical *Die neue Bücherschau*, whereupon the communist members of the editorial committee, the poet Johannes R. Becher and the journalist Egon Erwin Kirsch (known as the 'rasende Reporter'), resigned in indignation. Benn's essay in reply, *Über die Rolle des Schriftstellers in dieser Zeit*, which clearly outlined his anti-socialist standpoint as an aristocratic artist and defender of 'absolute Dichtung', was a conscious provocation of the writers of the left. On 23 March 1931 Benn made a sensational speech at a banquet of the Schutzverband Deutscher Schriftsteller in honour of Heinrich Mann's sixtieth birthday. In it he lauded the exemplary qualities of the poet and artist, but he made no mention of Heinrich Mann's political engagement in the aims of democracy and socialism. The waves rose higher and the architect Werner Hegemann compared him with Hitler and denounced him as an outlaw in a crass article in the left democratic weekly *Das Tagebuch*. Benn was roused to a caustic reply in the *Vossische Zeitung*. Perhaps these unpleasant experiences with socialist and communist writers unconsciously paved the way for Benn's enigmatic and dubious behaviour in 1933–4 after Hitler's seizure of power. In a radio dialogue which Benn held in 1930 with the poet Oscar Loerke (1884–1941) on the question 'Can poets change the world?', he satirized once more the politico-social engagement of the artist from his pessimistic philosophy of history. This also formed the basic theme of his oratorio *Das Unaufhörliche*, set to music by Paul Hindemith and first performed in 1931 by the Berlin Philharmonia under Otto Klemperer. A climax in Benn's life was finally reached with the public recognition of his poetic achievements when he was admitted to the poetry section of the Prussian

Academy of Arts on the suggestion of Oskar Loerke. The president of this section was Heinrich Mann, and the most famous members were Thomas Mann, Alfred Mombert, Alfred Döblin, Max Halbe, Theodor Däubler, Georg Kaiser, Ricarda Huch, Hermann Stehr, Franz Werfel, and others. Also admitted at the same time as Benn were Rudolf G. Binding, Max Mell, Rudolf Pannwitz, Alfons Paquet, and Ina Seidel. At the formal ceremony on 5 April 1932 Benn gave his *Akademie-Rede*, in which he formulated the programme of his poetic work and the principles of his view of art; he spoke of the 'form-fordernde Gewalt des Nichts' and portrayed the contemporary artist as the conqueror of nihilism. He felt his election to be 'eine außerordentliche Ehre, die größte, die einem Schriftsteller innerhalb des deutschen Sprachraums zuteil werden konnte'.[1]

This climax in his life was very quickly followed by a disastrous fall, and what has been called Benn's 'Verrat am Geist'. Immediately after Hitler had been named German Chancellor by the German President von Hindenburg on 30 January 1933, the persecution of liberal and socialist authors and poets began. As early as 15 February 1933 Heinrich Mann was removed by the National Socialists from his position as president of the poetry section of the Prussian Academy of Arts; together with the painter Käthe Kollwitz he had voiced his opposition to the new totalitarian regime in a passionate appeal, and warned against relapse into barbarism. When he and Käthe Kollwitz were forced to leave the Academy, they were followed by the majority of the most famous members of the section who had resigned (Ricarda Huch, Thomas Mann, Alfred Döblin) or who had been suspended (Franz Werfel, Leonhard Frank, Georg Kaiser, Bernhard Keller-

[1] *GW* IV, p. 86.

mann, Alfred Mombert, René Schickele, Fritz von Unruh, etc.), and Benn was appointed provisional leader of the poetry section in conjunction with Oskar Loerke in order to maintain continuity. Yet he did not protest at the disgraceful treatment of Heinrich Mann, whom he had praised so highly the year before, nor did he draw his own conclusions from the persecution of his colleagues. Soon, however, both he and the secretary Oskar Loerke were superseded by new members appointed by the authorities, and he had less and less to do with the Academy. Nevertheless he gave the funeral oration on the death of the president of the Academy, the composer Max von Schillings (27 July 1933), but he was not allowed to give his address on the death of Stefan George (who died on 4 December 1933), which had been commissioned by the new president of the 'German Academy of Poetry', the Nazi poet Hanns Johst, since the funeral ceremony was banned.

Benn knew that writers such as Thomas Mann, Alfred Döblin, Klaus Mann, and many others were leaving Germany and emigrating, since they saw themselves threatened by the new dictators. He himself experienced Jewish persecution in his own house and was struck off the list of certified doctors by the Nazi medical federation, since he was suspected of being a Jew—an accusation in which the ballad-writer Börries von Münchhausen, newly elected to the Academy, played a major role. In spite of all this, from 1933 to 1934 Benn supported the new totalitarian state of the National Socialists in essays and talks, most radically in his broadcast 'Der neue Staat und die Intellektuellen' (24 April 1933), in which, as Oskar Loerke noted with anger and grief, Benn argued 'stramm für die heroische Unterdrückung der Intellektuellen', and demanded the sacrifice of intellectual freedom for the sake of the new state and the future of the German people. In reply to this Klaus Mann sent him a long letter from abroad in May 1933, in which he justifiably reproached his behaviour, at the same time assuring him of his admiration for his work. In his *Antwort an die literarischen Emigranten*, Benn showered Klaus Mann with scorn and ridicule. In a radio talk 'Zucht und Zukunft' in October 1933, which was to be his last, Benn espoused the National Socialist doctrine and its breeding plans. When the German PEN club broke up and was replaced under Hitler by a 'Union Nationaler Schriftsteller', Benn accepted the post of vice-president under the president Hanns Johst (8 January 1934). As such on 29 March 1934 he entertained at a banquet the former futurist Marinetti, then president of the fascist writers' union in Italy, and took the opportunity to express his admiration for the 'Führer', who had called upon writers to work together for his 'neues Reich'. It is clear that after this, all those German writers who had emigrated regarded Benn as a Nazi writer and despised him as a traitor. Understandably, after 1945 Johannes R. Becher and Alfred Döblin tried to prevent new editions of his work from appearing.

Nevertheless, Benn still found himself obliged to defend himself and was soon required to retire completely from public life, since he was increasingly under attack and had been deprived of the basis of his bourgeois existence. He found it necessary to prove his Aryan extraction and investigate his family background, since Börries von Münchhausen had called him a 'reinblütiger Jude' in a letter that was published, and refused him entry into the Union Nationaler Schriftsteller, of which he was the director. In self-defence Benn published in 1934 his *Lebensweg eines Intellektualisten*, the title of which was itself provocative, since the National Socialists despised all intellectuals and used the term as an expression of abuse. The article appeared in a volume called *Kunst und Macht*, in which Benn repeated, in addition to his avowed loyalty to the new totalitarian state, his appeals in defence of modern art, particularly his own style, expressionism. These appeals were quickly attacked by the National Socialists as 'artfremd' and decadent; his claim of the *Eigengesetzlichkeit der Kunst* and his *Bekenntnis zum Expressionismus* were pilloried by a speaker for the party as cultural Bolshevism. But even his most significant attempt to demonstrate the relationship between the totalitarian state and absolute art (as seen in the example of Greek antiquity, Sparta and Athens), his important essay *Dorische Welt. Eine Untersuchung über die Beziehung von Kunst und Macht* led him to the conclusion that the state can indeed further art and make the individual receptive to it, but that there remains between state and art an unbridgeable gulf: 'Sie können beide gemeinsame Erlebnisse mythischen, volkhaften, politischen Inhalts haben, aber die Kunst bleibt für sich die einsame hohe Welt. Sie bleibt eigengesetzlich und drückt nichts als sich selbst aus.'[1]

His eyes were opened to the true character of the National Socialist regime by Hitler's crushing of the alleged plot amongst his highest SA leaders, the so-called 'Röhmputsch': more than a hundred SA leaders, the Generals von Schleicher and von Bredow, and several Catholic politicians were murdered, an action which was then sanctioned by law on 3 July 1934 as 'Staatsnotwehr'. Benn wrote on 27 August 1934 to Ina Seidel: 'Ich lebe mit vollkommen zusammengekniffenen Lippen, innerlich und äußerlich. Ich kann nicht mehr mit. Gewisse Dinge haben mir den letzten Stoß gegeben. Schauerliche Tragödie! Das Ganze kommt mir allmählich vor wie eine

[1] *GW* I, p. 290.

Schmiere, die fortwährend "Faust" ankündigt, aber die Besetzung langt nur für "Husarenfieber". Wie groß fing das an, wie dreckig sieht es heute aus. Aber es ist noch lange nicht zu Ende.'[1]

Benn immediately drew his conclusions and went back to active service as a medical officer in the army, which was still regarded at that time as a refuge from the Nazi terror. It was then that he coined the arrogant-sounding dictum: 'Die Armee ist die aristokratische Form der Emigration', which soon became proverbial. Oskar Loerke, to whom Benn spoke frankly, wrote of him in his diary on 21 November 1934: 'Ei, wie der schimpfte — ein Hymnus gegen Cäsarenwahn und Mord', and established that he had 'völlig zurückgekehrt in eine vernünftige Denkweise' (31 January 1935). With the help of friends from his student years he finally succeeded in being reinstated as surgeon-major at the army recruiting centre in Hanover, where he moved on 31 March 1935. At the same time he resigned from the Deutsche Akademie der Dichtkunst and the 'Union Nationaler Schriftsteller', giving as his reason that his entry into the armed forces made it necessary for him to retire completely from literary life and bodies of this kind.

If he thought that he was now safe from attack he was mistaken. On the occasion of his fiftieth birthday (2 May 1936), which was celebrated by a mere handful of courageous journalists, there appeared defamatory attacks in the SS weekly *Das Schwarze Korps* and in the official organ of the NSDAP, *Der Völkische Beobachter*. These were directed against his *Ausgewählte Gedichte, 1911–1936* which had just appeared and from which, on the instructions of Nazi censorship, Benn had to exclude the most violent of his early poems and to replace them by new 'statisch'

[1] *ABr.*, p. 58.

compositions. Wolfgang Willrich, a writer belonging to the SS, demanded in 1937 in his book *Säuberung des Kunsttempels* that Benn should be excluded from the German Chamber of Literature since he was a 'Kulturbolschewist' and as an action poet had 'Franz Pfemferts Vorbereitungen der bolschewistischen Revolution unterstützt'. Though Benn was supported and protected by his army superiors, his commanding officer in Hanover and the army medical chief in Berlin, advancement to positions of command and all influence on personnel were closed to him when, on 18 March 1938, the German Chamber of Literature forbade him to write anything further under threat of punishment and informed him of his suspension. Thus he was finally condemned to silence as an undesirable artist.

Benn had returned to Berlin by this time, having succeeded in 1937 in getting a transfer from Hanover, which he found too provincial. He then worked as surgeon-major at the headquarters of the Third Army Corps, and on 22 January 1938 married his second wife, Herta von Wedemeyer, whom he had met in Hanover where she had been his private secretary. After the outbreak of the Second World War he was moved to the army G.H.Q. in the Bendlerstraße, promoted to chief medical officer, and then transferred in September 1943 with his entire department, in which he was in charge of military injuries and army suicides, to Landsberg an der Warthe. There he composed up to the end of 1944, as previously in Berlin, a great number of poems and essays which criticized the Nazi movement in biting terms. Though Benn had been forbidden to write or publish anything, in August 1943 he distributed to his closest friends a private edition, *Zweiundzwanzig Gedichte*, which included a sharp account of the war and the Nazi terror in the poem *Monolog*. Then the German eastern front collapsed, and Benn and his wife had to walk by night in a snow-storm to Küstrin (on 28 January 1945) and flee to Berlin by train in an open cattle-truck. Here, in his half-empty flat in the Bozener Straße, he lived through the end of the war with all its terrors. His wife, whom he had sent for safety to the village of Neuhaus on the Elbe, committed suicide on 2 July 1945 when the Red Army moved in.

Once more Benn was alone and experienced a period of extreme suffering and loneliness, completely forgotten even by those interested in literature. However, he did not become apathetic and attempted as early as the summer of 1946 to publish the poems and essays which had been written in secret since 1936 and which had been preserved throughout the chaos of the war by his Bremen friend Dr. F. W. Oelze. The determined opposition of J. R. Becher in Berlin and of Alfred Döblin in south Germany made this impossible. On 18 December 1946 he married in a church ceremony the dentist Dr. Ilse Kaul (born 14 July 1913): 'Und dann fand ich noch in späten Jahren, nach viel Unglück und Tod und Trauer in dieser Richtung eine dritte Frau, eine Generation jünger als ich, die nun mit zarter und kluger Hand die Stunden und die Schritte und in den Vasen die Astern ordnet.'[1]

A Swiss publisher, Peter Schifferli in Zürich, was the first to have the courage to present the 'undesirable' author Gottfried Benn to the German public after 1945, which several German publishers, who were subject to the censorship of the allied occupation, had been afraid to do. When Benn's *Statische Gedichte* appeared from the Arche Verlag in Zürich in 1948, they aroused great attention, and it was then that Benn found in Max Niedermayer, who had founded the progressive Limes Verlag in

[1] *Doppelleben* (1950), *GW* IV, p. 170.

Wiesbaden after the war, a congenial publisher who took over his entire work. In the years that followed, during which Benn experienced a new period of creative work, Niedermayer published not only all his previous work including the early writings, but also the three new collections of poems that he wrote, radio plays, essays, and lectures. Benn suddenly became the most important German poet and essayist since the death of Rilke and found many admirers and imitators in the younger German post-war generation. His lecture 'Probleme der Lyrik', which he gave on 21 August 1951 to the international vacation course at Marburg University, remained for a long time the real *ars poetica* of young German poetry, and was even echoed abroad in T. S. Eliot's essay *The Three Voices of Poetry* (London, 1953). On 21 October 1951 the Deutsche Akademie für Sprache und Dichtung in Darmstadt awarded Benn the Georg Büchner Prize, and on his sixty-seventh birthday he received from the German President Theodor Heuss the Cross of the Order of Merit of the German Federal Republic. In the intervening year he took part in the European poetry assembly, the Biennale Internationale de Poésie in Knokke in Belgium, where on 12 September 1952 he reiterated in French the main points of his Marburg lecture, 'Probleme der Lyrik'. He was also a member of the awarding committee of the European Prize for Culture in Geneva, where in March 1953 his candidate was successful, and he gave the address when the prize was awarded to the German author Werner Warsinsky. He had now gained official international recognition, despite much sharp criticism of his conduct during the Nazi period and argument over the importance of his poetic work.

During the last years of his life he retired from medical practice as a skin specialist which he had taken up after

1945 near his wife's dental practice. Yet he remained creatively active and summarized his final questions and findings in his long essay 'Altern als Problem für Künstler' (1954), which he gave on the South German radio and in the Bavarian Academy for Fine Arts in Munich. On 15 November 1955 he held with Reinhold Schneider, a professed Catholic writer, a public radio discussion on the theme 'Soll die Dichtung das Leben bessern?', a question which he abruptly rejected and answered thus: 'Die Dichtung bessert nicht, aber sie tut etwas viel Entscheidenderes: sie verändert.'[1] Shortly afterwards Benn became very ill; with a very great physical effort he was able to receive the many honours which his seventieth birthday brought him in Berlin, but he died after a lengthy and unsuccessful convalescence in Bad Schlangenbad on 7 July 1956 in the Oskar Helene-Heim in Dahlem in the presence of his wife. He was buried on 12 July in the Neue Waldfriedhof in Berlin-Dahlem.

Benn's Work

When Benn's early *Morgue* poems burst upon the Berlin literary scene in 1912, a revolution had already begun in all spheres of German art. This new 'expressionism' marks the real beginning of modern art in Germany, and created the climate in which Benn's early poems, dramatic sketches, and prose works were able to be written and understood. The Expressionists had become bored with the aesthetic refinement and hypersensibility which had accompanied Viennese and south German impressionism and symbolism since 1890. They were beginning to replace this impressionism, which aimed at finely differentiated and subdued language and images, the too

[1] *GW* I, p. 593.

highly stylized symbolism of Stefan George, and the neo-classicism of Paul Ernst by a new, energetic expressionism, which embraced all spheres of life and was often crudely naturalistic. It consciously picked up where the social naturalism of 1885 had left off, but clothed it in a new artistic form which took its inspiration from both the French poets Charles Baudelaire and Arthur Rimbaud and the flowing free rhythms of the American Walt Whitman. The real breakthrough to new poetic themes and forms of expression is seen in two volumes of poems which appeared in 1911: Franz Werfel's *Der Weltfreund*, which introduced the ecstatically optimistic *O Mensch* poems of expressionism, and Georg Heym's *Der ewige Tag*, followed in 1912 by his posthumous collection of poems *Umbra vitae*, both of which contained gloomy visions of destruction and macabre images of death. A decisively new trend was also set by Else Lasker-Schüler's collection *Meine Wunder* (1911) and *Hebräische Balladen* (1913), characterized by her passionate oriental-Jewish imagination and religious longing.

It was not until his student years in Marburg and Berlin that the young Benn was able to study modern German poetry in greater depth, for at that time this was not taught as part of a classical education. The most notable writers he read included the highly sensual Impressionist Detlev von Liliencron (1844–1909), with his fleeting visual images which were the beginning of a telegrammatic lyrical style, his rigidly constructed stanzas and Sicilianas, filled with melancholy and the fear of death; the young Hugo von Hofmannsthal (1874–1929), whose collected symbolist poems and lyrical dramas appeared in 1903; and finally the sentimental, affected poems of the early Rilke (1875–1926), whose *Neue Gedichte* (1906–8) with their rigid forms Benn did not discover until later.

Of the poems which he sent to a Berlin magazine whilst

he was in Marburg, only to have them returned with the comment 'freundlich in der Gesinnung, schwach im Ausdruck',[1] none has been preserved. Two of his poems from the period 1910–11 (*Rauhreif*, *Herbst*) reproduce the melancholic descriptions of nature in the style of the early Rilke and are totally indistinguishable from other verse of that period. The same is true of another poem published in 1910, *Gefilde der Unseligen*, in the title of which there is for the first time a hint of parody, but which in every other respect betrays the influence of Rilke in the superabundance of enjambment and the dactylic adjectival end-rhymes. The new and completely individual note which Benn struck in his cycle *Morgue und andere Gedichte*, published in March 1912 as a *Flugblatt*, was therefore all the more surprising. And yet in his middle period in Paris Rilke had already treated the theme of the *Morgue* (1906) and the *Leichen-Wäsche* (1908) in his *Neue Gedichte*, which anticipate expressionism. Georg Heym had already preceded Benn in his description of clinical anatomy in his sketch for a short story *Die Sektion* (1911) and his cycle of poems *Das Fieberspital* (1910), but despite all the boldness of the imagery he still retained rigid and traditional poetic forms and language. Benn, on the other hand, inspired by the crude naturalism of Liliencron, used a completely new language, the cynical jargon of the medical student and the callous anatomist. This language alone seemed to him to express adequately the inner emotion he felt at the sight of the bodies of those who had drowned, dissected drunks, prostitutes, and negroes, those suffering from cancer or in the waiting-room at the women's hospital. His poems are mostly written in unrhymed free verse or very free rhymes, with crassly naturalistic images, conscious ridicule and parody of popular greeting-card verses

[1] *Probleme der Lyrik*, *GW* I, p. 532.

celebrating human happiness in images which had become meaningless clichés. They reveal in typical Berlin style an unmistakable sympathy for the suffering and the dead behind the apparent cynicism. One of the few critics to recognize this was Ernst Stadler, who matured early as an expressionist poet and was the first to point out the importance and individuality of Benn's *Morgue* poems.

But in his second collection of poems, dedicated to Else Lasker-Schüler, *Söhne. Neue Gedichte* (1913), Benn put aside this theme, although he in fact retained and developed it up to his Brussels period. Expressly denying the artistic ideals of impressionism, he proclaimed in his programmatic poem *Der junge Hebbel* that the poet must strive for a new art form, born out of passionate self-analysis, justifying his provocative attacks on the deceitful bourgeois world by reference to Schiller's revolutionary drama *Die Räuber*. We see here for the first time, in the pathos of the language and the visions of an imaginary South carried aloft by a nihilistic-dionysiac feeling of joy, the importance for Benn of the poems of the philosopher Friedrich Nietzsche, more particularly his *Dionysos Dithyrambs*. Benn's total view of the world, history, and aesthetics, which he discussed in several essays and lectures, is influenced by Nietzsche. The main theme is the father–son problem, the abrupt rejection of the older generation of the 'Fathers' and the passionate proclamation of the unlimited right to existence of the 'Sons', a typically expressionistic motif which became familiar to a wider public through Walter Hasenclever's drama *Der Sohn* (1914) and which can be traced as late as Bert Brecht's early dramas. The problem of modern city life and man's dubious existence there is the subject of sceptical-ironic or even dithyrambic-affirmative poems (cf. No. 2, *D-Zug*, No. 4, *Englisches Café*, No. 5, *Untergrundbahn*).

Benn's third collection of poems, *Fleisch. Gesammelte Lyrik*, which was published in 1917 by the 'Aktion' Verlag, included in the second and third parts poems written after 1914, which reflected in the opposing and uneven nature of their form and content a soul deeply wounded by war and inhumanity, whose cry became famous in the introductory poem *Der Arzt*, 'Die Krone der Schöpfung, das Schwein, der Mensch'. This horror at man's imprisonment by his physical, sensual nature and his slavery to death is expressed in a series of obscene and macabre poems, whose cry of accusation is intensified beyond limits and breaks all aesthetic bounds. These poems, contemporary in form and expression, contrast with monologues by the lonely lyrical ego, which is ecstatically identified with Icarus in a dionysiac feeling for life (No. 6, *Ikarus*), and with visions of the south (No. 7, *Reise*) and classical sensuality and *joie de vivre* (No. 8, *Kretische Vase*).

Analogous with the general development of expressionism, which declined during the twenties and gave way to the 'Neue Sachlichkeit', there followed in Benn's poetic creativity a period of reflectiveness and intellectual struggle with the findings of modern anthropology, psychoanalysis, ethnology, and philosophy of history, where he sought a mythical and historical basis for the problems of modern man. The result of this deepening of his knowledge and extension of his historical horizon is reflected in his essays *Das moderne Ich* (1920) and *Das letzte Ich* (1921), and also in the more concentrated lyrical form of the cycle of poems *Der späte Mensch* (cf. No. 10, *Das späte Ich*), which was written at the same time and which marks a new stage in his lyrical work. A new tendency and the rejection of expressionist formlessness can also be seen in a preference for rigid verse forms (cf. No. 11, *Schädelstätten*, which is modelled on Hebbel's poem *An die Jünglinge*).

The collections of poems *Schutt* (1924), *Betäubung* (1925), and *Spaltung. Neue Gedichte* (1925), which he published in 1927 in one 188-page volume of his *Gesammelte Gedichte*, also containing the early poems (1912–20), comprise a wealth of important and formally perfected poems which raised Benn to the top rank of modern poets beside the late Rilke and Brecht in the *Hauspostille* (1927). The great thematic breadth of these mostly very long poems, made up of from four to six eight-line rhyming strophes, can only be outlined here: they range from the love poems from his meeting with the 'Dänin' Ellen Overgaard (No. 12, *Nebel*) to poems of contemporary criticism (No. 11, *Schädelstätten*) and to his cultural, philosophical observations on the origin of human myths (No. 15, *Theogonien*) and their importance in the present (No. 19, *Orphische Zellen*), which is always pictured as night-time and an epoch of destruction. Benn was also beginning to write 'absolute Poesie' in the cycle of poems *Betäubung* (cf. No. 13, *Entwurzelungen*), in which he demonstrates the creative process in its various phases of 'Selbsterregung' and intensification, and thereby realizes his theory of the poetic which he had developed in his essays of that period. His new concept of the modern poet, in contrast to the poets of previous epochs, is reflected in his programme poem *Der Sänger* (No. 14), with which he prefaced his collection of poems *Spaltung* and the second part of his *Gesammelte Gedichte*. His 'hyperämische Metaphysik' of the poetic appears concentrated in the poem *Trunkene Flut* (No. 22), which was later used as the title of an anthology of his poems after the Second World War containing very many poems written during the twenties. Almost all his poems written in this rigid form (cf. Nos. 16 ff.) reflect his gloomy view of life, which, to use Oswald Spengler's phrase, saw the West threatened by destruction, and overshadowed by nihilism in the Nietzschean sense. Again and again the problem of death is central to his lyrical reflections (No. 23, *Aus Fernen, aus Reichen*, No. 27, *Immer schweigender*, No. 28, *Ein Land*, etc.); it overshadows the absolute loneliness of the lyrical ego (No. 26, *Du mußt dir alles geben*), which gives itself up to dreams of salvation from the terrors of the world of consciousness and historical evolution and longs to return to the primeval depths of the soul and life (No. 3, *Gesänge*, No. 25, *Regressiv*).

At the end of the twenties Benn came into conflict with the theory, put forward by the socialist intellectuals of the left, that the modern poet is sociologically restricted, obliged to take a stand in class conflict and to place art at the service of politics and efforts to change the world. This theory, which was then taken up in a perverted form after 1933 by National Socialism, placing the 'Volksgemeinschaft' above the individual and demanding the renunciation of intellectual freedom, did not fail to have an influence on Benn's lyrical work. But it is to be noted that in the period 1933–4, in which he pledged himself absolutely to the totalitarian state and Hitler's new regime in essays and lectures, he never exploited his poetry for political ends but rather maintained the purity of the inner realm of his poetic work. The poems written after 1932/3, which arise from the existential sense of life as heroic nihilism and individualism, still in reverence for Friedrich Nietzsche (cf. No. 29, *Dennoch die Schwerter halten*), are not only thematically distinct from those written in the twenties, but are also distinguished by their shorter form. Benn now preferred simple, four-line rhyming verses with three to four main stresses, which express the strain and pressure of his situation and portray the tragedy of historical events in terms of gloomy pessimism (No. 30, *Durch jede Stunde —*). The poet turns away from the man who sees himself in irrevocable opposition to the world of power, and withdraws to the realm of absolute intellect and autonomous art (No. 31, *Am Brückenwehr*, I–IV).

This is the transition to the 'statisches Gedicht' which became the characteristic lyrical form in Benn's late period from 1936 onwards. For him it marked the 'phase II' of expressionism, which he terms a new 'classicism'. For him it stood for both the late, ideological-religious work of the mature Goethe and the strict priestly-prophetic poetry of Stefan George, with its judgement of the contemporary world. It was not until the death of George, who had rejected so forcefully the barbarism of National Socialism in a letter to the propaganda minister Goebbels, that his work became important to Benn. There is, too, a discernible echo of the later poetry of Rainer Maria Rilke, whose *Duineser Elegien* and *Sonette an Orpheus* (1922) once more aroused topical interest and importance through the publication of his *Späte Gedichte* by the Insel Verlag in 1934. In January 1936 Benn published fourteen new poems in the series *Das Gedicht. Blätter für die Dichtung*, issued by the Hamburg publisher Heinrich Ellermann. The second series was entitled *Gedichte* and clearly reveals his pessimistic attitude towards the domination of the contemporary scene by the world of power politics and history (cf. No. 33, *Die weißen Segel*). Art, sharply distinct from the realm of mere living, has the task of 'transforming' the earthly into the spiritual, as in Rilke's late work. The poet sees himself as a tragic being who is not understood by his fellow men and subject to all the harshness of fate (cf. No. 34, *Das Ganze*). His opposition to the official party optimism of the National Socialists is expressed in the introductory poem *Valse triste*, which he used as the prologue to his *Ausgewählte Gedichte, 1911–1936*, published in

1936 and also containing parts of his oratorio *Das Unaufhörliche.* On the orders of the Nazi censorship he was obliged, in order to get the book published, to omit from this collection the five most offensive early poems (including No. 1, *Krebsbaracke*, No. 2, *D-Zug*, No. 5, *Untergrundbahn*), and to replace them with other 'static' poems from this period which were not open to objection. But his final poem, *Sieh die Sterne, die Fänge* (No. 24), leaves no doubt that he had no enthusiasm for contemporary belief in the future; he regarded his era rather as the evening of history and thought his own end had come. Since this book could only be sold 'stillschweigend und ohne Propaganda', little further attention was paid to him, and from then onwards Benn belonged to those who had been forgotten, whose existence and work were known only to their closest friends.

These years of extreme loneliness and obscurity were, however, creatively very productive: in Hanover Benn wrote his important review of the contemporary scene, his essay *Weinhaus Wolf* (1937), in addition to a large number of tense and emotional *Lehrgedichte* in the style of the late Goethe and George. In these he celebrates the magical power of the poetic word and the poem (cf. No. 42, *Gedichte*, No. 44, *Ein Wort*), which, however, cannot conceal the existential tragedy of the artistic genius and his work (cf. No. 43, *Bilder*, No. 45, *Abschied*). In the form of his poems this period marks the transition to long rhyming verses which were more suited to the breadth of the lyrical themes of this 'absolute Poesie' than were the short-lined rhyming verses of the early thirties. In August 1943 Benn ventured to distribute to his closest friends a private edition of the poems he wrote chiefly in Berlin and Landsberg, under the title *Zweiundzwanzig Gedichte 1936–1943*, in order to show them, above all in the long poem of accusation *Monolog*, how absolutely he rejected Hitler's gangster regime and into what inner conflicts the progress of the war had thrown him. These poems include the great poem of 1943 which is still quoted to excess today, above all in sermons:

Verlorenes Ich

Verlorenes Ich, zersprengt von Stratosphären,
Opfer des Ion —: Gamma-Strahlen-Lamm —
Teilchen und Feld —: Unendlichkeitschimären
auf deinem grauen Stein von Notre-Dame.

After portraying the hopeless situation of modern man in his disillusion, Benn concludes with a backward glance of longing to the Middle Ages, when all, even the 'verlorenes Ich', still had a religious focus and sacramental communion in the Eucharist:

Ach, als sich alle einer Mitte neigten
und auch die Denker nur den Gott gedacht,
sie sich den Hirten und dem Lamm verzweigten,
wenn aus dem Kelch das Blut sie rein gemacht,

und alle rannen aus der einen Wunde,
brachen das Brot, das jeglicher genoß —
o ferne zwingende erfüllte Stunde,
die einst auch das verlorne Ich umschloß.

In this Landsberg period of very great seclusion, when Benn realized more and more that the war had been lost and would end in unimaginable chaos and defeat for Germany, he turned, on the inspiration of Dostoyevsky's novel *Crime and Punishment* and the religious poems of Goethe's late period, to the problem of Christianity and Christian love for one's neighbour. In his free-verse poem *St. Petersburg — Mitte des Jahrhunderts* he expresses this love for his fellow men as his own vocation in opposition to the raging hatred and contempt for mankind during the war:

> Jeder, der einem anderen hilft,
> ist Gethsemane,
> jeder, der einen anderen tröstet,
> ist Christi Mund . . .

This critical conflict with the figure and doctrine of Christ permeates all Benn's late work, reaching its climax in the radio play *Die Stimme hinter dem Vorhang* (1951), in which he emphasizes the distance between man and the dark, invisible divinity, and clearly indicates, as in his essays, that he does not believe in the spiritual restoration of ecclesiastical Christianity. His reflective cycle of poems *V. Jahrhundert* (No. 47), written in Landsberg, gives additional proof that he was seeking the solution to the problem of death in connection with the rites, mysteries, and myths of Greek antiquity—a problem that had pursued him all his life—not in any metaphysical religious proclamation of the resurrection of the dead, but in the aesthetic free play of art. The influence of the Chinese philosophers of 'Tao' (the Way), Lao-tse, and Confucius on his outlook in later life can be seen in the poem *Statische Gedichte* (No. 48), written at the end of his stay in Landsberg shortly before his escape at the end of the war. It was used as the title for Benn's collection of poems 1935–45, five copies of which were published privately on 2 May 1946 and distributed to his few remaining friends, since he had once again been forbidden to publish, this time by the allied forces of occupation.

The publication of his *Statische Gedichte* by the Arche Verlag in Zürich in 1948, in defiance of all opposition, gave the public a picture of the poet from which were omitted such essential features as his blunt polemic against National Socialism and the political impotence of the

Germans: Benn's deserving publisher, Peter Schifferli, had excluded from the volume 'alles Düstere und Kalte' and turned Benn into a 'sanfter Heinrich', as the poet wrote sarcastically to his former publisher Erich Reiss, who was in New York.[1] Since he valued very highly the 'Tragik und Schärfe' in his work which was not welcome in Switzerland, he included in the German version of his *Statische Gedichte* (1949) three melancholy poems which portray the deaths of Rembrandt and Shakespeare, overshadowed by tragedy and resignation and containing a vision of death. In his two new volumes of poems, *Fragmente* (1951) and *Destillationen* (1953), he reverted quite consciously to the provocative slang and jargon of his earlier free-verse poems of social criticism, in order to shock the post-war public. The title poem *Fragmente* ends with a cynical definition of his contemporary modern man:

Ausdruckskrisen und Anfälle von Erotik:
das ist der Mensch von heute,
das Innere ein Vakuum,
die Kontinuität der Persönlichkeit
wird gewahrt von den Anzügen,
die bei gutem Stoff zehn Jahre halten.

Der Rest Fragmente,
halbe Laute,
Melodienansätze aus Nachbarhäusern,
Negerspirituals
oder Ave Marias.

But side by side with this outbreak of contempt for man, Benn expresses in typically contrasting softer tones his understanding for the humble existence of those who serve unnoticed (cf. No. 51, *Denk der Vergeblichen*). Both these

[1] 5 Mar. 1949, *ABr.*, p. 139.

and his last collection of poems *Aprèslude* have a general quality of deep disillusion, with respect both to the potentialities of art, which Benn saw only in formal terms (cf. No. 52, *Satzbau*), and to the existence of the poet, his relationship with his material and language (cf. No. 54, *Nur zwei Dinge*, No. 55, *Worte*), and his feeling of loneliness and exclusion from all that is human. This feeling also colours his religious ideas (cf. No. 53, *Die Gitter*), which, in the cycle of poems *Der Dunkle I–IV*, places the life of the individual and the epochs of human history in the power of the unknowable Old Testament *deus absconditus*. Although Benn was still to write a series of important poems, these last three collections are essentially reminiscences and encores, for which he coined the neologism 'Aprèslude' as the opposite of the French word 'Prélude' which Chopin used.

His most important poetic achievements in the last decade of his life were rather in the field of prose and radio plays. His *Roman des Phänotyp. Landsberger Fragment 1944* was an important early experiment in 'absolute Prosa', in fact an anti-novel without connected action, a series of monologues by a radical nihilist who recognizes the 'Disharmonie als Gesetz des Alls' and, as a result of his impressions of the last year of the war, regards all values as ambivalent and hovers between the pros and cons of ultimate indecision. From the 'Phänotyp', the 'Individuum, das die charakteristischen Züge dieser Epoche evident zum Ausdruck bringt, mit dieser Epoche identisch ist, das sie representiert',[1] the figure of the 'Ptolemäer' was developed after 1945, and portrayed by Benn in his story *Der Ptolemäer. Berliner Novelle, 1947*, a sharp criticism of the attempts at intellectual revival in the ruins of postwar Berlin. Benn's aesthetic philosophy is expressed by

[1] *GW* IV, pp. 143–4.

the 'Glasbläser', a foil to the 'Ptolemäer', a figure standing for the modern artist who proclaims Benn's principles of existence:

> Erstens: erkenne die Lage. Zweitens: rechne mit deinen Defekten, gehe von deinen Beständen aus, nicht von deinen Parolen. Drittens: vollende nicht deine Persönlichkeit, sondern die einzelnen deiner Werke. Blase die Welt aus Glas, als Hauch aus einem Pfeifenrohr: der Schlag, mit dem du alles löst: die Vasen, die Urnen, die Lekythen — dieser Schlag ist deiner und er entscheidet . . .[1]

This radical matter-of-factness and his fanatical adherence to an ethos of artistic workmanship, found also in his essay *Der Radardenker* (1949) and his lecture *Probleme der Lyrik* (1951), gained for Benn an influence which cannot be overstated on the intellectual climate of the fifties and sixties, a period in which many younger writers took his lyrics and prose style as a model and expressed their agreement with or criticism of his aesthetics of modern creative writing. Ideological and religious problems are treated also in his two late radio plays, *Drei alte Männer* (1948) and *Die Stimme hinter dem Vorhang* (1951), in which God, the 'Großer Unbekannte', angrily condemns the wretchedness of the contemporary human world and proclaims as his last maxim the thesis which determines all Benn's work: 'im Dunkel leben, im Dunkel tun, was wir können — *das soll sein.*'[2]

[1] *GW* II, p. 232.

[2] Ibid., p. 440. Cf. Benn's elucidation of this 'moralische Forderung' in his letter of 18 May 1953 to Friedrich Siems, *ABr.*, pp. 249–51.

MAIN DATES IN THE LIFE OF GOTTFRIED BENN

1886 Born Mansfeld (2 May).

1903 Leaves Friedrich Gymnasium (11 Sept.).
Student of theology and German philology, Marburg (1903–4).

1904 Transfers to Berlin.

1905 Medical student, Kaiser Wilhelm Academy of Army Medicine (Oct.).

1906 First period of military service (1 Apr.–30 Sept.).

1908 Preliminary medical examination.

1910 House physician, Berlin Charité Hospital (1 Oct. 1910–1 Oct. 1911).

1911 Receives prize for medicine, Berlin University.

1912 Doctorate, Berlin University (26 Feb.).
First collection of poems, *Morgue und andere Gedichte*.

1913 Second collection of poems, *Söhne. Neue Gedichte*.

1914 Travels to N. America as ship's doctor.
Locum tenens, Fichtelgebirge Sanatorium.
First short story, *Gehirne*.
Meets Edith Brosin on Hiddensee Island (summer).
Recalled to active service in army (1 Aug.).
Marries (1) Edith Brosin and adopts her son, Andreas (1 Aug.).
Takes part in siege of Antwerp (8 Oct.).

1915 Daughter Nele born (8 Sept.).
Member of court martial for Edith Cavell (autumn).
First play, *Etappe*.

1916 Poems, *Rönne Novellen* (*Gehirne Novellen*).

1917 Returns to Berlin.
Plays, *Etappe*, *Der Vermessungsdirigent*, *Karandasch*.
Medical practice in Berlin (to 1935).

1922 First wife Edith dies (19 Nov.).
Gesammelte Schriften.
Daughter goes to Denmark.

1924 Visits Paris and later France and Spain (1924–7).

1924–7 Various essays.

1929 Lilly Breda's suicide.

1930 Adopted son Andreas dies.
Radio dialogue with Oskar Loerke.

1931 Holiday with Reiss in Schwarzburg.
Oratorio, *Das Unaufhörliche*.

1932 Admitted to Prussian Academy of Arts.
Essay, *Goethe und die Naturwissenschaften*.

1933 Hitler German Chancellor. Heinrich Mann removed from Prussian Academy.
Benn appointed provisional leader, Prussian Academy.
Struck off medical register as suspected Jew (1 Apr.).
Gives funeral oration, Max von Schillings (27 July).

1933–4 Essays and talks in honour of National Socialism.

1934 Accepts vice-presidency, Hitler's 'Union Nationaler Schriftsteller' (8 Jan.).
Praises Hitler at banquet in honour of Marinetti.
Lebensweg eines Intellektualisten.
Dorische Welt.
Attacked as intellectual.

1935 Returns to army as Surgeon-Major, Army Recruitment Centre, Hanover (31 March).

1936 Poems, *Ausgewählte Gedichte.*
Fiftieth birthday (2 May); attacked in Nazi press for his poems *Ausgewählte Gedichte.*

1937 Returns to Berlin, Surgeon-Major to G.O.C. Third Army Corps.

1938 Marries (2) Herta von Wedemeyer (22 Jan.).
Forbidden to write (18 Mar.).

1939 Second World War. Promoted Chief M.O. Transferred to Landsberg an der Warthe.
Clandestine edition *Zweiundzwanzig Gedichte.*

1945 Eastern front collapses; flees to Berlin and sends wife to country.
Second wife Herta commits suicide in Neuhaus on day Russians enter.

1946 Attempts unsuccessfully to publish war essays.
Marries (3) Dr. Ilse Kaul (18 Dec.).

1948 *Statische Gedichte* (Zürich).

1951 Lectures vacation course, Marburg University.
Probleme der Lyrik.
Receives Georg Büchner Prize.

1952 Biennale Internationale de Poésie, Knokke.

1953 Receives Cross of Order of Merit of Federal Republic.

1954 Essay, *Altern als Problem für Künstler.*

1955 Radio discussion, *Soll die Dichtung das Leben bessern?.*

1956 Dies at Bad Schlangenbad (7 July); buried in Berlin at the Neue Waldfriedhof (12 July).

SELECT BIBLIOGRAPHY

1. *Works*

Gottfried Benn, *Gesammelte Werke*, Vols. I–IV (*GW*), ed. by Dieter Wellershoff, Wiesbaden, Limes Verlag, 1958–61. Vol. I: *Essays, Reden, Vorträge*, 1959, 2nd edn. 1964; Vol. II: *Prosa und Szenen*, 1958; Vol. III: *Gedichte*, 1960, 2nd edn. 1963; Vol. IV: *Autobiographische und vermischte Schriften*, 1961 (with index).

—— *Primäre Tage. Gedichte und Fragmente aus dem Nachlaß*, ed. by Marguerite Schlüter, Wiesbaden, Limes Verlag, 1958.

—— *Den Traum alleine tragen. Neue Texte, Briefe, Dokumente*, ed. by Paul Raabe and Max Niedermayer, Wiesbaden, Limes Verlag, 1966.

2. *Letters*

Gottfried Benn, *Ausgewählte Briefe* (mit einem Nachwort von Max Rychner), (*ABr.*), Wiesbaden, Limes Verlag, 1957, 2nd edn. 1959.

—— *Briefe an Ernst Jünger, E. R. Curtius, Max Rychner u. a.*, Zürich, Verlag der Arche, 1960, Nos. 311–12.

—— *Das gezeichnete Ich. Briefe aus den Jahren 1900–1956*, München, Deutscher Taschenbuch-Verlag, 1962, No. 89.

3. *Selections*

Gottfried Benn, *Lyrik und Prosa, Briefe und Dokumente. Eine Auswahl*, ed. by Max Niedermayer, Wiesbaden, Limes Verlag, 1962.

—— *Auswahl aus dem Werk*, ed. by Dieter Wellershoff, Darmstadt, Moderner Buch-Club, 1962.

4. *Critical works*

Reinhold Grimm, *Gottfried Benn. Die farbliche Chiffre in der Dichtung* (Erlanger Beiträge zur Sprach- und Kunstwissenschaft I), Nürnberg, Verlag Hans Carl, 1958, 2nd edn. 1962.

Ernst Nef, *Das Werk Gottfried Benns*, Zürich, Verlag der Arche, 1958.

Dieter Wellershoff, *Gottfried Benn. Phänotyp dieser Stunde. Eine Studie über den Problemgehalt seines Werkes*, Köln, Berlin, Kiepenheuer & Witsch, 1958.

Nele P. Soerensen, *Mein Vater Gottfried Benn*, Wiesbaden, Limes Verlag, 1960.

Else Buddeberg, *Gottfried Benn*, Stuttgart, J. B. Metzlersche Verlagsbuchhandlung, 1961.

Edgar Lohner, *Passion und Intellekt. Die Lyrik Gottfried Benns*, Neuwied, Luchterhand, 1961.

Gerhard Loose, *Die Ästhetik Gottfried Benns*, Frankfurt am Main, Vittorio Klostermann, 1961.

Else Buddeberg, *Probleme um Gottfried Benn* (*Die Benn-Forschung 1950–60*), Stuttgart, J. B. Metzlersche Verlagsbuchhandlung, 1962.

Helmut Kaiser, *Mythos, Rausch und Reaktion. Der Weg Gottfried Benns und Ernst Jüngers*, Berlin, Aufbau-Verlag, 1962.

Walter Lennig, *Gottfried Benn in Selbstzeugnissen und Dokumenten* (rowohlts monographien 71), Reinbeck bei Hamburg, Rowohlt, 1962.

Friedrich Wilhelm Wodtke, *Gottfried Benn* (Sammlung Metzler M 26), Stuttgart, J. B. Metzlersche Verlagsbuchhandlung, 1962, 2nd edn. 1970.

Beda Allemann, *Gottfried Benn. Das Problem der Geschichte*, Pfullingen, Verlag Günther Neske, 1963.

Friedrich Wilhelm Wodtke, *Die Antike im Werk Gottfried Benns*, Wiesbaden, Limes Verlag, 1963.

Else Buddeberg, *Studien zur lyrischen Sprache Gottfried Benns* (Beihefte zur Zeitschrift *Wirkendes Wort* 8), Düsseldorf, Pädagogischer Verlag Schwann, 1964.

Hans-Dieter Balser, *Das Problem des Nihilismus im Werke Gottfried Benns* (Abhandlungen zur Kunst-, Musik- und Literaturwissenschaft 29), Bonn, H. Bouvier & Co. Verlag, 1965.

Jürgen P. Wallmann, *Gottfried Benn*, Mühlacker, Stieglitz-Verlag E. Händle, 1965.

Bruno Hillebrand, *Artistik und Auftrag. Zur Kunsttheorie von Benn und Nietzsche* (Sammlung Dialog 7), München, Nymphenburger Verlagshandlung, 1966.

5. *Critical articles*

Max Rychner, 'Gottfried Benn. Züge seiner dichterischen Welt', in *Merkur* 3, 1949, pp. 781–93, 872–90. More recently in *Gottfried Benn: Lyrik und Prosa*, Wiesbaden, 1962, p. xxiii–lviii.

Fritz Martini, 'Gottfried Benn. Der Ptolemäer', in F. Martini, *Das Wagnis der Sprache. Interpretationen deutscher Prosa von Nietzsche bis Benn*, Stuttgart, Ernst Klett Verlag, 1954, pp. 468–517.

Michael Hamburger, 'Gottfried Benn', in M. Hamburger, *Reason and Energy. Studies in German Literature*, London, Routledge & Kegan Paul, 1957, pp. 273–312.

Albrecht Schöne, 'Überdauernde Temporalstruktur. Gottfried Benn', in A. Schöne, *Säkularisation als sprachbildende Kraft* (Palaestra 226), Göttingen, Vandenhoeck & Ruprecht, 1958, pp. 190–226.

Ingo Seidler, 'Statische Montage: zur poetischen Technik im Spätwerk Gottfried Benns', in *Monatshefte* (Wisconsin) 52, 1960, pp. 321–30.

Clemens Heselhaus, 'Die rhythmische Ausdruckswelt von Gottfried Benn', in C. Heselhaus, *Deutsche Lyrik der Moderne von Nietzsche bis Yvan Goll. Die Rückkehr zur Bildlichkeit der Sprache*, Düsseldorf, August Bagel Verlag, 1961, pp. 258–85.

Reinhold Grimm, Wolf-Dieter Marsch (eds.), 'Die Kunst im Schatten des Gottes. Für und wider Gottfried Benn' (articles by D. Wellershoff, R. Grimm, E. Lohner, L. Perlitt, N. Hinske), Göttingen, Sachse & Pohl Verlag, 1962.

Joachim Möller, 'Zur Thematik der Bennschen Lyrik', in *Der Deutschunterricht* 14, 1962, pp. 60–75.

Paul Requadt, 'Gottfried Benn und das südliche Wort', in P. Requadt, *Die Bildersprache der deutschen Italiendichtung von Goethe bis Benn*, Bern, München, Francke Verlag, 1962, pp. 282–302.

Hunter G. Hannum, 'George and Benn: the autumnal vision', in *PMLA* 78, 1963, pp. 271–9.

Paul Böckmann, 'Gottfried Benn und die Sprache des Expressionismus', in *Der deutsche Expressionismus. Formen und Gestalten*, ed. by Hans Steffen, Göttingen, Vandenhoeck & Ruprecht, 1965, pp. 63–87.

Rudolf Erckmann, 'Jazz und Lyrik. Erarbeitung Benn'scher Dichtung von der Schallplatte her', in *Der Deutschunterricht* 17, 1965, pp. 97–117.

Christoph Eyckmann, 'Die Funktion des Häßlichen in der Lyrik Heyms, Trakls und Benns. Zur Krise der Wirklichkeitserfahrung im deutschen Expressionismus' (*Bonner Arbeiten zur deutschen Literatur* 11), Bonn, H. Bouvier & Co., 1965, pp. 135–260.

Edgar Lohner, 'Gottfried Benn', in *Deutsche Dichter der Moderne. Ihr Leben und Werk*, ed. by Benno von Wiese, Berlin, Bielefeld, München, Erich Schmidt Verlag, 1965, pp. 479–99.

Eva M. Lüders, 'Das lyrische Ich und das gezeichnete Ich. Zur späten Lyrik Gottfried Benns', in *Wirkendes Wort* 15, 1965, pp. 361–85.

Peter Uwe Hohendahl, 'Die Rezeption Gottfried Benns in den Vereinigten Staaten und Frankreich. Ein kritischer Vergleich', in *DVjs.* 41, 1967, pp. 233–57.

Friedrich Wilhelm Wodtke, 'Gottfried Benn', in *Expressionismus als Literatur*, Bern-München 1969, pp. 309–32.

For further information on texts, books, and articles see:

Edgar Lohner, *Gottfried Benn Bibliographie 1912–1956*, Wiesbaden, Limes Verlag, 2nd edn. 1958.

Friedrich Wilhelm Wodtke, *Gottfried Benn* (Sammlung Metzler M 26), Stuttgart, J. B. Metzlersche Verlagsbuchhandlung, 1962 (2nd edn. in preparation).

POEMS

I

Mann und Frau gehn durch die Krebsbaracke

Der Mann:
Hier diese Reihe sind zerfallene Schößе
und diese Reihe ist zerfallene Brust.
Bett stinkt bei Bett. Die Schwestern wechseln stündlich.

Komm, hebe ruhig diese Decke auf.
Sieh, dieser Klumpen Fett und faule Säfte,
das war einst irgendeinem Mann groß
und hieß auch Rausch und Heimat.

Komm, sieh auf diese Narbe an der Brust.
Fühlst du den Rosenkranz von weichen Knoten?
Fühl ruhig hin. Das Fleisch ist weich und schmerzt nicht.

Hier diese blutet wie aus dreißig Leibern.
Kein Mensch hat so viel Blut.
Hier dieser schnitt man
erst noch ein Kind aus dem verkrebsten Schoß.

Man läßt sie schlafen. Tag und Nacht. — Den Neuen
sagt man: hier schläft man sich gesund. — Nur sonntags
für den Besuch läßt man sie etwas wacher.

Nahrung wird wenig noch verzehrt. Die Rücken
sind wund. Du siehst die Fliegen. Manchmal
wäscht sie die Schwester. Wie man Bänke wäscht.

Hier schwillt der Acker schon um jedes Bett.
Fleisch ebnet sich zu Land. Glut gibt sich fort.
Saft schickt sich an zu rinnen. Erde ruft.

2

D-Zug

Braun wie Kognak. Braun wie Laub. Rotbraun. Malaien-
gelb.
D-Zug Berlin-Trelleborg und die Ostseebäder.

Fleisch, das nackt ging.
Bis in den Mund gebräunt vom Meer.
Reif gesenkt, zu griechischem Glück.
In Sichel-Sehnsucht: wie weit der Sommer ist!
Vorletzter Tag des neunten Monats schon!

Stoppel und letzte Mandel lechzt in uns.
Entfaltungen, das Blut, die Müdigkeiten,
die Georginennähe macht uns wirr.

Männerbraun stürzt sich auf Frauenbraun:

Eine Frau ist etwas für eine Nacht.
Und wenn es schön war, noch für die nächste!
Oh! Und dann wieder dies Bei-sich-selbst-Sein!
Diese Stummheiten! Dies Getriebenwerden!

Eine Frau ist etwas mit Geruch.
Unsägliches! Stirb hin! Resede.
Darin ist Süden, Hirt und Meer.
An jedem Abhang lehnt ein Glück.

Frauenhellbraun taumelt an Männerdunkelbraun:

Halte mich! Du, ich falle!
Ich bin im Nacken so müde.
Oh, dieser fiebernde süße
letzte Geruch aus den Gärten.

3

Gesänge

I

O daß wir unsere Ururahnen wären.
Ein Klümpchen Schleim in einem warmen Moor.
Leben und Tod, Befruchten und Gebären
glitte aus unseren stummen Säften vor.

Ein Algenblatt oder ein Dünenhügel,
vom Wind Geformtes und nach unten schwer.
Schon ein Libellenkopf, ein Möwenflügel
wäre zu weit und litte schon zu sehr.

II

Verächtlich sind die Liebenden, die Spötter,
alles Verzweifeln, Sehnsucht, und wer hofft.
Wir sind so schmerzliche durchseuchte Götter
und dennoch denken wir des Gottes oft.

Die weiche Bucht. Die dunklen Wälderträume.
Die Sterne, schneeballblütengroß und schwer.
Die Panther springen lautlos durch die Bäume.
Alles ist Ufer. Ewig ruft das Meer —

4
Englisches Café

Das ganze schmalschuhige Raubpack,
Russinnen, Jüdinnen, tote Völker, ferne Küsten,
schleicht durch die Frühjahrsnacht.

Die Geigen grünen. Mai ist um die Harfe.
Die Palmen röten sich. Im Wüstenwind.

Rahel, die schmale Golduhr am Gelenk:
Geschlecht behütend und Gehirn bedrohend:
Feindin! Doch deine Hand ist eine Erde:
süßbraun, fast ewig, überweht vom Schoß.

Freundlicher Ohrring kommt. In Charme d'Orsay.
Die hellen Osterblumen sind so schön:
breitmäulig gelb, mit Wiese an den Füßen.

O Blond! O Sommer dieses Nackens! O
diese jasmindurchseuchte Ellenbeuge!
Oh, ich bin gut zu dir. Ich streichle
dir deine Schultern. Du, wir reisen:

Tyrrhenisches Meer. Ein frevelhaftes Blau.
Die Dorertempel. In Rosenschwangerschaft
die Ebenen. Felder
sterben den Asphodelentod.

Lippen, verschwärmt und tiefgefüllt wie Becher,
als zögerte das Blut des süßen Orts,
rauschen durch eines Mundes ersten Herbst.

O wehe Stirn! Du Kranke, tief im Flor
der dunklen Brauen! Lächle, werde hell:
die Geigen schimmern einen Regenbogen.

5
Untergrundbahn

Die weichen Schauer. Blütenfrühe. Wie
aus warmen Fellen kommt es aus den Wäldern.
Ein Rot schwärmt auf. Das große Blut steigt an.

Durch all den Frühling kommt die fremde Frau.
Der Strumpf am Spann ist da. Doch, wo er endet,
ist weit von mir. Ich schluchze auf der Schwelle:
laues Geblühe, fremde Feuchtigkeiten.

Oh, wie ihr Mund die laue Luft verpraßt!
Du Rosenhirn, Meer-Blut, du Götter-Zwielicht,
du Erdenbeet, wie strömen deine Hüften
so kühl den Gang hervor, in dem du gehst!

Dunkel: nun lebt es unter ihren Kleidern:
nur weißes Tier, gelöst und stummer Duft.

Ein armer Hirnhund, schwer mit Gott behangen.
Ich bin der Stirn so satt. Oh, ein Gerüste
von Blütenkolben löste sanft sie ab
und schwölle mit und schauerte und triefte.

So losgelöst. So müde. Ich will wandern.
Blutlos die Wege. Lieder aus den Gärten.
Schatten und Sintflut. Fernes Glück: ein Sterben
hin in des Meeres erlösend tiefes Blau.

6

Ikarus

I

O Mittag, der mit heißem Heu mein Hirn
zu Wiese, flachem Land und Hirten schwächt,
daß ich hinrinne und, den Arm im Bach,
den Mohn an meine Schläfe ziehe —
o du Weithingewölbter, enthirne doch
stillflügelnd über Fluch und Gram
des Werdens und Geschehns
mein Auge.
Noch durch Geröll der Halde, noch durch Land-aas,
verstaubendes, durch bettelhaft Gezack
der Felsen — überall
das tiefe Mutterblut, die strömende
entstirnte
matte
Getragenheit.

Das Tier lebt Tag um Tag
und hat an seinem Euter kein Erinnern,
der Hang schweigt seine Blume in das Licht
und wird zerstört.

Nur ich, mit Wächter zwischen Blut und Pranke,
ein hirnzerfressenes Aas, mit Flüchen
im Nichts zergellend, bespien mit Worten,
veräfft vom Licht —
o du Weithingewölbter,
träuf meinen Augen eine Stunde
des guten frühen Voraugenlichts —

schmilz hin den Trug der Farben, schwinge
die kotbedrängten Höhlen in das Rauschen
gebäumter Sonnen, Sturz der Sonnen-sonnen,
o aller Sonnen ewiges Gefälle —

II

Das Hirn frißt Staub. Die Füße fressen Staub.
Wäre das Auge rund und abgeschlossen,
dann bräche durch die Lider süße Nacht,
Gebüsch und Liebe.
Aus dir, du süßes Tierisches,
aus euern Schatten, Schlaf und Haar
muß ich mein Hirn besteigen,
alle Windungen,
das letzte Zwiegespräch —

III

So sehr am Strand, so sehr schon in der Barke,
im krokosfarbnen Kleide der Geweihten
und um die Glieder schon den leichten Flaum —
ausrauschst du aus den Falten, Sonne,
allnächtlich Welten in den Raum —
o eine der vergeßlich hingesprühten
mit junger Glut die Schläfe mir zerschmelzend,
auftrinkend das entstirnte Blut —

7
Reise

O dieses Lichts! Die Insel kränzt
sternblaues Wasser um sich her,
am Saum gestillt, zu Strand ergänzt,
und sättigt täglich sich am Meer.

Es muß nichts zueinander hin,
die Alke, das gelappte Laub
erfüllen sich; es liegt ihr Sinn
im Mittelpunkt, den nichts beraubt.

Auch ich zu: braun! Ich zu: besonnt!
Zu Flachem, das sich selbst benennt!
Das Auge tief am Horizont,
der keine Vertikale kennt.

Schon schwindet der Verknüpfungsdrang,
schon löst sich das Bezugssystem,
und unter dunklem Hautgesang
erhebt sich Blut-Methusalem.

8

Kretische Vase

Du, die Lippe voll Weingeruch,
blauer Ton-Zaun, Rosen-Rotte
um den Zug mykenischen Lichts,
Un-geräte, Tränke-Sehnsucht
weit verweht.

Lockerungen. Es vollzieht sich
Freigebärung. Lose leuchtend
Tiere, Felsen, Hell-Entzwecktes:
Veilchenstreifen, laue Schädel
wiesenblütig.

Welle gegen Starr und Stirn,
Glüher tiefer Bacchanale
gegen die Vernichtungsmale:
Aufwuchs und Bewußtseinshirn,

spüle, stäube — Knabenhände,
Läuferglieder, raumumschlungen
stranden dich zu Krug und Hang,
wenn bei Fischkopf, Zwiebel, Flöten
Leda-Feste rosenröten
Paarung, Fläche, Niedergang.

9
Pappel

Verhalten,
ungeöffnet in Ast und Ranke,
um in das Blau des Himmels aufzuschrein —:
nur Stamm, Geschlossenheiten,
hoch und zitternd,
eine Kurve.

Die Mispel flüchtet,
Samentöter,
und wann der Blitze segnendes Zerbrechen
rauschte um meinen Schaft
enteinheitend,
weitverteilend
Baumgewesenes?
Und wer sah Pappelwälder?

Einzeln,
und an der Kronenstirn das Mal der Schreie,
das ruhelos die Nächte und den Tag
über der Gärten hinresedeten
süßen aufklaffenden Vergang,
was ihm die Wurzel saugt, die Rinde frißt,
in tote Räume bietet
hin und her.

10

Das späte Ich

I

O du, sieh an: Levkoienwelle,
der schon das Auge übergeht,
Abgänger, Eigen-Immortelle,
es ist schon spät.

Bei Rosenletztem, da die Fabel
des Sommers längst die Flur verließ —
moi haïssable,
noch so mänadisch analys.

II

Im Anfang war die Flut. Ein Floß Lemuren
schiebt Elch, das Vieh, ihn schwängerte ein Stein.
Aus Totenreich, Erinnern, Tiertorturen
steigt Gott hinein.

Alle die großen Tiere: Adler der Kohorten,
Tauben aus Golgathal —
alle die großen Städte: Palm- und Purpurborden —
Blumen der Wüste, Traum des Baal.

Ost-Gerölle, Marmara-Fähre,
Rom, gib die Pferde des Lysippus her —
letztes Blut des weißen Stiers über die schweigenden Altäre
und der Amphitrite letztes Meer —

Schutt. Bacchanalien. Propheturen.
Barkarolen. Schweinerein.
Im Anfang war die Flut. Ein Floß Lemuren
schiebt in die letzten Meere ein.

III

O Seele, um und um verweste,
kaum lebst du noch und noch zuviel,
da doch kein Staub aus keinen Feldern,
da doch kein Laub aus keinen Wäldern
nicht schwer durch deine Schatten fiel.

Die Felsen glühn, der Tartarus ist blau,
der Hades steigt in Oleanderfarben
dem Schlaf ins Lid und brennt zu Garben
mythischen Glücks die Totenschau.

Der Gummibaum, der Bambusquoll,
der See verwäscht die Inkaplatten,
das Mondchâteau: Geröll und Schatten
uralte blaue Mauern voll.

Welch Bruderglück um Kain und Abel,
für die Gott durch die Wolken strich —
kausalgenetisch, haïssable:
das späte Ich.

II

Schädelstätten

Schwer von Vergessen
und ach so hangend schon,
aus Unermessen
Ton um Ton,
und Schattenmale
des letzten Lichts,
o Finale,
Nächte des Nichts.

Die Welten halten,
Äonen-Bann.
Schwer das Erkalten
fühlt nur der Mann,
Wälder zu schweigen
und Waidmannsruh —
wenn wir uns neigen,
wer warst du,
du?

Punisch in Jochen,
Heredität,
kranke Knochen
von Philoktet,
Fratze der Glaube,
Fratze das Glück,
leer kommt die Taube
Noahs zurück.

Schädelstätten,
Begriffsmanie,
kein Zeitwort zu retten
noch Historie —
allem Vergessen,
allem Verschmähn,
dem Unermessen
Panathenän —

in Heiligtumen
tyrrhenischer See
Stier unter Blumen
an Danaë,
in Leuenzügen
Mänadenklang,
und Götter fügen
den Untergang.

12

Nebel

Ach, du zerrinnender
und schon gestürzter Laut,
eben beginnender
Lust vom Munde getaut,
ach so zerrinnst du,
Stunde, und hast kein Sein,
ewig schon spinnst du
weit in die Nebel dich ein.

Ach, wir sagen es immer,
daß es nie enden kann,
und vergessen den Schimmer
Schnees des Neige d'antan,
in das durchküßte, durchtränte
nächtedurchschluchzte Sein
strömt das Fließend-Entlehnte,
spinnen die Nebel sich ein.

Ach, wir rufen und leiden
ältesten Göttern zu:
ewig über uns beiden
„immer und alles: du",
aber den Widdern, den Zweigen,
Altar und Opferstein,
hoch zu den Göttern, die schweigen,
spinnen die Nebel sich ein.

13

Entwurzelungen

Vage Entwurzelungen,
Lösungszwänge, wer heilt
Tage und Alterungen
dessen, der ahnt und eilt,
der seine Stirne den Keulen
aller Zersprengungen gab
von den punischen Säulen
bis an Astartes Grab.

Selber wo Balustraden
mit Levkoien, auch Gras
zu Verfallungen laden,
niemals geschieht es, daß —
niemals die Lippen kosten
dessen, was sich verheißt,
dunkler als Kreuz ein Pfosten
trägt die Worte: „Du weißt."

Niemand ist alles auf Erden.
In die Blüte des Lichts,
in die Aue des Werden
strömt die Seele ihr Nichts,
vom Acheron getrunken,
in Kraut, in pythischer Nacht
wie von Mord gesunken,
wie mit Tod verbracht.

14

Der Sänger

Keime, Begriffsgenesen,
Broadways, Azimut,
Turf- und Nebelwesen
mischt der Sänger im Blut,
immer in Gestaltung,
immer dem Worte zu
nach Vergessen der Spaltung
zwischen ich und du.

Neurogene Leier,
fahle Hyperämien,
Blutdruckschleier
mittels Koffein,
keiner kann ermessen
dies: dem einen zu,
ewig dem Vergessen
zwischen ich und du.

Wenn es einst der Sänger
dualistisch trieb,
heute ist er Zersprenger
mittels Gehirnprinzip,
stündlich webt er im Ganzen
drängend zum Traum des Gedichts
seine schweren Substanzen
selten und langsam ins Nichts.

15

Theogonien

Theogonien —
von den Dingen der Welt
ziehn Melancholien
an der Sterne Zelt,
weben Götter und Drachen,
singen Brände und Baal,
sinnvoll zu machen
Knechtschaft und Qual.

Fährt Er mit leuchtender Barke
über das Himmelsmeer,
ist Er der Widder, der Starke,
von Sonnen und Monden schwer,
naht Er sich in Gewittern,
als der die Felsen verschiebt,
und von den Bösen, den Bittern
die Kühe den Priestern gibt.

Ach, um Fluten, um Elche
rankt sich die Traurigkeit:
sie fahren; Stürme; welche
tauchen, das Land ist weit,
da: ihrem Möwentume
stäubt sich ein Körnchen schwer,
und Er macht aus der Krume
eine Insel auf dem Meer.

Wie mußten sie alle leiden,
um so zum Traum zu fliehn,
und sein des Kummers Weiden
wie hier die Algonkin!

Auch anderen Tieren, Steinen
vertrauten sie ihren Tod
und gingen hin zu weinen
die Völker, weiß und rot.

16

Schleierkraut

Schleierkraut, Schleierkraut rauschen,
rausche die Stunde an,
Himmel, die Himmel lauschen,
wer noch leben kann,
jeder weiß von den Tagen,
wo wir die Ferne sehn:
Leben ist Brückenschlagen
über Ströme, die vergehn.

Schleierkraut, Schleierkraut rauschen,
es ist die Ewigkeit,
wo Herbst und Rosen tauschen
den Blick vom Sterben weit,
da klingt auch von den Meeren
das Ruhelose ein,
von fahlen Stränden, von Schären
der Woge Schein.

Schleierkraut, Schleierkraut neigen
zu tief Musik,
Sterbendes will schweigen:
Silence panique,
erst die Brücken geschlagen,
das Blutplateau,
dann, wenn die Brücken tragen,
die Ströme — wo?

17

Levkoienwelle

„O du, sieh an, Levkoienwelle,
der schon das Auge übergeht“ —
von früher her — es ist die Stelle,
wo eine alte Wunde steht;
denn wieder ist es in den Tagen,
wo alles auf das Ende zielt,
„mänadisch analys“ und Fragen,
das sich um Rosenletztes spielt.

Man träumt, man geht in Selbstgestaltung
aus Selbstentfaltung der Vernunft;
man träumte tief; die falsche Schaltung:
das Selbst ist Trick, der Geist ist Zunft —
verlerne dich und jede Stelle,
wo du noch eine Heimat siehst,
ergib dich der Levkoienwelle,
die sich um Rosenletztes gießt,

die Bildungen der Zweige reifen,
es ist ein großes Fruchtbemühn,
die Seen dämmern hin wie Streifen,
die Gärten, welch ein quellend Glühn,
das ist lernäisches Gelände
und eine Schar Gestalten winkt,
die mähet Blut und säet Ende,
bis sie ans Herz der Schatten sinkt!

18

Dunkler —

Dunkler kann es nicht werden
als diese Stunde, die sinkt,
mit allen Lasten der Erden
in fremder Nacht ertrinkt,
enteignen sich die Figuren
zu einer großen Gestalt,
drohen die Lemuren
aus dem Schattenwald.

Löst du dich von den Dingen,
trägst du fahles Los:
Trauermäntel schwingen
dir um Mund und Schoß —
faltest du die Blätter
jedes Einzelbaums,
bist du kein Verketter
deines Trance-Traums.

In Bewußtseinsbresche
über Ahnung still
steht die Weltenesche
Yggdrasil,
steht auch Aarons Rute
trocken eingestückt,
dann mit Wunderblute
Israel beglückt —

Dir nur sich enthüllte
bis zum Schlunde leer
ewig unerfüllte
Promesse du bonheur,

dir nur kann es nicht werden,
jede Stunde, die sinkt,
mit allen Lasten der Erden
in fremder Nacht ertrinkt.

19
Orphische Zellen

Es schlummern orphische Zellen
in Hirnen des Okzident,
Fisch und Wein und Stellen,
an denen das Opfer brennt,
die Esse aus Haschisch und Meten
und Kraut und das delphische Lied
vom Zuge der Auleten,
wenn er am Gott verschied.

Wer nie das Haupt verhüllte
und niederstieg, ein Stier,
ein rieselnd Blut erfüllte
das Grab und Sargrevier,
wen nie Vermischungslüste
mit Todesschweiß bedrohn,
der ist auch nicht der Myste
aus der phrygischen Kommunion.

Um Feuerstein, um Herde
hat sich der Sieg gerankt,
er aber haßt das Werde,
das sich dem Sieg verdankt,
er drängt nach andern Brüsten
nach andern Meeren ein,
schon nähern sich die Küsten,
die Brandungsvögel schrein.

Nun mag den Sansibaren
der Himmel hoch und still,
eine Insel voll Nelkenwaren
und der Blüte der Bougainville,
wo sie in Höfen drehen
die Mühlen für Zuckerrohr,
nun mag das still vergehen —:
Er tritt als Opfer vor.

Und wo Vergang: in Gittern,
an denen der Mörder weint,
wo sonst Vergang, ach Zittern
löst schon die Stunde, die eint —:
ihm beben Schmerz und Schaden
im Haupt, das niemand kennt,
die Brandungsvögel baden,
das Opfer brennt.

20

Wie lange noch

„Wie lange noch, dann fassen
wir weder Gram noch Joch,
du kannst mich doch nicht lassen,
du weißt es doch,
die Tage, die uns einten,
ihr Immer und ihr Nie,
die Nächte, die wir weinten,
vergißt du die?

Wenn du bei Sommerende
durch diese Landschaft gehst,
die Felder, das Gelände
und schon im Dämmer stehst,

ist es nicht doch die Leere,
das Dunkel, das du fliehst,
ist es nicht doch das Schwere,
wenn du mich gar nicht siehst?

Die Falten und der Kummer
auf meinen Zügen tief,
das ist doch auch der Schlummer,
den hier das Leben schlief,
die eingeglühten Zeichen,
die Male dort und hier
sind doch aus unseren Reichen,
die litten wir.

Ja, gehst du denn zu Grabe,
daß es nun gar nichts gibt,
so gehe — ach, ich habe
dich so geliebt,
doch ist es eine Wende,
vergiß auch nie,
es gibt ein Sommerende
und Nächte, die

das Herz umfassen
mit Gram und Joch
— die du verlassen,
sie atmen noch —,
mit Schmerzen, hämmernden
Verlusten, wo
du suchst die dämmernden
Entfernten so!“

21

Dir auch —

Dir auch —: tauschen die Nächte
dich in ein dunkleres Du,
Psyche, strömende Rechte
schluchzend dem andern zu,
ist es auch ungeheuer
und du littest genug:
Liebe ist Wein ins Feuer
aus dem Opferkrug.

Selbst du beugst dich und jeder
meint, hier sei es vollbracht,
ach, in Schattengeäder
flieht auch deine, die Nacht,
wohl den Lippen, den Händen
glühst du das reinste Licht,
doch die Träume vollenden
können wir nicht.

Nur die Stunden, die Nächte,
wo dein Atem erwacht,
Psyche, strömende Rechte,
tiefe tauschende Nacht,
ach, es ist ungeheuer,
ach, es ist nie genug
von deinem Wein im Feuer
aus dem Opferkrug.

22

Trunkene Flut

Trunkene Flut,
trance- und traumgefleckt,
o Absolut,
das meine Stirne deckt,
um das ich ringe,
aus dem der Preis
der tiefen Dinge,
die die Seele weiß.

In Sternenfieber,
das nie ein Auge maß,
Nächte, Lieber,
daß man des Tods vergaß,
im Zeiten-Einen,
im Schöpfungsschrei
kommt das Vereinen,
nimmt hin — vorbei.

Dann du alleine
nach großer Nacht,
Korn und Weine
dargebracht,
die Wälder nieder,
die Hörner leer,
zu Gräbern wieder
steigt Demeter,

dir noch im Rücken,
im Knochenbau,
dann ein Entzücken,
ein Golf aus Blau,

von Tränen alt,
aus Not und Gebrest
eine Schöpfergestalt,
die uns leben läßt,

die viel gelitten,
die vieles sah,
immer in Schritten
dem Ufer nah
der trunkenen Flut,
die die Seele deckt
groß wie der Fingerhut
sommers die Berge fleckt.

23

Aus Fernen, aus Reichen

Was dann nach jener Stunde
sein wird, wenn dies geschah,
weiß niemand, keine Kunde
kam je von da,
von den erstickten Schlünden
von dem gebrochnen Licht,
wird es sich neu entzünden,
ich meine nicht.

Doch sehe ich ein Zeichen:
über das Schattenland
aus Fernen, aus Reichen
eine große, schöne Hand,
die wird mich nicht berühren,
das läßt der Raum nicht zu:
doch werde ich sie spüren,
und das bist du.

Und du wirst niedergleiten
am Strand, am Meer,
aus Fernen, aus Weiten:
„— erlöst auch er;“
ich kannte deine Blicke
und in des tiefsten Schoß
sammelst du unsere Glücke,
den Traum, das Los.

Ein Tag ist zu Ende,
die Reifen fortgebracht,
dann spielen noch zwei Hände
das Lied der Nacht,
vom Zimmer, wo die Tasten
den dunklen Laut verwehn,
sieht man das Meer und die Masten
hoch nach Norden gehn.

Wenn die Nacht wird weichen,
wenn der Tag begann,
trägst du Zeichen,
die niemand deuten kann,
geheime Male
von fernen Stunden krank
und leerst die Schale,
aus der ich vor dir trank.

24

Sieh die Sterne, die Fänge

Sieh die Sterne, die Fänge
Lichts und Himmel und Meer,
welche Hirtengesänge,
dämmernde, treiben sie her,

du auch, die Stimmen gerufen
und deinen Kreis durchdacht,
folge die schweigenden Stufen
abwärts dem Boten der Nacht.

Wenn du die Mythen und Worte
entleert hast, sollst du gehn,
eine neue Götterkohorte
wirst du nicht mehr sehn,
nicht ihre Euphratthrone,
nicht ihre Schrift und Wand —
gieße, Myrmidonc,
den dunklen Wein ins Land.

Wie dann die Stunden auch hießen,
Qual und Tränen des Seins,
alles blüht im Verfließen
dieses nächtigen Weins,
schweigend strömt die Äone,
kaum noch von Ufern ein Stück —
gib nun dem Boten die Krone,
Traum und Götter zurück.

25
Regressiv

Ach, nicht in dir, nicht in Gestalten
der Liebe, in des Kindes Blut,
in keinem Wort, in keinem Walten
ist etwas, wo dein Dunkel ruht.

Götter und Tiere — alles Faxen.
Schöpfer und Schieber, ich und du —
Bruch, Katafalk, von Muscheln wachsen
die Augen zu.

Nur manchmal dämmert's: in Gerüchen
vom Strand, Korallenkolorit,
in Spaltungen, in Niederbrüchen
hebst du der Nacht das schwere Lid:

am Horizont die Schleierfähre,
stygische Blüten, Schlaf und Mohn,
die Träne wühlt sich in die Meere —
dir: thalassale Regression.

26

Du mußt dir alles geben

Gib in dein Glück, in dein Sterben,
Traum und Ahnen getauscht,
diese Stunde, ihr Werben
ist so doldenverrauscht,
Sichel und Sommermale
aus den Fluren gelenkt,
Krüge und Wasserschale
süß und müde gesenkt.

Du mußt dir alles geben,
Götter geben dir nicht,
gib dir das leise Verschweben
unter Rosen und Licht,

was je an Himmeln blaute,
gib dich in seinen Bann,
höre die letzten Laute
schweigend an.

Warst du so sehr der Eine,
hast das Dumpfe getan,
ach, es zieht schon die reine
stille gelöschte Bahn,
ach, schon die Stunde, jene
leichte im Spindellicht,
die von Rocken und Lehne
singend die Parze flicht.

Warst du der große Verlasser,
Tränen hingen dir an,
und Tränen sind hartes Wasser,
das über Steine rann,
es ist alles vollendet,
Tränen und Zürnen nicht,
alles wogengeblendet
dein in Rosen und Licht.

Süße Stunde. O Altern!
Schon das Wappen verschenkt:
Stier unter Fackelhaltern
und die Fackel gesenkt,
nun von Stränden, von Liden,
einem Orangenmeer
tief in Schwärmen Sphingiden
führen die Schatten her.

Gabst dir alles alleine,
gib dir das letzte Glück,
nimm die Olivenhaine
dir die Säulen zurück,

ach, schon lösen sich Glieder
und in dein letztes Gesicht
steigen Boten hernieder
ganz in Rosen und Licht.

27

Immer schweigender

Du in die letzten Reiche,
du in das letzte Licht,
ist es kein Licht ins bleiche
starrende Angesicht,
da sind die Tränen deine,
da bist du dir entblößt,
da ist der Gott, der eine,
der alle Qualen löst.

Aus unnennbaren Zeiten
eine hat dich zerstört,
Rufe, Lieder begleiten
dich, am Wasser gehört,
Trümmer tropischer Bäume,
Wälder vom Grunde des Meer,
grauendurchrauschte Räume
treiben sie her.

Uralt war dein Verlangen,
uralt Sonne und Nacht,
alles: Träume und Bangen
in die Irre gedacht,
immer endender, reiner
du in Fernen gestuft,
immer schweigender, keiner
wartet und keiner ruft.

28

Ein Land

Ein Land, ein dunkles Meer,
und dann ein Reich, das endet
so fern, daß nie sich wendet
ein Strahl hierher.

Ein Tag, ein zwitternd Licht,
Urängste, Todesdränge:
das Land der Untergänge:
kennst du es nicht?

Auf Sänften und auf Truhn,
da lagern die Gestalten,
die Schweigenden, die Alten
und künden —: ruhn.

Die nur durch Tränen sahn
das tägliche Vernichten,
doch auch die Frein, die Lichten:
sie spähn, sie nahn.

29

Dennoch die Schwerter halten

Der soziologische Nenner,
der hinter Jahrtausenden schlief,
heißt: ein paar große Männer
und die litten tief.

Heißt: ein paar schweigende Stunden
in Sils-Maria-Wind,
Erfüllung ist schwer von Wunden,
wenn es Erfüllungen sind.

Heißt: ein paar sterbende Krieger
gequält und schattenblaß,
sie heute und morgen der Sieger —:
warum erschufst du das?

Heißt: Schlangen schlagen die Hauer,
das Gift, den Biß, den Zahn,
die Ecce-homo-Schauer
dem Mann in Blut und Bahn —

heißt: so viel Trümmer winken:
die Rassen wollen Ruh,
lasse dich doch versinken
dem nie Endenden zu —

und heißt dann: schweigen und walten,
wissend, daß sie zerfällt,
dennoch die Schwerter halten
vor die Stunde der Welt.

30

Durch jede Stunde —

Durch jede Stunde,
durch jedes Wort
blutet die Wunde
der Schöpfung fort,

verwandelnd Erde
und tropft den Seim
ans Herz dem Werde
und kehret heim.

Gab allem Flügel,
was Gott erschuf,
den Skythen die Bügel
den Hunnen den Huf —

nur nicht fragen,
nur nicht verstehn;
den Himmel tragen,
die weitergehn,

nur diese Stunde
ihr Sagenlicht
und dann die Wunde,
mehr gibt es nicht.

Die Äcker bleichen,
der Hirte rief,
das ist das Zeichen:
tränke dich tief,

den Blick in Bläue,
ein Ferngesicht:
das ist die Treue,
mehr gibt es nicht,

Treue den Reichen,
die alles sind,
Treue dem Zeichen,
wie schnell es rinnt,

ein Tausch, ein Reigen,
ein Sagenlicht,
ein Rausch aus Schweigen,
mehr gibt es nicht.

31

Am Brückenwehr

I

„Ich habe weit gedacht,
nun lasse ich die Dinge
und löse ihre Ringe
der neuen Macht.

Gelehnt am Brückenwehr —
die hellen Wasser rauschen,
die Elemente tauschen
sich hin und her.

Der Lauf ist schiefergrau,
der Ton der Urgesteine,
als noch das Land alleine
im Schichtenbau.

Des Sommers Agonie
gibt auch ein Rebgehänge,
Kelter- und Weingesänge
durchstreifen sie.

Wessen ist das und wer?
Dessen, der alles machte,
dessen, der es dann dachte
vom Ende her?

Ich habe weit gedacht,
ich lebte in Gedanken,
bis ihre Häupter sanken
vor welcher Macht?"

II

„Vor keiner Macht zu sinken,
vor keinem Rausch zur Ruh,
du selbst bist Trank und Trinken,
der Denker, du.

Du bist ja nicht der Hirte
und ziehst nicht mit Schalmein,
wenn der, wie du, sich irrte,
ist nie Verzeihn.

Du bist ja nicht der Jäger
aus Megalith und Ur,
du bist der Formenpräger
der weißen Spur.

So viele sind vergangen
im Bach- und Brückenschein,
wer kennt nicht das Verlangen
zum Urgestein —:

Doch dir bestimmt: kein Werden,
du bleibst gebannt und bist
der Himmel und der Erden
Formalist.

Du kannst es keinem zeigen
und keinem du entfliehn,
du trägst durch Nacht und Schweigen
den Denker — ihn."

III

„Doch wenn dann Stunden sind,
wo ohne Rang und Reue
das Alte und das Neue
zusammenrinnt,

wo ohne Unterschied
das Wasser und die Welle,
das Dunkle und das Helle
das eine Lied,

ein Lied, des Stimme rief
gegen Geschichtsgewalten
das in sich selbst Gestalten
asiatisch tief —

ach, wenn die Stunden dann kommen
und dichter werden und mehr
Sommer und Jahre verglommen,
singt man am Brückenwehr:

laß mich noch einmal reich sein,
wie es die Jugend gedacht,
laß mich noch einmal weich sein
im Blumengeruch der Nacht,

nimm mir die Hölle, die Hülle,
die Form, den Formungstrieb,
gib mir die Tiefe, die Fülle,
die Schöpfung — gib!“

IV

„Bist du auf Grate gestiegen,
sahst du die Gipfel klar:
Adler, die wirklichen, fliegen
schweigend und unfruchtbar.

Kürzer steht es in Früchten,
früher, daß es verblich,
nahe am Schöpfer züchten
wenige Arten sich.

Ewig schweigend das Blaue,
wer noch an Stimmen denkt,
hat schon den Blick, die Braue
wieder in Sehnsucht gesenkt.

Du aber dienst Gestalten
über dem Brückenwehr,
über den stumpfen Gewalten
Völker und Schnee und Meer:

formen, das ist deine Fülle,
der Rasse auferlegt,
formen, bis die Hülle
die ganze Tiefe trägt,

die Hülle wird dann zeigen,
und keiner kann entfliehn,
daß Form und Tiefe Reigen,
durch den die Adler ziehn."

32

Einsamer nie —

Einsamer nie als im August:
Erfüllungsstunde — im Gelände
die roten und die goldenen Brände,
doch wo ist deiner Gärten Lust?

Die Seen hell, die Himmel weich,
die Äcker rein und glänzen leise,
doch wo sind Sieg und Siegsbeweise
aus dem von dir vertretenen Reich?

Wo alles sich durch Glück beweist
und tauscht den Blick und tauscht die Ringe
im Weingeruch, im Rausch der Dinge —:
dienst du dem Gegenglück, dem Geist.

33
Die weißen Segel

Die weißen Segel, die Bogen,
an Bord die leuchtende Fahrt
sind eine Art von Wogen
und eine Segel-Art.

Des hohen Tiers, des Einen
zentaurisch, ohne Qual,
der frühen Welt, der seinen
bei Rauch und Widdermahl.

Der Kiel im Elemente,
der Bug in Wurf und Wehr,
wer da noch Fragen kennte,
was ist wohl der —?

Wo Spill und Tau am Lager,
der Topp sich dreht im Nu,
wer spräche da dem Frager
wohl Wesen zu?

Und doch vor Flagg' und Fahnen
erhebe dich gedämpft:
auch dein Gefühl hat Ahnen,
du hast es dir erkämpft.

Keiner kann dich beschenken
weder mit Brot noch mit Wein,
dein ist Leiden und Denken:
so empfängst du das Sein.

Östliche Ströme durchschwimmen
uralte, zaubergebleicht,
westlich die Höhe bestimmen
selber, in die man reicht.

Wachen und immer bereit sein
dem, was Verwandlung verheißt,
bald wird die Erde so weit sein,
zu dir zu steigen als Geist.

34
Das Ganze

Im Taumel war ein Teil, ein Teil in Tränen,
in manchen Stunden war ein Schein und mehr,
in diesen Jahren war das Herz, in jenen
waren die Stürme — wessen Stürme — wer?

Niemals im Glücke, selten mit Begleiter,
meistens verschleiert, da es tief geschah,
und alle Ströme liefen wachsend weiter
und alles Außen ward nur innen nah.

Der sah dich hart, der andre sah dich milder,
der wie es ordnet, der wie es zerstört,
doch was sie sahn, das waren halbe Bilder,
da dir das Ganze nur allein gehört.

Im Anfang war es heller, was du wolltest
und zielte vor und war dem Glauben nah,
doch als du dann erblicktest, was du solltest,
was auf das Ganze steinern niedersah,

da war es kaum ein Glanz und kaum ein Feuer,
in dem dein Blick, der letzte, sich verfing;
ein nacktes Haupt, in Blut, ein Ungeheuer,
an dessen Wimper eine Träne hing.

35

Leben — niederer Wahn

Leben — niederer Wahn!
Traum für Knaben und Knechte,
doch du von altem Geschlechte,
Rasse am Ende der Bahn,

was erwartest du hier?
immer noch eine Berauschung,
eine Stundenvertauschung
von Welt und dir?

Suchst du noch Frau und Mann?
ward dir nicht alles bereitet,
Glauben und wie es entgleitet
und die Zerstörung dann?

Form nur ist Glaube und Tat,
die erst von Händen berührten,
doch dann den Händen entführten
Statuen bergen die Saat.

36

Wer allein ist —

Wer allein ist, ist auch im Geheimnis,
immer steht er in der Bilder Flut,
ihrer Zeugung, ihrer Keimnis,
selbst die Schatten tragen ihre Glut.

Trächtig ist er jeder Schichtung
denkerisch erfüllt und aufgespart,
mächtig ist er der Vernichtung
allem Menschlichen, das nährt und paart.

Ohne Rührung sieht er, wie die Erde
eine andere ward, als ihm begann,
nicht mehr Stirb und nicht mehr Werde:
formstill sieht ihn die Vollendung an.

37

Auf deine Lider senk ich Schlummer

Auf deine Lider senk ich Schlummer,
auf deine Lippen send ich Kuß,
indessen ich die Nacht, den Kummer,
den Traum alleine tragen muß.

Um deine Züge leg ich Trauer,
um deine Züge leg ich Lust,
indes die Nacht, die Todesschauer
weben allein durch meine Brust.

Du, die zu schwach, um tief zu geben,
du, die nicht trüge, wie ich bin —
drum muß ich abends mich erheben
und sende Kuß und Schlummer hin.

38

Anemone

Erschütterer —: Anemone,
die Erde ist kalt, ist nichts,
da murmelt deine Krone
ein Wort des Glaubens, des Lichts.

Der Erde ohne Güte,
der nur die Macht gerät,
ward deine leise Blüte
so schweigend hingesät.

Erschütterer —: Anemone,
du trägst den Glauben, das Licht,
den einst der Sommer als Krone
aus großen Blüten flicht.

39
Astern

Astern — schwälende Tage,
alte Beschwörung, Bann,
die Götter halten die Waage
eine zögernde Stunde an.

Noch einmal die goldenen Herden
der Himmel, das Licht, der Flor,
was brütet das alte Werden
unter den sterbenden Flügeln vor?

Noch einmal das Ersehnte,
den Rausch, der Rosen Du —
der Sommer stand und lehnte
und sah den Schwalben zu,

noch einmal ein Vermuten,
wo längst Gewißheit wacht:
die Schwalben streifen die Fluten
und trinken Fahrt und Nacht.

40
Tag, der den Sommer endet

Tag, der den Sommer endet,
Herz, dem das Zeichen fiel:
die Flammen sind versendet,
die Fluten und das Spiel.

Die Bilder werden blasser,
entrücken sich der Zeit,
wohl spiegelt sie noch ein Wasser,
doch auch dies Wasser ist weit.

Du hast eine Schlacht erfahren,
trägst noch ihr Stürmen, ihr Fliehn,
indessen die Schwärme, die Scharen,
die Heere weiterziehn.

Rosen und Waffenspanner,
Pfeile und Flammen weit —:
die Zeichen sinken, die Banner —:
Unwiederbringlichkeit.

41

Wenn dir am Ende —

„Wenn dir am Ende der Reise
Erde und Wolke verrinnt,
sie nur noch Laute, leise,
vom Himmel gefallene sind,

und nur noch Farben, getönte
aus einem wechselnden Reich,
nicht bittere, nicht versöhnte,
Austausch alles und gleich,

wenn dir die Blicke nach oben
und dir die Blicke zu Tal
schweigend das Nämliche loben,
schweigend die nämliche Qual,

schließen sich die Gesichte
über der lastenden Flut:
ach, die vielen Gewichte,
doch die Waage, sie ruht."

42
Gedichte

Im Namen dessen, der die Stunden spendet,
im Schicksal des Geschlechts, dem du gehört,
hast du fraglosen Aug's den Blick gewendet
in eine Stunde, die den Blick zerstört,
die Dinge dringen kalt in die Gesichte
und reißen sich der alten Bindung fort,
es gibt nur ein Begegnen: im Gedichte
die Dinge mystisch bannen durch das Wort.

Am Steingeröll der großen Weltruine,
dem Ölberg, wo die tiefste Seele litt,
vorbei am Posilip der Anjouine,
dem Stauferblut und ihrem Racheschritt:
ein neues Kreuz, ein neues Hochgerichte,
doch eine Stätte ohne Blut und Strang,
sie schwört in Strophen, urteilt im Gedichte,
die Spindeln drehen still: die Parze sang.

Im Namen dessen, der die Stunden spendet,
erahnbar nur, wenn er vorüberzieht
an einem Schatten, der das Jahr vollendet,
doch unausdeutbar bleibt das Stundenlied —
ein Jahr am Steingeröll der Weltgeschichte,
Geröll der Himmel und Geröll der Macht,
und nun die Stunde, deine: im Gedichte
das Selbstgespräch des Leides und der Nacht.

43
Bilder

Siehst du auf Bildern in den Galerien
verkrümmte Rücken, graue Mäuler, Falten
anstößiger gedunsener Alten,
die schon wie Leichen durch die Dinge ziehn,

brüchige Felle, Stoppeln, käsiger Bart,
blutunterflossenes Fett von Fuselräuschen,
gewandt, für Korn zu prellen und zu täuschen,
den Stummel fischend und im Tuch verwahrt;

ein Lebensabend, reichliches Dekor,
Reichtum an Unflat, Lumpen, Pestilenzen,
ein Hochhinauf wechselnder Residenzen;
im Leihhaus tags und nachts im Abflußrohr,

siehst du auf Bildern in den Galerien,
wie diese Alten für ihr Leben zahlten,
siehst du die Züge derer, die es malten,
du siehst den großen Genius — Ihn.

44
Ein Wort

Ein Wort, ein Satz —: aus Chiffren steigen
erkanntes Leben, jäher Sinn,
die Sonne steht, die Sphären schweigen
und alles ballt sich zu ihm hin.

Ein Wort — ein Glanz, ein Flug, ein Feuer,
ein Flammenwurf, ein Sternenstrich —
und wieder Dunkel, ungeheuer,
im leeren Raum um Welt und Ich.

45
Abschied

Du füllst mich an wie Blut die frische Wunde
und rinnst hernieder seine dunkle Spur,
du dehnst dich aus wie Nacht in jener Stunde,
da sich die Matte färbt zur Schattenflur,
du blühst wie Rosen schwer in Gärten allen,
du Einsamkeit aus Alter und Verlust,
du Überleben, wenn die Träume fallen,
zuviel gelitten und zuviel gewußt.

Entfremdet früh dem Wahn der Wirklichkeiten,
versagend sich der schnell gegebenen Welt,
ermüdet von dem Trug der Einzelheiten,
da keine sich dem tiefen Ich gesellt;
nun aus der Tiefe selbst, durch nichts zu rühren,
und die kein Wort und Zeichen je verrät,
mußt du dein Schweigen nehmen, Abwärtsführen
zu Nacht und Trauer und den Rosen spät.

Manchmal noch denkst du dich —: die eigene Sage —:
das warst du doch —? ach, wie du dich vergaßt!
war das dein Bild? war das nicht deine Frage,
dein Wort, dein Himmelslicht, das du besaßt?

Mein Wort, mein Himmelslicht, dereinst besessen,
mein Wort, mein Himmelslicht, zerstört, vertan —
wem das geschah, der muß sich wohl vergessen
und rührt nicht mehr die alten Stunden an.

Ein letzter Tag —: spätglühend, weite Räume,
ein Wasser führt dich zu entrücktem Ziel,
ein hohes Licht umströmt die alten Bäume
und schafft im Schatten sich ein Widerspiel,
von Früchten nichts, aus Ähren keine Krone
und auch nach Ernten hat er nicht gefragt —
er spielt sein Spiel, und fühlt sein Licht und ohne
Erinnern nieder — alles ist gesagt.

46

Wenn etwas leicht

Wenn etwas leicht und rauschend um dich ist
wie die Glyzinienpracht an dieser Mauer,
dann ist die Stunde jener Trauer,
daß du nicht reich und unerschöpflich bist,

nicht wie die Blüte oder wie das Licht:
in Strahlen kommend, sich verwandelnd,
an ähnlichen Gebilden handelnd,
die alle nur der eine Rausch verflicht,

der eine Samt, auf dem die Dinge ruhn
so strömend und so unzerspalten,
die Grenze ziehn, die Stunden halten
und nichts in jener Trauer tun.

47
V. Jahrhundert

I

„Und einer stellt die attische Lekythe,
auf der die Überfahrt von Schlaf und Staub
in weißen Grund gemalt als Hadesmythe,
zwischen die Myrte und das Pappellaub.

Und einer steckt Zypresse an die Pfosten
der lieben Tür, mit Rosen oft behängt,
nun weißer Thymian, Tarant und Dosten
den letztesmal Gekränzten unterfängt.

Das Mahl. Der Weiheguß. Die Räucherschwaden.
Dann wird ein Hain gepflanzt das Grab umziehn
und eine Flöte singt von den Zykladen,
doch keiner folgt mir in die Plutonien.“

II

Das Tal stand silbern in Olivenzweigen,
dazwischen war es von Magnolien weiß,
doch alles trug sich schwer, in Schicksalsschweigen,
sie blühten marmorn, doch es fror sie leis.

Die Felder rauh, die Herden ungesegnet,
Kore geraubt und Demeter verirrt,
bis sich die beiden Göttinnen begegnet
am Schwarzen Felsen und Eleusis wird.

Nun glüht sich in das Land die ferne Küste,
du gehst im Zuge, jedes Schicksal ruht,
glühst und zerreißest dich, du bist der Myste
und alte Dinge öffnen dir dein Blut.

III

Leuké — die weiße Insel des Achill!
Bisweilen hört man ihn den Päan singen,
Vögel mit den vom Meer benetzten Schwingen
streifen die Tempelwand, sonst ist es still.

Anlandende versinken oft im Traum.
Dann sehn sie ihn, er hat wohl viel vergessen,
er gibt ein Zeichen, zwischen den Zypressen,
weiße Zypresse ist der Hadesbaum.

Wer landet, muß vor Nacht zurück aufs Meer.
Nur Helena bleibt manchmal mit den Tauben,
dann spielen sie, an Schatten nicht zu glauben:
„— Paris gab dem den Pfeil, den Apfel der —"

48

Statische Gedichte

Entwicklungsfremdheit
ist die Tiefe des Weisen,
Kinder und Kindeskinder
beunruhigen ihn nicht,
dringen nicht in ihn ein.

Richtungen vertreten,
Handeln,
Zu- und Abreisen
ist das Zeichen einer Welt,
die nicht klar sieht.
Vor meinem Fenster
— sagt der Weise —

liegt ein Tal,
darin sammeln sich die Schatten,
zwei Pappeln säumen einen Weg,
du weißt — wohin.

Perspektivismus
ist ein anderes Wort für seine Statik:
Linien anlegen,
sie weiterführen
nach Rankengesetz —
Ranken sprühen —,
auch Schwärme, Krähen,
auswerfen in Winterrot von Frühhimmeln,

dann sinken lassen —

du weißt — für wen.

49
Nasse Zäune

Nasse Zäune
über Land geweht,
dunkelgrüne Stakete,
Krähenunruhe und Pappelentblätterung
als Umwelt.

Nasse Zäune,
Gartenabgrenzung,
doch nicht für Abkömmlinge
der berühmten Tulpe Semper Augustus,
die Paris im siebzehnten Jahrhundert mit unerhörten Preisen
bezahlte
oder die Hyazinthe „Bleu Passe"
(1600 fl. anno 1734),

man trug seinen Namen in ein Buch ein,
erst mehrere Tage später
führte einen ein Gartendirektor vorbei —
vielmehr für die alten bewährten Ranunkeln Ostades.

Nasse Zäune,
Holzfäulnis und Moosansatz
in der Stille der Dörfer,
kleine Ordnungszeile
über Land geweht,
doch Schnee und Salze sammeln sich,
rinnen Verfall —
die alten Laute.

50

Orpheus' Tod

Wie du mich zurückläßt, Liebste —
von Erebos gestoßen,
dem unwirtlichen Rhodope
Wald herziehend,
zweifarbige Beeren,
rotglühendes Obst —
Belaubung schaffend,
die Leier schlagend
den Daumen an der Saite!

Drei Jahre schon im Nordsturm!
An Totes zu denken, ist süß,
so Entfernte,
man hört die Stimme reiner,
fühlt die Küsse,
die flüchtigen und die tiefen —
doch du irrend bei den Schatten!

Wie du mich zurückläßt —
anstürmen die Flußnymphen,
anwinken die Felsenschönen,
gurren: „im öden Wald
nur Faune und Schratte, doch du,
Sänger, Aufwölber
von Bronzelicht, Schwalbenhimmeln —
fort die Töne —
Vergessen —!“

— drohen —!

Und eine starrt so seltsam.
Und eine Große, Gefleckte,
bunthäutig („gelber Mohn“)
lockt unter Demut, Keuschheitsandeutungen
bei hemmungsloser Lust — (Purpur
im Kelch der Liebe —!) vergeblich!

— drohen —!

Nein, du sollst nicht verrinnen,
du sollst nicht übergehn in
Iole, Dryope, Prokne,
die Züge nicht vermischen mit Atalanta,
daß ich womöglich Eurydike
stammle bei Lais —

— doch: drohen —!

und nun die Steine
nicht mehr der Stimme folgend,
dem Sänger
mit Moos sich hüllend,
die Äste laubbeschwichtigt,
die Hacken ährenbesänftigt —:
nackte Haune —!

nun wehrlos dem Wurf der Hündinnen,
der wüsten —
nun schon die Wimper naß,
der Gaumen blutet —
und nun die Leier —
hinab den Fluß —

die Ufer tönen —

51
Denk der Vergeblichen

Wenn ein Verzweifeln
— der du doch große Stunden hattest
und sicher gingst und viele Beschenkungen
aus Rausch und Morgenröten und Wendungen,
unerwarteten,
dir pflegen konntest —
wenn ein Verzweifeln,
selbst mit Zerstörung und Endverglimmen
aus dem Unergründlichen
in seine Macht dich will:

denk der Vergeblichen,
die zarter Schläfe, inngewendeten Gesichts
in der Erinnerungen Treue,
die wenig Hoffnung ließen,
doch auch nach Blumen fragten
und still Verschwiegenes
mit einem Lächeln von wenig Ausdruck
in ihren kleinen Himmel hoben,
der bald verlöschen sollte.

52
Satzbau

Alle haben den Himmel, die Liebe und das Grab,
damit wollen wir uns nicht befassen,
das ist für den Kulturkreis besprochen und durchgearbeitet.
Was aber neu ist, ist die Frage nach dem Satzbau
und die ist dringend:
warum drücken wir etwas aus?

Warum reimen wir oder zeichnen ein Mädchen
direkt oder als Spiegelbild
oder stricheln auf eine Handbreit Büttenpapier
unzählige Pflanzen, Baumkronen, Mauern,
letztere als dicke Raupen mit Schildkrötenkopf
sich unheimlich niedrig hinziehend
in bestimmter Anordnung?

Überwältigend unbeantwortbar!
Honoraraussicht ist es nicht,
viele verhungern darüber. Nein,
es ist ein Antrieb in der Hand,
ferngesteuert, eine Gehirnlage,
vielleicht ein verspäteter Heilbringer oder Totemtier,
auf Kosten des Inhalts ein formaler Priapismus,
er wird vorübergehn,
aber heute ist der Satzbau
das Primäre.

„Die wenigen, die was davon erkannt"— (Goethe) —
wovon eigentlich?
Ich nehme an: vom Satzbau.

53
Die Gitter

Die Gitter sind verkettet,
ja mehr: die Mauer ist zu —:
du hast dich zwar gerettet,
doch wen rettetest du?

Drei Pappeln an einer Schleuse,
eine Möwe im Flug zum Meer,
das ist der Ebenen Weise,
da kamst du her,

dann streiftest du Haar und Häute
alljährlich windend ab
und zehrtest von Trank und Beute,
die dir ein anderer gab,

ein anderer — schweige — bitter
fängt diese Weise an —
du rettetest dich in Gitter,
die nichts mehr öffnen kann.

54
Nur zwei Dinge

Durch so viel Formen geschritten,
durch Ich und Wir und Du,
doch alles blieb erlitten
durch die ewige Frage: wozu?

Das ist eine Kinderfrage.
Dir wurde erst spät bewußt,
es gibt nur eines: ertrage
— ob Sinn, ob Sucht, ob Sage —
dein fernbestimmtes: Du mußt.

Ob Rosen, ob Schnee, ob Meere,
was alles erblühte, verblich,
es gibt nur zwei Dinge: die Leere
und das gezeichnete Ich.

55
Worte

Allein: du mit den Worten
und das ist wirklich allein,
Clairons und Ehrenpforten
sind nicht in diesem Sein.

Du siehst ihnen in die Seele
nach Vor- und Urgesicht,
Jahre um Jahre — quäle
dich ab, du findest nicht.

Und drüben brennen die Leuchten
in sanftem Menschenhort,
von Lippen, rosigen, feuchten
perlt unbedenklich das Wort.

Nur deine Jahre vergilben
in einem anderen Sinn,
bis in die Träume: Silben —
doch schweigend gehst du hin.

56
Nike

Die Nike opfert — was enthält die Schale:
Blut oder Wein — ist das ein Siegesschluß,
wenn sie am Abend sich vom Liebesmahle
erhebt und schweigt und steht und opfern muß?

Sie senkt auf dieser attischen Lekythe
die Stirn, hat Pfeil und Messer abgetan,
wo blickt sie hin, erblickt sie schon die Mythe
vom Heiligen mit Pfeil: — Sebastian?

Sie schlug mit Zeus die Heere der Titanen
und stieß den Fels gen Kronos in der Schlacht,
Apollon, Kore zogen dann die Bahnen —
wem opfert sie — was sieht sie in der Nacht?

57
Kann keine Trauer sein

In jenem kleinen Bett, fast Kinderbett, starb die Droste
(zu sehn in ihrem Museum in Meersburg),
auf diesem Sofa Hölderlin im Turm bei einem Schreiner,
Rilke, George wohl in Schweizer Hospitalbetten,
in Weimar lagen die großen schwarzen Augen
Nietzsches auf einem weißen Kissen
bis zum letzten Blick —
alles Gerümpel jetzt oder gar nicht mehr vorhanden,
unbestimmbar, wesenlos
im schmerzlos-ewigen Zerfall.

Wir tragen in uns Keime aller Götter,
das Gen des Todes und das Gen der Lust —
wer trennte sie: die Worte und die Dinge,
wer mischte sie: die Qualen und die Statt,
auf der sie enden, Holz mit Tränenbächen,
für kurze Stunden ein erbärmlich Heim.

Kann keine Trauer sein. Zu fern, zu weit,
zu unberührbar Bett und Tränen,
kein Nein, kein Ja,
Geburt und Körperschmerz und Glauben
ein Wallen, namenlos, ein Huschen,
ein Überirdisches, im Schlaf sich regend,
bewegte Bett und Tränen —
schlafe ein!

NOTES

1. Mann und Frau gehn durch die Krebsbaracke

The seventh poem of the cycle *Morgue und andere Gedichte* appeared in March 1912, just before Benn passed his final medical examinations; the cycle caused sensation and scandal and made Benn famous overnight. His account of the composition of this series of poems reads: 'Als ich die *Morgue* schrieb, mit der ich begann und die später in so viele Sprachen übersetzt wurde, war es abends, ich wohnte im Nordwesten von Berlin und hatte im Moabiter Krankenhaus einen Sektionskurs gehabt. Es war ein Zyklus von 6 Gedichten, die alle in der gleichen Stunde aufstiegen, sich heraufwarfen, dawaren, vorher war nichts von ihnen da; als der Dämmerzustand endete, war ich leer, hungernd, taumelnd und stieg schwierig hervor aus dem großen Verfall' (*GW* IV, p. 45).

In this poem Benn is concerned to expose the medical lie which glosses over and renders harmless the horror of dying from cancer. A similar theme is found in the first Rönne story, *Gehirne* (1915): 'Wer glaubt, daß man mit Worten lügen könne, könnte meinen, daß es hier geschähe' (*GW* II, p. 13).

l. 10. By using the religious symbol of the rosary for the soft cancerous nodules in the dying woman's breast, Benn rejects all religious-transcendental solace, as he does in the other *Morgue* poems and the even more aggressive poems written during the First World War in Brussels (1914–17).

ll. 22 ff. The poem ends in the stoic resignation of biological naturalism, but parodies the biblical words: 'Von Erde bist du genommen, zu Erde sollst du wieder werden' (Genesis 3^{19}). 'Benn escapes from physical decay to the "superindividuality" of the organic, of the life force' (Hamburger, *Reason*, p. 281).[1]

[1] Michael Hamburger, *Reason and Energy* (London, 1957).

2. D-Zug

This poem was also written in 1912, and belongs to his collection of poems *Söhne* (1913), which was dedicated to the expressionist poet Else Lasker-Schüler (1869–1945). The poem is characteristic of Benn's dionysiac-orgiastic sense of life, 'a hedonism of the imagination as much as of the senses' (Hamburger, *Reason*, p. 285), and shows the influence which Friedrich Nietzsche's *Dionysos Dithyrambs*, with their visions of southern bucolic happiness, had on Benn as a young man. For him the modern civilized world is also stirred by this longing for *griechisches Glück*, for *Süden*, *Hirt und Meer*, the modern world as it appears in the express train which links Berlin to the Baltic resorts and the ferry port of Trelleborg in southern Sweden. This feeling is increased still further by the sight of the last days of summer, and the fields through which the train travels, where the corn has been cut and cleared away. Benn's awareness of the dying autumnal season appears from the exact dating of his journey back to Berlin—29 September. A typically expressionist feature is the identification of mankind with the tanned skins of those who have been on the Baltic, and the standardization of I and Thou in terms of *Männerbraun* and *Frauenbraun*, *Frauenhellbraun* and *Männerdunkelbraun*. By this means the individual sense of life becomes generalized and, particularly at the end, raised to a universal level, where the ego is eliminated.

l. 6. *Sichel-Sehnsucht*: neologism: longing for maturity, fulfilment, conclusion; 'yearning for the scythe' (Hamburger, *Reason*, p. 284). The scythe is the implement used for cutting grass, with which the prophet compares human life (Isaiah 40^{6}).

l. 8. *Stoppel und letzte Mandel*: the picture of a field where the corn has been cut and where, apart from the stubble, only one shock of corn is left standing.

l. 9. *Entfaltungen*: love unfolds one human being to another.

l. 10. *Georginen-Nähe*: neologism: the many colours of the autumn-flowering dahlia provide an external symbol for the inner passion of love.

ll. 12–15. Benn's typical dialectic: cynical longing for sexual union followed by the return to solitude of the artist who is dedicated to his work.

l. 17. *Resede*: the flower mignonette, perhaps used here as an imperative, which asks to be transformed into the scent of flowers.

3. Gesänge I–II

(First published in the leading expressionist periodical *Die Aktion* on 26 Feb. 1913, then in the collection of poems *Fleisch* in 1917.)

The first poem treats for the first time in Benn's poetry the motif of 'thalassale Regression' (from Greek *thalassa*, the sea; see poem No. 25, *Regressiv*), that is to say the longing to escape from modern existence, with its conflicts and excess of suffering, from the world of consciousness (*Bewußtseinswelt*) back to the primitive roots of biological life—a leitmotif of his middle poetry up to about 1932. His withdrawal from the world of consciousness into the silent world of the unconscious is expressed as a radical demand that the subjective consciousness should be transcended. He does not romantically turn to the animal kingdom, which 'in its suffering seems too close to man's existence, but to protoplasm, marine vegetation, and the mineral world.

The second poem condemns all impulses of the human emotions and spirit (love, mockery, despair, longing, hope) as *verächtlich*, but in suffering, on the other hand, he sees the distinctive characteristic of man, which links him with the divine. Though the mythical name is not mentioned, the image of the god with the panther evokes the myth and cult of Dionysus, where man is freed from his suffering and relieved of his individuality through ecstasy. In the final stanza the visions of Dionysus are linked with the motif of 'thalassale Regression', which can be achieved through dionysiac ecstasy, understood here only as an intellectual process. The significance of the Mediterranean, with its mysteries and myths, the 'griechisches Glück', is thus deepened in Benn's early poetry. The realm of the south and the realm of the unconscious, which is achieved through regression, are shown to be already identical here.

4. Englisches Café

(Publ. 26 Mar. 1913.)

In his early period the *demi-monde* of the Berlin late-night cafés with their dubious lady clients is portrayed in a series of cyclically arranged poems, of which he later rejected all but two: *Nachtcafé* (*GW* III, pp. 18–19), which, like all the others, criticizes the contemporary scene and anticipates the grotesque anti-bourgeois caricatures of the painter George Grosz, who later portrayed 'Dr. Benn' sitting in these surroundings, and *Englisches Café*. It celebrates the dionysiac-sensual ecstasy which is possible even in such encounters with women of easy virtue, whilst the sixth verse is illuminated by a great vision of the south. The journey he suggests is not real but imaginary, leading into the unknown and to be experienced in sexual union.

l. 7. A typical antithesis at this period between sex and brain, consciousness and sensuality.

l. 10. *Charme d'Orsay*: type of material (*Charmeuse* = silk or artificial silk)? Or a perfume? Perhaps freely invented by Benn.

l. 11. *Osterblumen*: daffodils. This refers to the pattern on the material which the woman referred to as *Ohrring* is wearing.

l. 14. *jasmindurchseucht*: neologism: 'filled with the scent of jasmine' ('durchseuchen': 'to permeate with disease or weakness'). Cf. *D-Zug* (No. 2): 'Eine Frau ist etwas mit Geruch'.
Ellenbeuge: the inside of the elbow.

l. 18. *In Rosenschwangerschaft*: neologism: 'filled, pregnant with roses'.

l. 20. *Asphodelentod*: neologism: in classical mythology the asphodel is the flower of death, which grows and flowers in Hades.

5. Untergrundbahn

(Publ. May 1913.)

Together with *D-Zug* and *Englisches Café* this poem is concerned with the problem of portraying the break-through of the dionysiac in modern civilization. The dionysiac experience of pleasure takes place in the journey by underground train, which is conceived as representing the journey both into Hades and into the darkness of the unconscious.

The point of departure is the experience of spring (verse 1), when the powers of nature stir anew, and from which even man cannot escape. For the 'lyrisches Ich' that is speaking here, these powers are embodied in the appearance of the *fremde Frau* (verse 2); she is praised in mythical and antithetical images, since in her the human is combined in essence with the vegetative, raising her, as female in contrast to male, into the ambiguous higher spheres of the *Götter* (verse 3). The journey of the underground train into the darkness of the tunnel finally breaks all connection with reality, and evokes a vision of an excursion into a vague, shadowy land of dionysiac release from the pangs of consciousness. Here Benn tersely poses the problem which tortured him all his life and which is closely connected with the problem of consciousness: the question of the existence and meaning of God: *Ein armer Hirnhund, schwer mit Gott behangen. / Ich bin der Stirn so satt.* Finally the accent is placed once more on 'thalassale Regression', sinking into the *Blau* (Benn originally wrote *Blut*) of the sea, whence the woman who is praised as *Meer-Blut* originates.

l. 1. *Blütenfrühe*: neologism for spring, 'early bloom' (*MGP*, p. 73).[1]

l. *Rot*: for Benn the colour of sensuality. His favourite flower was the red poppy. Identical with the *großes Blut* which rises in springtime.

l. 5. *Spann*: upper part of the human foot. In 1913 women were still wearing ankle-length clothes.

l. 7. *Geblühe*: neologism: a noun formed from the verb *blühen*, in praise of the beauty of the woman.

l. 9. *Rosenhirn*: neologism. In the woman, nature (roses) and intellect (*Hirn*) combine in indissoluble union, in contrast to the man, the *Hirnhund* (*l.* 14).

Meer-Blut: neologism; cf. *Erdenbeet* (*l.* 10), praising the unified natural qualities of the woman, for which the man longs. An indirect allusion to the myth of Aphrodite, who was born from the sea. Cf. Rilke's poem *Die Geburt der Venus* in *Neue Gedichte.*

Götter-Zwielicht: neologism: of the gods who vanished with the dawn of Christianity, there is only a faint trace remaining, here embodied in the woman.

l. 14. *Hirnhund*: neologism for the pain of consciousness. Cf. No. 6, *Ikarus* I, *l.* 21.

6. Ikarus I–III

(Publ. May 1915.)

A great trilogy composed during the First World War. It follows the tradition of the Icarus poems of Charles Baudelaire (*Les Plaintes d'un Icare*, translated by Rilke), Stefan George, and others, and more recently continued by W. H. Auden. It may have been inspired by the picture in the Brussels museum, *Landscape with Icarus falling* by

[1] *Modern German Poetry*, ed. M. Hamburger and C. Middleton (London, 1962).

Pieter Breughel the Elder. Benn reverses the classical myth of Icarus by not portraying his death as the result of his wicked flight into the heavens, a forbidden venture into the sphere of the gods, so that his punishment does not represent the condemnation of human *hubris* by the gods. For Benn, Icarus is the prototype of the 'modernes Ich', which can draw on the forces of nature but no longer on divine power. Icarus stands for the problem that was critical for Benn at that time, the attempt to free himself from his own ego in order to escape through voluntary self-destruction and self-sacrifice from the sphere of consciousness into the realm of the unconscious.

I. Icarus is lying stretched out in the midday sun in a meadow and picks a poppy, the symbol of dionysiac ecstasy. The 'panic hour' of noon arrives, as in Nietzsche's *Also sprach Zarathustra*, when individuality disappears in nature, into which Icarus *hinrinnt*, the time when the ego is freed from the world of reason and the categories of space and time. Benn's Icarus strives after 'Enthirnung' through the agency of the noontide, the *Weithingewölbter*, which he beseeches so earnestly; its burning heavens are identified with the sun, and he hopes to become part of nature itself (*das tiefe Mutterblut*). Man, now described more precisely as *hirnzerfressenes Aas*, is sharply contrasted with the animal world and with organic and inorganic life; he finds himself in a position of absolute nihilism: *mit Flüchen / im Nichts zergellend*. He longs for a prehistoric age to return (*Voraugenlicht*), when there was no human eye, no individual colours, but only the mighty power of the sun. As the world collapses, the *kotbedrängte Höhlen*, i.e. human eyes that have grown dim with the burden of the experience of life, should be absorbed and fused into it.

l. 5. *Weithingewölbter*: neologism for the vault of the heavens, adj. used as a noun.
enthirne . . . mein Auge: only by loss of the brain ('decerebralization'), of consciousness, is it possible to rise into the light and be saved from the suffering of this world. Lines 25–30 return to this image.

l. 6. *stillflügelnd*: neologism: 'gently soaring'; 'mutely winging' (*MGP*, p. 69).

l. 9. *Land-aas*: neologism: the arid, poor Mediterranean countryside, which appears as dead as an *Aas* ('carrion'), is nevertheless permeated by the *tiefes Mutterblut* of the powers of nature, in contrast with mankind, which has lost touch with them.

l. 13. *entstirnt*: neologism: 'decerebralized', formed from the prefix 'ent-' and 'Stirn'. For Benn 'Stirn' is identical with 'Gehirn'. Inorganic nature is fortunate in having no consciousness, but rather *Getragenheit* (*l.* 15); it reposes with itself. Cf. *Ikarus* III, *l.* 8.

ll. 18–19. Benn contrasts the vain curses of man, *im Nichts zergellende,* with the silence of the mountainside, which answers the sunlight with flowers. Like man and animals, the slope, too, is transitory.

l. 20. *Wächter*: the consciousness ('Gehirn') of man, which destroys his unity.

l. 21. *hirnzerfressen*: neologism: 'destroyed by consciousness'.

l. 22. *zergellend*: neologism: 'resounding, dying away'; 'plunged into annihilation' (*MGP*, p. 69).

l. 23. *veräfft*: 'derided, mocked'; 'guyed' (*MGP*, p. 69).

l. 26. *Voraugenlicht*: neologism. The light of prehistory, to which no human eye responded, since man did not then exist.

l. 29. *Sonnen-sonnen*: like the preceding image *das Rauschen / gebäumter Sonnen* and the last line, this repetition expresses the strength and power of the cosmic light, which surpasses the light of the earthly sun and in which Icarus soars and perishes.

II forms an antithesis to this: it introduces a retardation in this process and emphasizes once more the force of gravity and the bondage of man to his consciousness. The path to inner depths, the mystical closing of the eyes appears as a means of experiencing ecstatic union with nature and the absolute. This is preceded, however, by a final dialogue between the Ego and its Self, which must once again rise from the sphere of the 'süßes Tierische' of sensuality, into which it has allowed itself to slide, in order to transcend the world of consciousness.

III portrays the death of Icarus, his fall to earth, as a synthesis, a dionysiac mystery of death. Icarus now wears the *krokosfarbnes Kleid der Geweihten* like the priests of Dionysus in classical antiquity, and finds himself in the *Barke*, which symbolizes the boat of Charon. As one who has been transformed by the Mystery, who has escaped from life and the world of consciousness, he now possesses the plumes (*leichter Flaum*) which will carry him up until he falls into one of the burning stars which have been formed by cosmic light. His death in the flames brings about the desired unity with the absolute.

In all three poems Benn separates the lines with dashes, rather than commas and full stops, in order to emphasize the flowing action of this inner impetus as it opens itself up to the absolute.

l. 4. *ausrauschst*: neologism for the formation of new stars from the sun.
l. 8. Cf. *Ikarus* I, *ll.* 9 ff. The freed ego has become part of nature.

7. Reise

(Publ. 20 May 1916.)

In Benn's early poetry the island is often the place of sensual happiness, of release from the torments of the world of consciousness and of longed-for unity of man with nature, the unconscious, and the absolute. A favourite name for this island is Ithaca, the island of Odysseus, which the ancient sufferer reached in sleep after the wars of Troy and his adventures, guided by Pallas Athene, who appears particularly in Benn's late work as the goddess of the intellectual. In this poem it is an island in the North Sea, as described in his highly autobiographical short story *Die Insel* (1916), which he composed about the same time and which is closely linked in theme with this poem. There are also echoes of Rilke's trilogy *Die Insel. Nordsee* (1906) from his collection *Neue Gedichte*. This island, surrounded by the sea, is by its very nature a place of perfection; it bears, like the animals and plants that live in it, *ihr Sinn / im Mittelpunkt, den nichts beraubt*, since it has no consciousness to produce logical connections. On it shines the cosmic light, for which Benn's Icarus longs. In the second half of the poem (verses 3 and 4), the 'lyrisches Ich', which lies stretched out on the shores of the island, like the other *braune* and *besonnte* people and natural phenomena (*Flaches, das sich selbst benennt*) achieves separation from the world of man, from consciousness, and achieves transition into the sphere of the 'Blut', unity with the 'Mutterblut' of nature.

l. 2. *sternblau*: neologism. Benn had a predilection for 'Blau' as a 'Südwort'.
l. 6. *Alke*: the auk, a North Sea bird of the guillemot family.
gelapptes Laub: perhaps seaweed with its feathery strands.
ll. 9–10. As in the poem *D-Zug*, adjectives such as 'braun' and 'besonnt' stand for the people on the beach. In his desire for syntactical brevity Benn frequently omits the verb; we must add: 'Auch ich (gehöre oder lege mich) zu: braun!'

ll. 11–12. Benn's preference for the horizontal, his dislike of everything vertical and rising, is particularly marked here. Cf. *Der Ptolemäer. Berliner Novelle, 1947*: 'alles Vertikale hätte mir nicht gelegen — für Ebene, Wasser, horizontale Situationen hätte ich manches beibringen können, für das Unterbewußte, das Schläfrige, das Panische, für Waben, Gärten, die Mittagsstunde' (*GW* II, p. 245).

l. 13. *Verknüpfungsdrang*: neologism: the irresistible thirst for knowledge, with its urge to create logical connections both within the world of natural phenomena and between it and the perceiving ego, as in Kantian philosophy which Benn detested. Benn embodied this urge to analyse and examine traditonal concepts in the figure of Pameelen in his 'erkenntnistheoretisches Drama' *Der Vermessungsdirigent* (Brussels, Mar. 1916, *GW* II, pp. 322–50), who is destroyed by his *Verknüpfungsdrang*, whilst his opposite number Picasso, the prototype of the sensual artist, triumphs. In his story *Die Insel* (*GW* II, pp. 40–1) Benn describes in detail the workings of perception, which he calls the 'dritter Trieb', as well as the disappearance of 'Bezugssysteme' and absorption into dionysiac-sensual ecstasy.

l. 15. *Hautgesang*: neologism for sensuality.

l. 16. *Blut-Methusalem*: neologism: the ancient power of sexuality (*Hautgesang*) through which the archaic experience of unity is achieved, as in the poem *Untergrundbahn*. This metaphor is connected with Rilke's 'verborgener schuldiger Fluß-Gott des Blutes' and 'des Blutes Neptun' in his third *Duino Elegy*, written in 1912/13, but still unpublished in 1916. Both Benn and Rilke show the influence of the psychoanalysis of Freud and Jung.

8. Kretische Vase

(Publ. 1916.)

Benn's description of the classical earthenware vessel from the dawn of human culture, a subject which was then beginning to occupy him more intensely, as is also shown by his anti-classicist poem *Karyatide* (1916), is not an objective picture of a static nature, as used by Rilke in the so-called 'Ding-' or 'Bildgedichte' of his *Neue Gedichte* to portray classical and modern works of art. Benn evokes his picture by indirect reference to a succession of loosely connected images and uses the vessel to stimulate poetic visions. These reach their climax in a classical bacchanalian revel, which is then transformed into intellectual actuality and envelops the poetic ego.

The first verse, which lauds the ancient drinking-vessel as *blauer Ton-Zaun, Rosen-Rotte / um den Zug mykenischen Lichts*, raises it out of the sphere of mere utility by calling it *Un-geräte*, which is only used for religious purposes. The *Tränke-Sehnsucht*, which is embodied in it, the longing for dionysiac ecstasy, is further described as *weit verweht*, existing far in the past.

But the second verse sets in motion the poetic process of *Lockerungen*, the destruction of reality and the intellectual excitement of the lyrical ego, which is illuminated by the true significance of the animals, rocks, and plants portrayed on the drinking-vessel. They represent the process of *Freigebärung*, the emancipation of the ego which takes place in the Mysteries of antiquity through rebirth, and union with nature and unconscious vegetative life: *laue Schädel / wiesenblütig*.

The third verse marks the sudden change from rhymeless free verse to rhymes, and brings with it a torrent of pictorial associations, into which the lyrical ego is drawn. It experiences a process of release in the bacchanalian revels of the *Leda-Feste* (an invention of Benn's), the mingling and pairing of the divine and human.

l. 2. *Ton-Zaun*: neologism, 'blue enclosure of clay' (Penguin, p. 93);[1] cf. No. 49, *Nasse Zäune*: the work of art as an enclosure, here of the light of antiquity.

l. 3. *Zug mykenischen Lichts*: Benn regards the Cretan (Minoan) and the Mycenean culture of the third and second millenia B.C. as a unity; the light of Mycenae shines forth out of the Cretan vessel.

l. 8. *Hell-Entzwecktes*: everything on the vessel which embodies the process of *Freigebärung* shines *hell*, and, like the chalice itself, previously described by the neologism *Un-geräte*, is itself free from all earthly, everyday aims and ends (*entzweckt*: Benn's neologism); 'bright unpurposed things' (Penguin, p. 94).

l. 11. *Welle gegen Starr und Stirn*: the sensual and intellectual dynamism which proceeds from the artistic form (*Welle* — often also called 'Strömen') opposes the torpor (Benn uses the adjective *starr* as a noun) of the modern world of consciousness (*Stirn* = brain, consciousness).

[1] *Twentieth Century German Verse*, ed. P. Bridgwater, Penguin, 1963.

l. 13. *Vernichtungsmale*: 'stigmata of annihilation' (Penguin, p. 94), the wounds inflicted upon life by the *Bewußtseinshirn* (*l.* 14), to which also belongs the process of becoming (*Aufwuchs, l.* 14), since Benn is convinced that it should have remained in the original state of being.

l. 19. *Leda-Feste*: not a classical reference. Benn wishes to convey that the divine reveals itself in the mortal, just as Zeus, in the form of a swan, fertilized Leda.

rosenröten: an expressionistic neologism, a verb formed from 'Rose' and 'Röte' by analogy with the 'rosenfingrige Eos' of Homer to describe the 'Morgenröte'. It implies a new beginning set in motion by the dionysiac experience of ecstasy.

9. Pappel

(Publ. 1917 in the collection *Fleisch.*)

The poplar is the only tree to which Benn devoted a whole poem. It is also mentioned in his late poems (No. 48, *Statische Gedichte*). He is drawn first to the rigid compactness of its form (verse 1), which rises slim and stiff into the heavens like a 'Schrei', and then to its solitude: it always stands alone, never in groups or even *Pappelwälder* (verse 2). Thus it becomes a symbol for the expressionist poet who finds himself in a position of nihilism, for whom the *Himmel* are only *tote Räume* (verse 3).

l. 7. *Mispel*: Benn means the parasitical plant mistletoe (*Viscum album*), since he calls it *Samentöter*, rather than the harmless medlar (*Mespilus rosacea*).

l. 11. *enteinheitend*: neologism: the unity of form of the tree is destroyed by the *segnende* flashes of lightning, which divide what once was a tree (*Baumgewesenes*).

l. 16. *Kronenstirn*: the crown of the tree and the human forehead (= brain, consciousness) are identified here.

l. 18. *hinresedeten*: neologism: a verb formed from the flower name 'Reseda' (mignonette) plus the prefix 'hin', indicating direction. Benn was especially fond of the scent of the mignonette, as already seen in the poem *D-Zug* (No. 2, *l.* 17).

l. 19. *Vergang*: neologism: 'passing away, disappearance'.

10. Das späte Ich

(Publ. 1921 under the title *Der späte Mensch.*)

As in his essays written at the same time, *Das moderne Ich* (1920) and *Das letzte Ich* (1921), Benn links in this trilogy the individual problems of modern man (I and III) with a survey of the history of mankind from its origins to its final destruction (II). It was written at a time when Benn could well have read Oswald Spengler's *Der Untergang des Abendlandes* (vol. i, 1919), which attracted much attention and was of great importance for Benn's work, as he himself attested. The title of the poem indicates the position in which modern man finds himself at the end of a civilization. 'Das Ich ist eine späte Stimmung der Natur und sogar eine flüchtige' (*GW* I, p. 78).

l. 1. *Levkoienwelle*: neologism. See *l.* 5.

l. 2. A reference to Goethe's poem *Der König von Thule*, where the death of the king is described with the words: 'Die Augen gingen ihm über'.

l. 3. *Abgänger*, *Eigen-Immortelle*: cf. Benn's letter to Edgar Lohner, who gave a penetrating interpretation of this poem in *Passion und Intellekt* (1961, pp. 93–124): '. . . das späte Ich ist ein einsames Ich, auf sich selbst gestellt und nur sich selbst erlebend. Das ist ja das Zeichen seiner extremen Lage. Also auch die Unsterblichkeit, die Immortalität, endet für dies Ich mit seinem Tode, eine allgemeine objektive Immortalität gibt es für ihn nicht, die allgemeine Immortalität ist ein ideologischer, bürgerlich-kultureller, von Wohlwollen der Nachwelt und von Todesangst der Mitwelt geprägter moralischer Begriff. Es gibt ihn nicht für den finalen Typ, der nur in sich selber lebt, nur sich selbst gestaltet und sein Schicksal und seine Unsterblichkeit mit hinabnimmt, wenn die Stunde schlägt. Alles dies soll in dem vielleicht nicht glücklichen Wort „Eigen-Immortelle" sich ausdrücken oder zumindest durchschimmern. In dieselbe Richtung zielt der reichlich unpassende Ausdruck „Abgänger" in der gleichen Strophe, d. h. der Mensch ist ein Samenerguß ohne Befruchtungswillen und Befruchtungsmöglichkeit, er geht in die Nacht, aus dem Traum, ins Nichts und kennt keine Gemeinschaft, auch keine geschlechtliche mehr. Liebe ist das Elysium der Unproduktiven, derer, die nicht denken und Ausdruck schaffen können. Der Extreme in seiner Finallage gibt auch die Liebe nicht mehr ab, er behält sie für sich selbst' (19 Feb. 1952, *ABr.*, pp. 227–8).

l. 5. *Rosenletztes*: neologism: the poet perceives a *Welle* of ecstasy coming from the stocks (cf. No. 17, *Levkoienwelle*, where Benn develops the theme which is only touched on here); the 'letzte Rose' (the title of a popular song) is the sign of death and destruction. Cf. *Das letzte Ich* (1921): 'O Rosenletztes und Levkoien-Welle, und Holz und Erde, alles ist vertilgt, es schweigt um dich, wie es nie schwieg: die Menschen, Götter und die Sterne, du bist dahin und von dir abgetan . . .' (*GW* II, p. 99). 'Blumen tragen die Sonne, den Sommer und die Nacht, ich empfinde sie als durchaus tragisch: sinnlos und schnell verblühend' (19 Apr. 1952 to Hans Egon Holthusen, *ABr.*, p. 230).

ll. 5–6. *Fabel des Sommers*: the summer appears as the mythical time of maturity, which has now passed.

l. 7. *moi haïssable*: a quotation from Pascal, *Fragment* 455, 'Le moi est haïssable . . .': Pascal's reason for this contention is that the ego has made itself the centre of everything out of false self-love; it is the enemy of everything else and would like to be all-dominant ('chaque moi c'est l'ennemi et voudrait être le tyran de tous les autres'). Benn's work lacks all moral-religious condemnation of self-love; he uses the quotation from Pascal in the sense of an objective situation, where the late ego, which thinks and writes only with reference to itself, ruthlessly analyses itself and the world, is not a pleasant ego, but detestable in every respect, a fate which links it with Cain (see III, *l.* 14) and which it obstinately takes upon itself. 'Vier Jahrtausende der Menschheit sind gewesen, und Glück und Unglück war immer gleich. Wende dich ab von deinem Nächsten, wird die Lehre sein, wenn jetzt die Memnonsäule klingt' (*Das moderne Ich*, *GW* I, pp. 15–19 on the ego, describing it as 'überreif, faulig, giraffig, unbeschneidbar: ohne Glauben und ohne Lehre, ohne Wissenschaft und ohne Mythe, nur Bewußtsein ewig sinnlos, ewig qualbestürmt').

l. 8. *mänadisch analys*: the analysis of the ego and the world, executed with the rage of the maenads, which can lead to self-destruction and self-hatred (cf. *GW* I, p. 19). In Goethe's *Faust II* (*l.* 8772) Phorkyas abusively describes the chorus of the captured women of Troy who accompany Helen as 'mänadisch wild'. Benn, who criticized 'Begriffsmanie' very strongly (*GW* III, p. 79), later took up again and explored the theme of self-analysis in the three-verse poem *Levkoienwelle* (No. 17), using literal quotations from *Das späte Ich* I.

II presents a survey, formed from fragmentary images and associations, of the development of mankind, at the end of which is found the 'spätes Ich'. In the essay written at the same time, *Das moderne Ich*, in which Benn attempts to give a 'Biographie des Ich', he differentiates between the following stages of development: (1) animism, (2) polytheism, and (3) monotheism, to which the origin and development of human feeling for life run parallel. The first verse of the poem begins with the Flood, into which everything flows again at the end of the poem. He represents the beginning of the world as a time of myth, peopled by primitive, ape-like men and the first animals. This is followed by the development of the idea of God, a theme which Benn also discussed in the poem *Theogonien* (No. 15, 1925). Here it is derived from the concept of death, recollection (Plato's anamnesis?), and animal sacrifices.

l. 1. *Im Anfang war die Flut*: cf. Genesis 1^1 ff. and the story of the Flood, Genesis 6–8, widely discussed by ethnologists at that time (Edgar Dacqué and others). Which myth Benn is referring to in *Ein Floß Lemuren / schiebt Elch, das Vieh, ihn schwängerte ein Stein* has so far not be explained. It is not syntactically clear as to who pushes whom.
Lemuren: in classical Rome the name of the spirits of the dead; in zoology the animal lemur which is related to the monkey family. Benn appears to be using the second of these two meanings, cf. *Der Garten von Arles* (1920): 'Aus Antithesen-Spalt, aus Hirn-Riß, aus Monistisch-Aufgesprungenem: Lemuren-Ich, gesalbt vom Rauch der Herden, Brotbaumtitanen, Affentranszendenzen . . .' (*GW* II, p. 91). In his essay *Zur Problematik des Dichterischen* (1930) Benn mentions the new theory of evolution, which, in opposition to Darwin's theory of the evolution of man from the apes, maintains that 'Der Homo sapiens ist der Primitive, Grundform (aquatile — weißer Mensch — Affe — Lemure ist die neue Skala) . . .' (*GW* I, pp. 70–1). In this poem he also means by *Lemuren* the ancestors of man in the Darwinian sense.

The second verse describes the history of man in terms of animals, and contrasts the warlike Roman empire (*Adler der Kohorten*) with the gospel of peace of Christianity (*Tauben aus Golgathal*). The picture is widened to include the rise of classical culture around the Mediterranean, the cities of the Roman empire. These are not given names, but are linked by poetic association with Asia Minor (Syria) and Africa (*Traum des Baal*). Benn changes Golgotha, the hill of the crucifixion of Christ, into a valley (*Golgathal*), not merely because of the rhyme, but because with the teaching of Christ he connects the concept of 'Tiefe': in *Gedichte* he speaks of the 'Ölberg, wo die tiefste Seele litt' (No. 42, *l.* 10).

In the third verse the glories of Rome give way to decadence, the transference of the power of Rome to Byzantium (*Ost-Gerölle, Marmara-Fähre*), which is accompanied by the movement of works of art from one Mediterranean kingdom to the other, and the end of classical culture and its mythical inspiration from nature.

l. 9. *Ost-Gerölle*: neologism, referring not to geological changes in the western Mediterranean, but to the historical transference of power from Rome to Byzantium, which indicates decline: cf. *Das späte Ich* III, *l.* 12, and No. 42, *Gedichte*, *l.* 9: 'Am Steingeröll der grossen Weltruine . . .'. The image of the *Marmara-Fähre* extends this idea: the ferry links the European shores of the Marmara sea, Propontis of classical times, with the Asian shores, where Byzantium, modern Istanbul, lies on both sides of the Bosporus.

The first version of part II, in *Der Anbruch*, IV. Jg., No. 4, 1921, reads:

Welke Imperien, fallende Armaden.
Pästen der Nacht und tödliches Lagun,
Fiebermaremmen, Vendramin-Arkaden,
Da hältst du gern, wo die auf Städten ruhn

Und vom Gebein verwehter Karawane
Am Wasserschlauch die tote Hand, vom See
Kaspischer Steppen und der Hindostane
Immer der Klang der späten Niobe.

l. 10. *Pferde des Lysippus*: a four-in-hand made by the court sculptor of Alexander the Great for the island of Rhodes; it became the property of Rome after the Macedonian war. Benn was also possibly thinking of the varied fate of the four Roman bronze horses over the portals of Saint Mark's in Venice. These first decorated the triumphal arches of Nero and Trajan in Rome

(A.D. 117), and were then brought by Emperor Constantine to the Hippodrome in Constantinople in A.D. 350. During the Fourth Crusade in 1204 they were removed by the Venetians to Venice, where, however, they did not come to rest: Napoleon ordered them to be taken to Paris, and they did not return to Venice until 1815.

l. 11. *Blut des weißen Stiers*: perhaps referring to the sacrifice of the bull in the cult of Mithras, practised by soldiers and colonists in the Roman empire, which disappeared with the coming of Christianity. It plays an important thematic role in Benn's poetry, at this period (cf. No. 19, *Orphische Zellen*).

l. 12. *Amphitrites letztes Meer*: the end of the classical myth, whereby the sea is the dominion of Poseidon and his wife Amphitrite.

The fourth verse scornfully condemns the history of mankind, which is nothing but senseless decline (*Schutt*), cyclic recurrence, and a succession of *Bacchanalien. Propheturen. / Barkarolen. Schweinerein.* It ends where it began: in the Flood. The higher development of man becomes regressive once more, the end returns to the beginning.

l. 13. *Bacchanalien*: Bacchanalia, the Roman name for the festival of Bacchus and dionysiac orgies, which for Benn have here a negative meaning.
Propheturen: a derogatory neologism for 'Prophetien', or the office of prophet, cf. 'Professur'.

III. The *Seele*, the true centre of being of the 'lyrisches Ich', appears already to bear the mark of death (*um und um verweste*); on the one hand it is scarcely alive, on the other still *noch zuviel*, as Benn shows in a series of scarcely comprehensible 'negative Ordnungen', as Edgar Lohner calls the negated images in lines 3–5, after Thibaudet's concept of 'ordres négatifs' in Mallarmé's poetry. In terms of nothingness, lack of life and abundance of life are seen to be identical for the disembodied soul, separated from the world, and a mere shadow. On this verse see Edgar Lohner, 'Welt und Ausdruck des späten Ich. Interpretation eines Gedichts von Gottfried Benn', in *Germanisch-romanische Monatsschrift* 41, 1960, pp. 305–25; and *Passion und Intellekt. Die Lyrik Gottfried Benns*, 1961, pp. 113–18; also Else Buddeberg, *Probleme um Gottfried Benn* (Die Benn-Forschung 1950–60), Stuttgart, 1962, pp. 90–100.

This dialectic negativism in the modern soul is contrasted in the second verse with the poetic vision achieved in sleep and dream, which conceives death and the *Totenschau*, the evocation of the dead and the past in poetry, as *mythisches Glück*, like Novalis in his *Lied der Toten*. As early as 1918 Benn said in his story *Querschnitt*, when depressed by the sight of death in the First World War: 'Wenn wir aber lehrten den Reigen sehen und das Leben formend überwinden, würde da der Tod nicht sein der Schatten blau, in dem die Glücke stehen?' (*GW* II, p. 77). Thus here too he implies that the negative (death, Hades) is turned into something positive.

The third verse gives an example of how the past can be recalled through *Totenschau*: the mythical world of Peru is seen again. Cf. *Der Garten von Arles* (1920): 'Überall, wohin ich sehe, ist Peru: mit den Dschungeln, die dampfen, und mit dem größten Gummiwald der Welt; da sind Wüsten, in denen es alle neun Jahre einmal regnet, da ist Völkerschaft, Inka oder aus Tahiti, verschollen, fortgewischt, vertrocknet oder ersoffen, in Tiahuanaco am Titicacasee; da ist der Tempel überlebensgroß, trümmernd, fladenhaft aus einem Menschheitsteil verkrümelter Gehänge, mit Sinnbildern unenträtselbar an einem Tempeltor —: da ist kein Laut, keine Sage, kein Klang, kein Zeichen — da ist der Tempel, einzig und verworren' (*GW* II, p. 93).

After rising to visionary scenes in the second and third verses, where death and the mythical past are seen as happiness and arouse 'finale Lust', the poem ends in the last verse in a mood of bitterness and resignation. It contrasts the state of primitive man with the contemporary situation, this time with reference to biblical myth. Compared with the negative, desperate situation of the self-hating *spätes Ich*, the hatred between Cain and Abel leading to fratricide was still a *Bruderglück*, especially since their rivalry related to a God who was still visibly present for them, but who has now vanished. Between Cain and Abel there was for Benn only an inessential difference: 'Kain und Abel, Klante und Zoroaster, lächerliche Nuancen der gleichen Clownerie' (*Alexanderzüge mittels Wallungen*, *GW* II, p. 106). He was also fond of claiming ironically that the modern 'lyrisches Ich' was descended from Cain, referring to Genesis 4^{21}, according to which the 'Geiger und Pfeifer' were Cain's descendants. In 1952 Benn declared that it was 'eher Kain als Abel': 'es ist nicht indifferent, aber es ist nicht brüderlich, nicht kollektiv, sondern anachoretisch, nicht religiös, sondern monoman' (*Vortrag in Knokke*, *GW* I, p. 546).

***l.* 6. *blau*: Benn's favourite colour which for him evokes the south.**

l. 7. *Oleanderfarben*: white and red. White is for Benn usually the colour of the dead (cf. No. 47, *V. Jahrhundert*, I–III). Red is the colour of blood and the realm of the unconscious, also of sensuality and sexuality.

l. 10. *Bambusquoll*: in the *Gesammelte Schriften* of 1922 this read: 'der Bambus quoll'; the linking up of the two words into a noun, which perhaps arose through a printing error, was allowed to stand and thereby sanctioned by Benn in several editions (*Trunkene Flut*, *Gesammelte Gedichte*).

l. 11. *Inkaplatten*: neologism for the terraces of the Peruvian Inca buildings.

l. 12. *Mondchâteau*: neologism for a castle seen in a dream, analogous with 'castles in Spain'.

l. 16. *kausalgenetisch*: the *späte Ich* no longer feels itself caused and directed by God, like the ego of Cain, but suffers deeply from its bondage to the laws of causality of modern science, which Benn had always detested. Cf. his tirade against the 'Träger der positiven Idee, den kausalgenetischen Denker'—a doctor, against whom he had defended the idea of the unity of life (*Urgesicht*, 1929, *GW* II, p. 112).

11. Schädelstätten

Published December 1922 under the title *Schwer*, as the final part of a trilogy consisting of the poems *Schutt* (originally *Spuk*) and *Palau* (originally *Rot*). This marks the beginning of a new poetic form which remained characteristic of Benn's writing up to 1932: a long poem of contemporary criticism made up of eight-line, mostly trochaic or iambic verses, with a falling rhythm and feminine–masculine or masculine–feminine alternating cross rhymes.

The title of the poem, taken from the beginning of the fourth verse, is in the singular the German translation of Golgotha, in the plural means total reality, of both the past and the present, a place of destruction and death. Compare the end of Hegel's *Phänomenologie des Geistes*, where he says of history and knowledge: 'beide zusammen, die begriffne Geschichte, bilden die Erinnerung und die Schädelstätte des absoluten Geistes, ohne den er (scil. der sich als Geist wissende Geist) das leblose Einsame wäre; nur — „aus dem Kelche dieses Geisterreiches / schäumt ihm seine Unendlichkeit“ [a quotation from Schiller's *Die Götter Griechenlands*].'

In the first verse the present is described as a *Finale*, as the end period directly before destruction comes to pass. The ego finds itself in the very oppressive state of consciousness when it will be emancipated, and be *Vergessen*; it faces dying and death (*hangen, sich neigen*), and therefore the absolute, the *Unermessenes* and the *letztes Licht*, beyond which there are only the *Nächte des Nichts*.

The second verse contrasts with the *Halten*, the apparent continuity (or cessation, halting?) of worlds which are subject to the *Äonen-Bann*, the historical law of the rise and fall of civilizations (Oswald Spengler), the human consciousness of downfall, which is characterized as a specifically masculine attribute. Here we see the beginning of Benn's 'heroischer Nihilismus', which developed further after 1933. He poses the question of the nature of man during this final period, but does not answer it.

l. 14. *Waidmannsruh*: the name given to huntsmen's huts, often the name of restaurants in the woods around Berlin. Here an ironic image for death which follows silence.

Instead of giving a direct answer, verses 3 and 4 present a series of fragmentary images, which on the one hand illuminate the problematic elements in the modern personality, and on the other criticize in terms of bitter nihilistic negation the present situation in the West as a time of suffering and unbelief.

l. 18. *Punisch in Jochen*: Benn is referring to the Roman custom of humiliating prisoners by making them pass under a yoke of lances (321 B.C., Caudine yoke, punishment by the Samnites). A symbol for the suffering and mortification of man.

l. 19. *Heredität*: heredity: for the individual the predetermination of man through inherited characteristics, historically speaking a reference to the relationship between antiquity and the present, which Oswald Spengler had strongly emphasized in his *Untergang des Abendlandes*. The Roman yoke, that once oppressed the Punic people, has been handed down into modern times and inflicts only suffering and repression, giving no real freedom for the individual.

ll. 20–1. *kranke Knochen von Philoktet*: the suffering of Philoctetes, who was left behind by the Greeks on the island of Lemnos because of a snake-bite he had received on the voyage to Troy, is still effective today. Cf. Sophocles' tragedy *Philoctetes*. The image refers to the frailty of the ego and the decadence and morbidity of the West, where there is no longer either faith or happiness in the real sense—these have become *Fratze*, caricatures.

ll. 24–5. *Taube Noahs*: a reference to the estrangement of the present God; the divine promise of a new earth (Genesis 8^{8-12}) has no meaning.

In the middle of verse 4, however, there is once more a shift from abrupt negation to a poetic standpoint. The negative character of the present is described as *Schädelstätten*; it springs from the over-emphasis of consciousness, which has become *Begriffsmanie*. Benn sees no means of salvation either in the *Zeitwort* (verb) as the dynamic expression of becoming, which he strongly criticizes, substituting for it the static 'Hauptwort' (noun) as an expression of being which reposes within itself; or in *Historie*, history as the essence and place of becoming. He thus takes up an opposing position to Hegel's thesis at the end of the *Phänomenologie des Geistes* quoted above, according to which the salvation of man and his relationship with the absolute proceed from the unity of history and knowledge, the 'begriffene Geschichte'. Benn remains close to Hegel, however, in his affirmation of negativity, nothingness, and death, and when he draws on images from classical myth and cult, and demands that celebrations (*Panathenäen*) be held for everything that is *Vergessen*, *Verschmähen*, and for the unknown absolute, the *Unermessenes*.

l. 33. *Panathenän*: the most important festival of the Athenians for Athene, held in the Erechtheum on the Acropolis.

The fifth verse increases the number of these mythical-cultic classical images and builds up a 'Südvision' of a clearly ecstatic, dionysiac character. By affirming *Untergang* as a fate sent by the gods, the poem, which began with an elegiac lament, ends in the affirmation of the 'finale Lust'.

l. 37. *Danaë*: the mother of Perseus, who received him from Zeus in a golden shower of rain. An image for the ecstatic overpowering of man by the divine. A bull is to be sacrificed to her.

l. 38. *Leuenzüge*: beasts of prey, here lions instead of panthers, which are led by the maenads in procession in the cult of Dionysus.

12. Nebel

(Publ. 1924 in the collection *Schutt.*)

A love poem, dating from Benn's friendship with the 'Dänin' (see the Introduction, 'Benn's Life', p. 17) and lamenting the transitory nature of love, both the experience itself and the words that are uttered. The mists are used as an image for the fleeting nature of existence as they envelop and conceal everything (verse 1). The second verse, which explores a quotation from Villon, takes up a theme from Rilke's first *Duino Elegy* where the poet comments on lovers who see eternity in their nocturnal embrace: 'Ach, sie verdecken sich nur mit einander ihr Los' (*l.* 22). In the third verse, however, despite this realization that in love, too, 'alles gleitet und vorüberrinnt' (Hofmannsthal, *Terzinen über Vergänglichkeit*) *I*, the experience of love is made subject to the overriding law of supra-individual experience, imposed on mankind by the 'älteste Götter' and therefore raising the individual experience of love to the universal. This is represented at the end of the poem by the cultic symbols *Widder, Zweige, Altar und Opferstein,* which give the meeting of the two lovers and their vow of constancy „*immer und alles: du*" the character of a mutual self-sacrifice which is at the same time a sacrifice of life to the silent gods, who rule the existence of mankind (for the idea of love as a sacrifice, cf. No. 21, *Dir auch —*).

l. 12. *Neige d'antan*: quotation from the *Ballade des dames du temps jadis* by François Villon (?1431–after 1463) which tells of the transitory nature of female beauty and closes each verse with the refrain: 'Mais où sont les neiges d'antan?'

l. 15. *das Fließend-Entlehnte*: the destiny imposed by the gods which is given to man, so that it is *entlehnt* by him; like the mist it flows through him and passes on to others (cf. No. 57, *Kann keine Trauer sein, ll.* 21 ff.).

13. Entwurzelungen

Published September 1925 as the third poem of the five-part cycle *Betäubung. Neue Gedichte,* in which Benn describes the numbing and stimulating effects of different narcotics on the creative power of the poet, his dreams and visions. The accent shifts more and more from drugs to the purely intellectual 'Selbsterregung' ('auto-excitement') or 'Selbstentzündung des dichterischen Bewußtseins', incisively concentrated in the last poem *Schweifende Stunde* in the final words 'trunken zerebral'.

The poem is an elegiac lament over the impossibility of finding, through poetic, intellectual stimulus, an answer to the problem of death, which makes the human soul aware of its own insignificance, since it is no longer able to believe in religious promises of survival and immortality. The first verse asks where the poet can obtain salvation from his suffering and the transitoriness of human existence (*Tage und Alterungen*), when his attempt to rise through intellectual ecstasy above oppressive reality and free himself from it (*Entwurzelungen, Lösungszwänge*) has proved to be unsatisfactory (*vage*). After praising, in the preceding poem *Selbsterreger* (*GW* III, p. 119), the intellectual fascination inspired by antiquity and the Mediterranean, here he even questions these *Zersprengungen* which do not extend beyond a 'Sternentraum'.

l. 1. *Entwurzelungen*: the release of the ego from the soil of reality, in which its 'Wurzeln' were once firmly planted.

l. 2. *Lösungszwänge*: neologism. Benn does not mean hallucinations induced by 'Lösungen' = narcotics, but rather, as with *Entwurzelungen*, an inner compulsion to raise one's existence out of the customary bondage to modern reality in order to find poetry and a meaning in life.

ll. 7–8. *von den punischen Säulen bis an Astartes Grab*: Benn's vision of the south comprises here the Mediterranean of classical times, from Carthage in the west to Syria in the east, where Astarte was worshipped as the goddess of love, whose cult is also found among the Phoenicians. The reference to the *Grab* of the goddess is a mythological invention of Benn's, meaning that the goddess of antiquity is no longer worshipped in modern times. By these *Zersprengungen* is meant erotic ecstasy.

The second verse extends this elegiac lament and describes even the realm of nature as a release from *Verfallungen*, ecstatic feelings, which are only momentary. Here Benn chooses the image of a garden with a terrace, of which the balustrades are planted with stocks. The intoxicating effect of the scent of stocks was used in the image of the 'Levkoienwelle' in *Spätes Ich* I (No. 10), from which sprang a complete poem in 1925, *Levkoienwelle* (see No. 17). Through the scent of the flowers the release of the ego and its regression into nature become possible—

but no more: and it is for this very 'more', which cannot be explained further, since it is not known, that Benn longs. It has been *verheißen*, but remains unobtainable. The end is death, as the final image indicates, a gloomy gravestone with the warning inscription „*Du weißt*". It was not until long afterwards that Benn explained this very puzzling image in the poem *Epilog IV* (1949, *GW* III, p. 345):

> Es ist ein Spruch, dem oftmals ich gesonnen,
> der alles sagt, da er dir nichts verheißt —
> ich habe ihn auch in dies Buch versponnen,
> er stand auf einem Grab: „tu sais" — du weißt.

In the third verse the poem dies away in negations, resigned to the conclusion that there is for man *auf Erden* no experience of totality, that *niemand* can absorb everything, embody everything, and therefore become *alles*. This is developed to the conclusion that the soul is *Nichts*, that it is not destined to add anything but this *Nichts* to the highest peaks of existence, which the soul experiences as the *Blüte des Lichts* and the *Aue des Werdens*. It is the soul that introduces the experience of death to the fullness of life in nature. Here the connection between consciousness—in this instance of *Mord* and death—and *Nichts* becomes apparent.

l. 21. *Acheron*: mythical river in the underworld of the dead which, according to the belief of ancient Greece, separated them from the upper world of the living. Even nowadays the name for hell in modern Greece.

l. 22. *Kraut*: magic plant and narcotic. In a late essay *Provoziertes Leben* (1943, *GW* I, pp. 332–43), where he argues once more that intellectual life requires stimulants, Benn refers in a list of narcotics to 'Kraut der Gräber' (p. 333).
pythische Nacht: the darkness out of which came the prophesying voice of Pythia, the visionary at the Oracle at Delphi, who spoke in an ecstasy brought about by vapours from the earth.

14. Der Sänger

(Publ. 1925 in the collection *Spaltung*.)

In this poem Benn differentiates categorically between the modern poet and the poet of earlier times. Nevertheless, he gives both of them the rather old-fashioned name of *Sänger*, though in verse 3 he characterizes the poet of the past as a 'dualist'. In Benn's opinion the contrast between the lyrical ego and the world, subject and object, man and nature, was not felt in the classical-romantic poem, and the soul was simply reflected in nature or the world. On this traditional poetic form, which for him was rather obsolete, Benn spoke much later in his famous lecture, 'Probleme der Lyrik' (1951): 'Wir haben also zwei Objekte. Erstens die unbelebte Natur, die angedichtet wird, und am Schluß die Wendung zum Autor, der jetzt innerlich wird oder es zu werden glaubt. Also ein Gedicht mit Trennung und Gegenüberstellung von angedichtetem Gegenstand und dichtendem Ich, von äußerer Staffage und innerem Bezug' (*GW* I, p. 503). The modern poet, however, Benn calls *Zersprenger mittels Gehirnprinzip*, since for him the creative process of *Gestaltung* consists of breaking through reality, bursting and destroying logical, scientific, historical, and all other relationships by means of his perceptive intellect. Then the dualistic *Spaltung zwischen ich und du* (Kant's basic division between subject and object, the perceiving consciousness and the thing-in-itself, which Benn loathed) also becomes irrelevant for him. But he is not only a *Zersprenger*, but also at the same time a synthesizer, who 'mingles everything in his blood', i.e. absorbs into himself and allows everything to penetrate his unconscious, so that everything external is transformed into the internal. The poem begins in the first verse with a list of disparate features in the modern world: biological (*Keime*), philosophical (*Begriffsgenesen*), actual (*Broadways*), astronomical (*Azimut*), sport (*Turf*), and nature (*Nebelwesen*)—a selection which is not random but programmatical. The modern poet should not exclude anything from the actuality of his environment; everything that he encounters, facts and phenomena, concepts and images, must be transmuted and included in his poetry. The free arrangement of nouns in the modern poem gives it a characteristic loosely assembled appearance ('Montage'). It is also emphasized that the poet must continually apply himself to the *Wort*, to language.

In verse 2 Benn repeats his thesis that lyrical poetry depends on a heightening of intellectual and spiritual consciousness, which he symbolizes here in the stimulant caffeine. The aim of the modern poet to achieve *Vergessen* of dualism and experience unity appears as an attitude which is incomprehensible to other people. The third verse follows the antithesis of the *Sänger* of the past and today with a picture of the creative process by which the poem arose. In his heightened state of consciousness the poet finds himself at the centre of the world—Benn also calls this condition 'Totalisation'—and creates a new synthesis in the poem, which thus arises from a dialectical process of bursting and mingling, in which the intellect and feeling, consciousness and ecstasy are equally involved. This tissue of images and visions created by the poet Benn calls a *Traum*, in the sense of Friedrich Nietzsche's aesthetics in his *Die Geburt der Tragödie aus dem Geiste der Musik* (1871), with its differentiation between the dionysiac 'Rauschkunst' (see verse 2) and the apollonian 'Traumkunst'. Finally Benn emphasizes from his own experience the infrequent and slow creation of modern poems and the heaviness of the *Substanzen* of the lyrical ego, which has to endure deep suffering and the experience of death before it can become creative. Added to this is the nihilistic situation in which lyrical poems are created today. The modern *Sänger* holds his poem out *ins Nichts* and answers the void in the form of a challenge. As late as 1952 Benn said: 'Kein Zweifel, das moderne Gedicht ist monologisch, es ist ein Gedicht ohne Glauben, ein Gedicht ohne Hoffnung, ein Gedicht aus Worten, die Sie faszinierend montieren. . . . Das Gedicht ist also absolut — gerichtet an das Nichts' (*Vortrag in Knokke*, *GW* I, pp. 547 ff.).

l. 1. *Keime*: the biological concept of the germ, here a substitute for the question of the origin of the world and man.
Begriffsgenesen: philosophical-ideological questions of the origin of human thought and consciousness.

l. 2. *Broadways*: image for the modern city. Benn liked to call himself a 'Citylyriker'.
Azimut: astronomical sector on the horizon between the observer's meridian and the vertical circle through a star. Here an image symbolizing the relationship of man to higher spheres of transcendence.

l. 3. *Turf*: 'racecourse'. By adding *wesen* he extends this to a general word for horse-racing.
Nebelwesen: cf. No. 12, *Nebel*.

l. 9. *Neurogene*: relating to the nerves.
Leier: from classical times an image for the lyrical poet.

l. 10. *Hyperämien*: increase in the blood-supply to a human organ or tissue, here to the poet's brain, which thus stimulates him into creativity.

l. 11. *Blutdruckschleier*: neologism. The taking of caffeine leads to an increase in blood-pressure (hypertonia) which 'verschleiert' the external view and turns one's attention to inner images.

l. 20. *Gehirnprinzip;* neologism. The analysing activity of the intellect.

15. Theogonien

(Publ. in 1925 in the collection *Spaltung*.)

For Benn the question of the 'Begriffsgenesen', which preoccupied him from 1920 onwards, was linked with the question of the origin of myths. This is the subject of this poem, which deals solely with the realm of actual human beliefs in nature of early polytheism. The concept of theogony, the origin of the gods, is derived from the Greek epic writer Hesiod (*c.* 700 B.C.), who wrote a didactic poem with this title on the gods which makes the attempt, characteristic of all polytheistic religions, to combine the multitude of divinities worshipped in different localities. Benn uses this word in the plural, since he extends his gaze beyond Mediterranean antiquity and the *weiße Völker* to include all the peoples of the earth and their myths, represented here by the *Rote* (Algonquin Indians).

The first verse develops from the resonant word *Theogonien* Benn's characteristic thesis that divine and mythical characters have been born out of human misery and grief. Men in the past, brought low by *Knechtschaft und Qual*, tried to give their life a meaning by projecting in the heavens divine figures filled with superhuman power and strength, as foils to their own existence. Benn's ideas are linked with those of the philosopher Ludwig Feuerbach (1804–72), according to whom God was the creation of man, in whom he embodied his own being and made it absolute. In contrast with the ethnologists, however, Benn does not derive these ideas about the gods from fear. In the second verse he describes the highest God of heaven, whom he calls the universally recognized *Er*, in images which depict him as the ruler of heaven and earth and the judge of the *Bösen*. In the third verse he also refers to the myths of the Flood and the migrations, a theme which he also treated in the same year in the poem *Meer- und Wandersagen* (*GW* III, pp. 66–7), which depicted particularly the South Seas (Polynesia). The fourth verse describes these myths, in a concluding mood of resignation, as an escape from the experience of pain and death into *Traum*, which today has lost all its reality and can only continue to exist in the 'Traum des Gedichts'.

l. 5. *Drachen*: the enemies of the gods in many religions; in the Old Testament, Leviathan (Job 41; Isaiah 27[1]), the personification of the primeval sea which encircles the earth.

l. 6. *Brände*: worship of fire (the myth of Prometheus), e.g. among the Persians and the Indian races of North America.

Baal: Semitic name, the lord of heaven, fire, and thunder, originally identical with the lustful, roaring bull, which was worshipped by the Babylonians, Syrians, and Phoenicians in orgiastic cults. In Israel he was known from the Canaanites (1 Kings 18[26]).

l. 11. *Widder*: ram, sacrificial animal.

l. 15. *den Bittern*: noun: those who offer pleas and prayers to the divinity in order to be spared, an attitude which Benn rejects as human arrogance. (Cf. the conversation piece *Die Stimme hinter dem Vorhang*, 1951, *GW* II, p. 440.)

l. 17. *Fluten, Elche*: cf. No. 10, *Das späte Ich* II, *ll.* 1–2, where the Flood and the elk are also named together as primeval beings.

l. 21. *Möwentum*: neologism, comparing primitive men who travel across the sea into the unknown with the seagulls: just as these seek a *Körnchen*, a *Krume* of bread, so men seek an *Insel auf dem Meer* where they can land, and which appears to them as a gift from the gods on high.

l. 27. *des Kummers Weiden*: metaphor: suffering mankind is the pasture-land on which the personified affliction feeds.

l. 28. *Algonkin*: great Indian language group which formerly inhabited the north-east of North America and the Atlantic coast. These tribes lived as maize farmers in the forests or as buffalo hunters; they believed in a 'großer Geist' or Manitu, who inhabits and rules everything, and reveals himself particularly in animals and men, who worship him through asceticism and ecstasy and acquire supernatural powers. Most of the images in verse 2 are derived from these myths. In his essay *Zur Problematik des Dichterischen* (1930) Benn referred to Manitu, and with total resignation with regard to the fate of the ancient myths in the present, he said: 'Es gibt nur den Einsamen und seine Bilder, seit kein Manitu mehr zum Clan erlöst' (*GW* I, p. 82).

l. 29. *Tiere*: reference to human animal cults. Benn usually has the worship of the bull in mind.

Steine: stone cults, as e.g. in the early history of Israel. Benn was particularly fascinated by the worship of the black stone of the Ka[a]ba in Mecca by the Arabs, the inscription on which he quotes with approval: 'Nimm uns im Schatten Deines Thrones auf an dem Tag, an dem kein anderer Schatten mehr sein wird als Dein Schatten' (*Roman des Phänotyp*, 1944, *GW* II, p. 163).

16. Schleierkraut

(Publ. 1925 in *Spaltung*.)

The white, pink, or red flowering shrub gypsophila is invoked, *die Stunde anzurauschen*, i.e. the *Stunde* of creation, in other words to invoke it as a state of ecstasy. But through this intoxication the gypsophila also awakens a sense of transitoriness, with which life is contrasted in the first verse. Benn uses the maxim *Brückenschlagen / über Ströme, die vergehn* to describe this life, contrasting the river which embodies transience and its bridge with all that is permanent and indestructible. Since Goethe's *Märchen* the bridge over the river has been a poetic symbol, and in Nietzsche's poem *Venedig* and Hofmannsthal's lyric drama *Das kleine Welttheater* it became the place where poetic consciousness of self was experienced (cf. No. 31, *Am Brückenwehr* I–IV, 1934). The second verse portrays the transformation into *Ewigkeit* of the autumnal moment of creation. The autumn and its flowers exchange glances which are far removed from the death that faces them, and eagerly await eternity, whilst from the sea, the symbol of the absolute (and unconscious), comes the *Ruhelose*, i.e. fate in the form of sound and light.

The third verse concludes with the motif of death: the *tief* melody of fate, the *Ruhelose*, ends the intoxication of the gypsophila, which also now wilts and dies; its place is taken by silence as a sign that fate has been fulfilled. The question of what follows a life that has been made complete through achievement remains unanswered.

l. 6. *die Ferne sehn*: by looking at things that are far away, distance from objects in the immediate environment is effected, awakening consciousness of the nature of existence. Cf. Rilke's *Sonette an Orpheus* II, 29, 'Stiller Freund der vielen Fernen . . .'.

l. 14. *das Ruhelose*: the law of change and fate which characterizes all life, the subject of Benn's oratorio *Das Unaufhörliche* (written in 1931 for Paul Hindemith).

l. 15. *Schären*: islands and cliffs on the Baltic coast of Sweden.

l. 20. *Silence panique*: 'panic silence', the stillness of noontide, when the ancient god of shepherds, Pan, is asleep and his pipes are silent. In his aphorism *Am Mittag* Nietzsche calls the experience of this moment a 'Tod mit wachen Augen', when man sees 'was er nie sah' and experiences 'ein schweres Glück' (*Menschliches, Allzumenschliches* II, No. 308).

l. 22. *Blutplateau*: neologism. Metaphor for the life for which space is created by building a poetic bridge, and which is thus extended beyond mortality.

17. Levkoienwelle

(Publ. 1925 in *Spaltung*.)

This poem is a variation on a theme already treated by Benn, for it begins with a quotation from *Das späte Ich* I (No. 10). The problems of the situation in which the ego finds itself in the final period are taken up again, but this time in a more conciliatory tone. The movement of the ego, which derives from the stocks and last roses, is described in images well known *von früher her*, and which reappear in autumn. *Die alte Wunde* reopens, the suffering of the ego from its own consciousness, the delusion of self-analysis („*mänadisch analys*"), and the unanswerable questions about the nature of the world and man. The second verse opposes the illusion that man is able from within himself to develop his *Selbst* to become a personality (*Selbstgestaltung*), simply by following his own reason as the highest power of his own intellect, unfolding and developing his own entelechy (*Selbstentfaltung der Vernunft*), as taught by the German idealists (Goethe, Schiller, Hegel), whose concepts Benn criticizes here. He describes this idea as a 'tiefer Traum', but denies any reality to it, and then rejects it as a foolish pattern of thought, unmasks the idea of human *Selbst* as a mere *Trick*, and calls the concept of *Geist* a mere convention of the philosophers (*Zunft*). This belief in the possibility of human self-determination, which he also declared to be out of date in his essays on the problem of the personality, is opposed by a demand for self-rejection: the rejection of the ego and its firm roots in a particular place in existence, and devotion to the intoxication which comes from nature, which leads to death, as the third verse shows.

l. 8. *sich um Rosenletztes spielt*: verbal neologism, analogous with 'sich um etwas drehen'. In the centre of the artistic activity of asking and forming, which Benn likes to call 'Spiel', stands the problem of transience and death.
Rosenletztes: cf. No. 10, *Das späte Ich* I, *l.* 5.

l. 11. *Schaltung*: technological image, here symbolizing the false pattern of thought which leads to a 'Kurzschluß'; Berlin slang expression: 'er hat falsch (oder: nicht) geschaltet' for 'er hat falsch (oder: nicht) verstanden'.

l. 12. *Zunft*: since the Middle Ages the name of the handworkers' guilds, here used negatively for university philosophers.

l. 21. *lernäisches Gelände*: a realm in which the highest ecstasy of life passes into death. Lerna is the name of a river and a very fertile marshy area twelve miles south of Argos in Argolis, with the Lernaean spring, where lived the nine-headed Hydra which Hercules killed. According to Pausanias this was the entrance to the underworld, which Pluto used after the rape of Persephone. Her mother Demeter Lernaia (Ceres) was worshipped there at the festival of the Lernaeae.

18. Dunkler

(Publ. 1925 in *Spaltung*.)

An evening hour, insurpassable in its gloom and gradually turning into complete darkness, leads to the experience of release from the world and the ego and the premonition of death, of sinking into nothingness. The first verse speaks of the heaviness of this unique hour, which is later made absolute, and which is drawn by *alle Lasten der Erde* into the finality of night which appears to man as a *fremd*, ruthless enemy power. In it everything that has been shaped, formed, and delimited (*Figuren*) loses its own being and melts indistinguishably into a single *große Gestalt*. At the same time the hands of death threaten man. The release of man from *Dinge*, the formless *Figuren* of the Western world, imposes on him, as the second verse describes, a *fahles Los*, so that he can only see things in the pale hues of death. The symbols of death are the *Trauermäntel* (Camberwell Beauties), dark butterflies that hover around the *Mund* of the poet and thus reduce him to silence, which paralyse his *Schoß*, his sensual powers, and make them impotent. Consciousness, which reduces everything to its basic components (*Einzelbaum*) and then analyses (*faltet*) the details (*Blätter*), is destructive, for a synthesis of things in the *Trance-Traum* of the poem is no longer possible: the poet cannot connect things any more, he is no longer a *Verketter*. The third verse summarizes these ideas in the image of the *Bewußtseinsbresche*, the gap which human thinking has left behind after it has violently broken through reality as it is. In this gap myth becomes visible once more, only to disappear from sight again: out of *Ahnung*, longing, rise silently the mythical symbols of a world that has been saved, in which God and man are firmly established, where God promises man salvation and eternal life: the Germanic ash-tree of the universe, Yggdrasil, and the rod of Aaron from the Old Testament. This promise of a happy life (*Promesse du bonheur*) has no longer any validity, as the fourth verse shows, for the lonely late ego which sees through the promise and realizes that it is totally empty and *ewig unerfüllt*. All that he knows is that not only this particular hour of darkness, which was the starting-point of the poem, but also *jede Stunde* will be hard and oppressive, when the unique, particular experience will be raised to the general.

l. 4. *fremde Nacht*: cf. Hölderlin's elegy *Brot und Wein* I, *ll.* 15–18:

> . . . die Schwärmerische, die Nacht kommt,
> Voll mit Sternen und wohl wenig bekümmert um uns
> Glänzt die Erstaunende dort, die Fremdlingin unter den Menschen,
> Über Gebirgeshöhn traurig und prächtig herauf.

l. 5. *sich enteignen*: the reflexive form is a neologism: 'to give up one's own being'.

l. 7. *Lemuren*: here clearly the ghosts of the dead in the Roman sense (cf. No. 10, *Das späte Ich* II, *l.* 1).

l. 8. *Schattenwald*: metaphor for the kingdom of the dead, Hades.

l. 10. *Los*: fate.

l. 11. *Trauermäntel*: *Nymphalis antiopa*, Camberwell Beauties, butterflies with dark brown, white, or yellow-bordered wings.

l. 14. *Einzelbaum*: symbol for details, separate items (cf. No. 9, *Pappel*).

l. 15. *Verketter*: neologism: the poet as synthesizer, 'coupler' (Penguin, p. 98) (cf. No. 14, *Der Sänger*).

l. 16. *Trance-Traum*: combination of ecstasy and dream in the creative process, which leads to the composition of the poem.

l. 17. *Bewußtseinsbresche*: neologism: the hole that the consciousness has violently torn in the relationships between the objects of the world and between the ego and the world.

ll. 19–20. *Weltenesche Yggdrasil*: in Norse mythology the tree of the universe which supports and holds together the heaven and the earth from the centre of the earth: 'immer in grünem Laub, über dem Brunnen der Urd' (the goddess of fate; from the Völuspá).

ll. 21–24. *Aarons Rute*: cf. Numbers 17^{1-13}, where Moses at God's command placed twelve dry rods in the sanctuary of the Ark. As a sign that Aaron and the Levites had been chosen, God made only Aaron's rod grow green, blossom, and bear almonds. This rod was placed in the Ark as a sign that the children of Israel would not die.

l. 23. *Wunderblut*: the sap which God awoke in the dry rod. Blood was the sign that Israel had been chosen (Exodus 12^{22} ff.).

l. 28. *Promesse du bonheur*: promise of happiness.

19. Orphische Zellen

(Publ. 1927 in *Gesammelte Gedichte.*)

The theme of this often-quoted poem is a double question about the nature of ancient sacrificial rites and the ecstatic cults surrounding the mysteries, which once gave man the experience of unity with the divine, and the possibility of a renewal of these experiences. Benn claims here that these archaic forms of experience, which gave life a higher consecration and are lacking in the modern world, to its detriment, can still be experienced again, since they merely lie dormant in the *orphische Zellen* of the human brain stem as 'Archetypen', primeval images, until the poet is able to awaken them again through introversion. Behind this lies the teaching of the psychoanalyst C. G. Jung, that the total spiritual and intellectual heritage of human evolution lies hidden in the 'kollektives Unbewußte', an archaic region of the soul which is present in all human beings, and can be reawakened by the language of art. In his essay *Der Aufbau der Persönlichkeit, Grundriß einer Geologie des Ich* (1930), Benn repeated the thoughts expressed in the first verse of this poem: 'Wir tragen die frühen Völker in unserer Seele, und wenn die späte Ratio sich lockert, in Traum und Rausch, steigen sie empor mit ihren Riten, ihrer prälogischen Geistesart und vergeben eine Stunde der mystischen Partizipation. Wenn der logische Oberbau sich löst, die Rinde [sc. des Großhirns], müde des Ansturms der vormondalten Bestände, die ewig umkämpfte Grenze des Bewußtseins öffnet, ist es, daß das Alte, das Unbewußte erscheint in der magischen Ichumwandlung, im frühen Erlebnis des Überall und des Ewigseins' (*GW* I, p. 99).

This longing for the dawn of humanity with its high intensity in relation to life and death is evoked in the first verse by a series of archetypal images of sacrificial rites and narcotics which produce ecstasies.

l. 1. *orphisch*: secret, in the sense of the ancient Orphic mysteries, in whose rites the experience of death was anticipated, and

their doctrine of salvation, which promised man deification through ecstasy.
Zellen: brain cells.

In Benn's late work, the conversation piece *Drei alte Männer* (1948), he repeated this idea: 'In unserem Gehirn liegt die Vorwelt gesammelt mit ihren verdeckten Kräften, aus seinen Nähten, Lötstellen, Rissen stößt sie gelegentlich vor: im Rausch, im Traum, in Trancezuständen, in gewissen Geisteskrankheiten — jedenfalls ist sie da, alle jene Zeiten und Zustände sind da, als Außen und Innen noch nicht getrennt waren, Gott und Nicht-Gott noch vereint, die unerträglich gewordene Spannung zwischen Ich und Welt noch unerklungen — sie ist da jene Prähistorie der Wirklichkeit, in der der akausale Beziehungswahn sein Arkadien feiert . . .' (*GW* II, pp. 403–4).

l. 2. *Okzident*: Europe in contrast to the Orient.

l. 3. *Fisch*: in classical times a sacrifice made to the gods of the underworld and an offering for the dead.
Wein: the libation of wine in connection with the cult of Dionysus, offered in classical times to the gods at every meal, and still found in Greece as an offering to the dead. This reference is found increasingly in Benn's poetry of the twenties as a cipher image for the self-sacrifice of the poet or the lover (cf. No. 21, *Dir auch*) and also for the evocation of the past in poetry (No. 24, *Sieh die Sterne, die Fänge*).

l. 5. *Esse*: here the hearth, place of sacrifice.
Haschisch: *Cannabis indica.*
Meten: mead, here probably derived from the Greek *methy* = wine; drink made of honey, herbs, and water.

l. 6. *Kraut*: narcotics, which produce intoxication and lead to a feeling of mystical unity with the divinity. Cf. *Drei alte Männer* (1948): 'Helena gibt den Helden Nepenthes beim Mahl, wenn die Stimmung sinkt, oder den Kriegern vor der Schlacht — im Träumer-Rancho von Chimbote, in Zelten, während der Zauberer die Trommel schlägt, erfolgt die Einverleibung der Fröhlichkeitspillen oder des Krautes der Gräber, das die Vereinigung mit den Geistern bringt. Die Lösungen quellen aus den Feldern, aus Kraut und Wurzeln, aus Pilzen und Blüten — ein Urtrieb, keineswegs aus entarteten, sondern ebenso von primitiven Völkern, steigt aus den verdeckten Zentren, rötet sie mit jener Grunddurchdringung, mit jenem Rausch, mit jenem Allgefühl — *Gott ist eine Droge*, ah, eine

Droge von Gottes Strauch —' (*GW* II, p. 406).
das delphische Lied: the competition between the Muses in singing and playing the flute, as described by Pausanias: 'it consisted of gloomy flute melodies and laments sung to flute accompaniment' (*Elegies*).

l. 7. *Auleten*: flute-players, from the Greek *aulos* = double flute, from Phrygia; associated with this was the Phrygian mode which aroused ecstasy.

l. 8. *am Gott verschied*: in the ecstasy of the cults of the mysteries the initiate experiences a 'mystischer Tod', a self-sacrifice by renunciation of the ego; he thus becomes one with the god and has a claim to eternity.

The second verse develops this picture of 'mystischer Tod' by showing that the initiate himself is the sacrificial animal, who experiences his own death. This experience of the unity of man with animal, which Benn calls *Vermischungslüste*, and which removes fear of death (*Todesschweiß*), is the prerequisite for 'mystische Partizipation' or *Kommunion* with being as a totality.

l. 10. *Stier*: Benn is referring to the late classical cult of Mithras, with its image of the killing of a bull by the god, often celebrated in crypts in the depths of the earth. The worship and sacrifice of bulls was widespread in classical times throughout the Mediterranean (cf. *Das späte Ich* II, *l.* 11).

l. 12. *Sargrevier*: neologism for graveyard: the catacombs and crypts of antiquity as places where secret cults took place.

l. 13. *Vermischungslüste*: in the cult of the mysteries the ecstatic union between animal, man, and the god.

l. 15. *Myste*: a person who has been initiated into the cult of the mysteries.

l. 16. *phrygische Kommunion*: the cult of Cybele, the great mother figure of the Mediterranean, closely linked with the cult of Dionysus.

The third verse, which turns to the subject of the present, criticizes the world of history and historical evolution, where man is proud of the higher development of humanity, and the use of the fire-stone and fire as the first *Sieg* of human civilization is celebrated. Benn opposes 'Werden' by 'Entwerden', the longing to return to the *Meer* of the absolute and the unconscious, for 'thalassale Regression' (cf. No. 25, *Regressiv*).

In the fourth verse the image of the island as the symbol of a happy human life returns once more, a picture so important in Benn's early period. Now, however, it is rejected as too idyllic, and with this sensual happiness is contrasted the tragedy of the poet who turns himself into an *Opfer*. This is the prerequisite for the experience of the *Stunde, die eint*, which in the fifth verse follows transience and fear of death, which even the murderer behind the prison bars feels. It *löst*, i.e. at the moment of creative ecstasy the lonely poetic ego, which sacrifices and yields up itself, rises beyond its own suffering and regains the ancient depths of the primeval soul. The symbols of this unity with the unconscious are the *Brandungsvögel* which swim in the sea, and the burning *Opfer*.

l. 25. *Sansibaren*: neologism: the plural form of the name of the island of Zanzibar off the east coast of Africa, whose main product is cloves (*Nelkenwaren*).

l. 26. After *still*, supply 'vergehen' (*l.* 31).

l. 28. *Bougainville*: the ornamental plant *Bougainvillea spectabilis*, with red or mauve flowers.

l. 33. *Vergang*: neologism: 'transience, death'.
Gitter: cf. No. 53, *Die Gitter*. The designation of the poet as a murderer comes from Rilke (*Le Magicien*, 12 Feb. 1924). Hans Bender has collected the interpretations of their own work by modern German poets in a volume entitled *Mein Gedicht ist mein Messer* (Heidelberg, 1955; München, List Bücher 187, 1961).

20. Wie lange noch

(Publ. 1927 in *Gesammelte Gedichte.*)

As the inverted commas which enclose the whole poem show, this is not the poet speaking, but a monologue by the woman who loves him, telling of the end of love and life. In her reproachful lament the motifs of love and death are combined, as in most of Benn's love poems at this period. In the face of the threatened separation of the lovers and the end of life, she recalls the unforgettable days and nights they shared in love (verse 1). In the man's turning away from her she sees an escape from the *Leere*, *Dunkel*, and *Schwere* of life (verse 2) and points to the marks of shared experiences and suffering on her face (verse 3). Finally she allows him to proceed on the path which leads him irresistibly to his death and sets him free, but calls this act an irrevocable turning-point; from now on he will seek in vain in hours of suffering for what he has abandoned and is for ever out of reach (verses 4 and 5).

21. Dir auch –

(Publ. 1927 in *Gesammelte Gedichte*.)

This love poem, in which the poet addresses both himself and his beloved, is in praise of the power of the ecstasy of love, recalling the classical myth of Eros and Psyche: the loved one is referred to as *Psyche*. In the nights of love, when the individual ego *strömt* across into the other, a transformation of the lovers into a *dunkleres Du* takes place; they experience a feeling of sinking into the depths of being. But this also brings pain and tears. Yet in this very experience that love is *ungeheuer* and transcends everyday life lies the reason why love can be praised here in a mythical image as a sacrificial offering, recalling Orphic sacrifices and mysteries. Goethe had the same experience that 'Liebesnächte' awaken a longing for 'Flammentod' and a desire for transfiguration to higher levels of existence. He expressed this in his famous poem *Selige Sehnsucht*, which Benn knew (in the poem *Wer allein ist*, No. 36, he quotes from it: 'Stirb und werde').

This praise of love, which is taken up again in the final verse, is contrasted in the second verse with a mood of resignation: love strives for completion and perfection, but even it is subject to the law of transience. Although the loved one pours *reinstes Licht* on the lover, even the night of love passes into the *Schattengeäder*, the kingdom of death, and although they have been transported up to a higher level of being, the lovers are denied a final fulfilment of their *Träume* of experiencing final unity.

The third verse, in its summary of all the themes in the preceding verses, affirms love as a necessity of life, despite its fleeting and transient nature, since in the ecstasy of love an intensification and transformation of the lyrical ego takes place, which, filled with the *Wein* of love and purified by the *Feuer* of the experience of love, becomes creative.

l. 3. *Psyche*: the ancient myth of Eros and Psyche is related by Apuleius in his *Metamorphoses* with many elaborations and additions. Because of her very great beauty, Psyche aroused the envy of Aphrodite, who sent Eros to kill her. But Eros fell in love with the mortal maiden and carried her off to an enchanted palace, where he visited her only by night without revealing his identity. Because of Psyche's curiosity their happiness was destroyed: as she looked at the sleeping Eros by the light of an oil-lamp, a hot drop of oil fell on him, so that he woke up and left her. After a series of tests which Psyche had to undergo, Zeus made her a goddess, and finally she and Eros were united. Benn's poem contains the essential images from this myth: the meeting of the lovers by night, transformation into a *dunkleres Du, reinstes Licht*, which illuminates the night (without, however, having a separating and threatening effect on love). Benn knew J. J. Bachofen's (1815–87) interpretation of the Psyche myth with its symbol of the oil-lamp, which represented for him two stages in the development of female existence: 'die tiefere des unreinen hetärischen Tellurismus und die höhere der zu ewiger Einheit mit dem Geliebten durchdringenden uranischen Existenz; dort die irdische, hier die himmlische Aphrodite . . . dort die unruhig flackernde Öllampe, deren überfließender Tropfen sich mit dem Herrn des Feuers zu verbinden strebt, hier das helle Licht des nicht brennenden Feuers' (*Das Mutterrecht*; from the selection appearing in 1926, *Der Mythus von Orient und Occident*, publ. by Manfred Schroeter, München, 1926, pp. 374–5, which was in Benn's library).

l. 11. *Schattengeäder*: neologism, presumably for the kingdom of death, where according to classical ideas men are only shadows. A similar image is found at the beginning of Rilke's poem *Orpheus. Eurydike. Hermes* (1902): 'Das war der Seelen wunderliches Bergwerk. / Wie stille Silbererze gingen sie / als Adern durch sein Dunkel . . .'

22. Trunkene Flut

(Publ. 1927 in *Gesammelte Gedichte*.)

In this programmatic lyric, which was used in 1949 as the title poem of a complete collection of his poems, Benn describes his relationship with the divine, the primordial *Absolutes*, out of which only can 'absolute Kunst' become possible, arise, and become justified. The image of the *trunkene Flut*, which arises from the depths of the soul (the 'kollektives Unbewußte' of Jung) and brings up out of it in trance and dream *die tiefen Dinge*, the archetypes of human consciousness, is closely linked here with the absolute for which the poet strives. 'Das Absolute ist der Traum,' he wrote in 1920 in the prose work *Der Garten von Arles* (*GW* II, p. 88). It *deckt* the *Stirne*, i.e. it is the central problem with which the poet's consciousness is concerned: in one of his early poems Benn called himself an 'armer Hirnhund, schwer mit Gott behangen' (No. 5, *Untergrundbahn*, *l.* 14). As in the late work of Rilke, poetry is the praise and honour of *Dinge*.

That the creative ecstasy of the poet is an immeasurably strong intellectual stimulus which derives from the absolute is represented in the second verse by the metaphor *Sternenfieber*. At night, whenever the poet finds himself face to face with the absolute, he is able to create a synthesis (*Einen*, *Vereinen*) of the most distant epochs of time; he feels himself raised above loneliness and pain and can forget that he is mortal. He himself becomes the Creator who utters the divine word of creation. But this synthesis in the words of poetry does not last for ever, even it is transitory, and goes *vorbei*.

Verses 3, 4, and 5 form a great syntactical unity and mark the turning-point into the existential, the state which follows creative ecstasy. The *große Nacht* is represented in mythical images from the mysteries of *Demeter* (Ceres) and Dionysus, and as in the poem *Orphische Zellen* (No. 19) the poet appears as an initiate and the artistic process as a sacrificial offering. The inner emptiness that follows is also reflected in mythical images from the same source: the barrenness which follows creative plenty (*Hörner*, *Wälder*) when the goddess Demeter (Ceres) descends into Hades in search of her daughter Core (Persephone), who has been abducted by Pluto, and therefore makes the earth barren. At the beginning of the fourth verse Benn refers in terms of realistic physiology to the physical feeling of a man who experiences relaxation after great inner excitement. But the poem does not end with this negative experience, and there follows once more a vision (*Entzücken*) of the south (*Golf aus Blau*) and of the great artistic genius, the *Schöpfergestalt*, which is the poet's ideal and makes life itself possible for him. Again Benn derives art and the existence of the great, exemplary artist from suffering, sickness, and distress; without these bitter experiences he cannot approach the *trunkene Flut*, which is compared with the gaily coloured foxglove that covers the mountains in summer with patches of colour, an image which brings the poem back again to the point where it began.

l. 2. *trance- und traumgefleckt*: neologism: in the *trunkene Flut* of the soul appear, like things floating in a river, trances and dreams, the states of the soul, which give rise to the poem. A concrete image of this is the final picture of the foxglove, which covers the mountains in summer with patches of colour.

l. 3. *Absolut*: in Christian theology God is the highest *absolutum*. As a metaphysical concept, 'das Absolute' in German idealistic philosophy means the divine spirit as the highest intelligence in the world (Hegel) or the final reality of being (Schelling), the predetermined nature of man, in contrast with all that is relative. For Benn 'das Absolute' was the final point of reference in his poetry, even in an era which declared with Friedrich Nietzsche that God was dead. But the precise meaning remains very vague and obscure and is usually expressed in such negative terms as the 'Unergründliches', 'Unbegreifliches', 'Unaufhörliches', 'Nichts'. Benn includes in this concept basically all metaphysical powers to which man has ever been subject in the course of history. Of the white man he says: 'er ist den Weg gegangen, den ihn jenes ,,Absolut-Reale", Götter, Vor-Götter, Ur, Vor-Ure, Ens realissimum, Natura naturans, mit einem Wort: das Herz der Finsternis getrieben hat — er trat heraus aus der Natur. Sein Ziel . . . lautet . . . Kunst' (*GW* I, p. 367). The highest task of art is a conflict with the absolute which can give it shape. For this reason he called the Expressionists, amongst whom he included himself, 'Gläubige einer neuen Wirklichkeit und eines alten Absoluten' (*GW* I, p. 247), and said of their achievement: 'da hämmert eine Gruppe das Absolute — ihm verfallend, aber es geistig überwindend — in abstrakte harte Formen: Bilde, Vers, Flötenlied' (*GW* I, p. 256). In this continual conflict with the *Absolutes* there arises what Benn calls 'absolute Kunst' or 'die Wortkunst des Absoluten' (*GW* I, p. 328).

l. 9. *Sternenfieber*: metaphorical neologism: the stars as representatives of the absolute in the cosmic night dispense *Fieber*, physical and intellectual excitement which leads to artistic creation, as in No. 24, *Sieh die Sterne, die Fänge*. In his *Akademie-Rede* (1932) Benn said: 'Aber wir kommen um die Frage nicht herum, was erleben wir denn in diesen Räuschen, was erhebt sich denn in dieser schöpferischen Lust, was gestaltet sich in dieser Stunde, was erblickt sie, auf welche Sphinx blickt denn ihr erweitertes Gesicht? Und die Antwort kann nicht anders lauten, sie erblickt auch hier am Grunde nur Strömendes hin und her, eine Ambivalenz, Bilden und Entformen, Stundengötter, die auflösen und gestalten, sie erblickt etwas Blindes, die Natur, erblickt das Nichts' (*GW* I, p. 437).

l. 11. *Lieber*: as with other monologues in Benn's poetry, not addressed to a friend but to the lyrical ego itself.

l. 13. *Zeiten-Einen*: neologism: the *Vereinen* (*l.* 15) of the most varied and furthest apart of human epochs in the work of art, in the poetic word which provides unity.

l. 14. *Schöpfungsschrei*: neologism: the Expressionists frequently called the poetic word, which was intensified to be most expressive, a *Schrei*. Benn adds to this the analogy between the divine word of creation (Genesis 1 ff.) and the word of the poet. Cf. No. 44, *Ein Wort*.

ll. 19–20. *Korn und Weine dargebracht*: the gifts of Demeter (Ceres) and Dionysus to man, which Hölderlin described in his elegy *Brot und Wein* (8, *ll.* 14–15): 'Brot ist der Erde Frucht, doch ists vom Lichte gesegnet, / Und vom donnernden Gott kommet die Freude des Weins.'

l. 22. *Hörner leer*: the image of the horn of plenty as a symbol for poetry, which Rilke used in a symbolist meaning in two poems, *Das Füllhorn* and *Corne d'abondance* (11 Feb. 1924). In classical times the horn of plenty of Amalthea was a metaphor for superfluity and an attribute of the goddess of the earth.

l. 24. *Demeter*: for Benn's expansion of the myth of Demeter (Ceres), Persephone, and Pluto cf. No. 47, *V. Jahrhundert*. 'She (Ceres) is the goddess who governs the fruits of the earth, especially, though not quite exclusively, bread-corn. She would appear to have thrown off very early a younger double of herself, the 'Virgin' (*Κόρη*), who . . . seems to be essentially the power which is in the corn itself and appears and disappears with it. . . . The Great Mysteries are in Boedromion . . . and connected with the return of Kore; the time is early autumn, when the fields are growing green again after the drought of summer. The Lesser Mysteries of Agrae are in Anthesterion; it is spring, and they lead up to the summer harvest and the following period of dryness, during which Kore, the young corn or seed-corn, is indeed under the earth, stored away in the great grain-jars. That the ritual of the Mysteries (which at Eleusis are even older than Demeter, being pre-Hellenic) had to do with the death and rebirth of the corn and that in time hopes of human immortality came to be read into this ritual is fairly clear, but the details remain extremely obscure' (*Oxford Classical Dictionary*, Demeter, p. 263).

l. 30. *Gebrest*: archaic word for sickness, infirmity (MHG *gebrest*).

l. 31. *Schöpfergestalt*: neologism for the creative artist or God as creator. Both meanings are found in Benn's work: in the poem *Dann gliederten sich die Laute* (6 Mar. 1939, *GW* III, pp. 430–1) he is referring to the artist: 'ich sehe am Ende / einen großen schweigenden Mann. // Der weiß, daß keinen Bitten / jemals ein Gott erscheint, / er hat es ausgelitten, / er weiß, der Gott verneint. // Er sieht den Menschen vergehen / und bildet seinen Traum.' In the conversation piece *Drei alte Männer* (1948, *GW* II, p. 397) he uses the term to mean the unknown, obscure God, Being itself: 'Ich wende mich nun dem Künstlerischen zu, dem Künstler, seinem eigentlichen Wesen, jedenfalls dem mit der heutigen Situation identischen Phänotyp. Nach außen starr sein und schweigen, jeden Zug des Gehabens, der mimischen Besonderung dämpfen und innen mit Kompressor arbeiten, schichten, schneiden, schälen, bis der Ausdruck dasteht, wie die verborgene, im Hintergrund wirkende, nie hervortretende, ewig unbekannt bleibende Gestalt es wollte, die Gestalt im Schatten, die von Schleiern umwogte anfängliche Figur, das gesichtslose, aber Züge entwickelnde Sein, das Urwort, das alte Wesen, die Hieroglyphe.'

l. 39. *Fingerhut*: foxglove, digitalis, the red and yellow flowering poisonous plant, here a conscious symbol for the ecstasy and dream (*trunkene Flut*) of expressionist poetry.

23. Aus Fernen, aus Reichen

(Publ. 1927 in *Gesammelte Gedichte.*)

In Benn's early poetry death meant the end of life and consciousness for man, and the Christian doctrine of salvation and the resurrection of man after death was sharply rejected. In this poem, which opens with the question of life after death, Benn's answer is still sceptical and resigned, but no longer so completely negative. The first verse recalls Hamlet's monologue, in which he speaks of 'the undiscover'd country from whose bourn / no traveller returns'; but for Benn, although death is synonymous with nothingness, it does not arouse any terror. He conceives it, as the second verse shows, as a *Schattenland* in the classical sense. There is indeed for him an unbridgeable gulf between the land of the living and the kingdom of shades, between life and death, but there is also for Benn, again in the sense of the classical belief that the gods speak to mortals through *Zeichen* and hints (Heraclitus), a message from the kingdom of death, which he pictures in a vision of a symbolic *große, schöne Hand*, a *pars pro toto* of the beloved. From her comes the message of salvation, which Benn expresses in the third verse in a quotation: „— *erlöst auch er*", a reference to a poem written before 1925 by Ina Seidel and addressed to Benn: 'Trunkener Bruder, rede, ich weiß, dass du reden mußt . . .'. In this poem she prophesies, on the basis of Benn's early *Morgue* poems, that he will find salvation from his suffering and misunderstanding of his poetry by others. It closes: 'Taumle, du wirst einst tanzen, lösender Gott und erlöst' (Albert Soergel, *Dichtung und Dichter der Zeit*, vol. ii, 1925, p. 826). But this 'Erlösung' still belongs to the inner world. Therefore the end of the third verse turns also to the experience of happiness in love, which anticipated such a fulfilment and salvation: the fourth verse describes the environment of Benn's Danish friend, the singer Ellen Overgaard, whom he met immediately after the death of his first wife in 1922. Most of his love poems at this period are dedicated to her, particularly the cycle *Die Dänin*, where she is portrayed in a house standing in a garden by the sea, a house filled with the *Lied der Nacht*—one of Chopin's nocturnes. The final verse, as it leads from the kingdom of night into the day of life, recasts the cipher image of *Zeichen* from the second verse in a negative sense: it is no longer the message of salvation which survives death, but points to suffering and death, by which both the 'You' and the lyrical ego are 'gezeichnet'. Both are united in the experience of death—this is expressed in the concluding image of the drink from the *Schale*, which united love, death, and oblivion in the poem *Lethe* by Conrad Ferdinand Meyer (1825–98) which Benn greatly admired: the dead beloved appears to the lover in a dream on Charon's boat and hands him a 'volle Schale' of 'Vergessen'. He snatches it away from her, but cannot save her from the kingdom of shades (cf. Benn's essay *Geliebte Gedichte* of 1953 (*GW* IV, pp. 327–8), in which he quotes and discusses this poem). The feelings and thoughts which gave rise to the poem *Aus Fernen, aus Reichen* in the twenties were formulated by Benn after the death of his publisher Erich Reiss, five years before his own death: 'Es ist immer wieder so schwer zu begreifen, daß ein Leben nun nicht mehr ist, mit dem man verbunden war — wenigstens nicht mehr in der Gestalt ist, in dem man an sie dachte und vor sich sah. Ich glaube ja an eine irgendwie geartete Weiterexistenz auch nach dem Tode, es ist kein Aufhören, die Toten bleiben bei uns und gehören dazu, trotzdem bleibt das Aufhören des Sichtbaren und Ansprechbaren eine große Erschütterung' (15 May 1951 to Lotte Reiss-Jacobi, *ABr.*, p. 217).

l. 5. *Schlünde*: 'throats'; the dead.
l. 10. *Schattenland*: the kingdom of the dead.
l. 26. *Reifen*: symbol for play on the beach? Or bracelets, which are taken off before playing the piano; 'hoops' (*MGP*, p. 81).
l. 29. *Tasten*: *pars pro toto*, the keys stand for the whole piano.
l. 32. *Norden*: from Benn's early work onwards the realm of rationality which is antagonistic to life, in contrast with the sensual south. It is used here apparently in a positive sense.
l. 39. *die Schale*: cf. Benn's poem *Die Schale* (1933, *GW* III, p. 154), in which it is the symbol of the unity of lovers.

24. Sieh die Sterne, die Fänge

(Publ. 1927 in *Gesammelte Gedichte.*)

Much like Hölderlin and Rilke, Benn felt the age in which he lived to be a final stage in time, *Nacht*, which in his opinion would not be followed by a new day of the gods which Hölderlin still hoped for. In this poem the lyrical ego first turns its attention to the sphere of the starlit heavens by night, and to the sea—both symbols for the transcendent and the absolute. Out of the tension of this relationship with the cosmic powers, which are later referred to as *Götter*, arises the question of whether these powers still evoke today *Hirtengesänge, / dämmernde* which relate stories about them (a syntactically obscure construction). When his Swiss interpreter Ernst Nef asked 'ob im zweiten und dritten Verse „welche Hirtengesänge, dämmernde, treiben sie her" — ob hier „Hirtengesänge" Satzsubjekt oder -objekt sei', Benn replied: 'Das bitte erlassen Sie mir. Keine Ahnung mehr' (Ernst Nef, p. 45). A similarly ambiguous formulation is found in line 5: *die Stimmen gerufen*, where it is not clear whether the lyrical ego has called the voices, or the voices have called it.

After this survey of the metaphysical powers of life both on high and beneath, the lyrical ego turns to itself and describes itself as a 'spätes Ich', which has fulfilled its task in life by evoking anew the *Stimmen* which echo out of the past, and by resolving its *Kreis*. By this he means not only the poet's immediate intellectual and material environment, but also the cultural environment to which he inescapably belongs. All that remains after this is silence and descent into night and death. The *Bote der Nacht*, whom he calls upon himself to follow, is not further clarified: he is reminiscent of Hermes Psychopompos in classical mythology, who guided souls into the night of Hades.

The second verse develops the theme of descent and departure and introduces a variation. The mood and the language become noticeably sharper and more resigned: it is the poet's task to question the real meaning of the old *Mythen und Worte* and to give them new vitality in his poetry. Myths and words are regarded here as equally valid, which is characteristic of Benn's concept of word and language as the instruments of the mythical. But Benn realizes also that this renewal of *Mythen und Worte* is simultaneously accompanied by an emptying of the senses, and recognizes the fact that outside poetry there can no longer be any real return of the gods. He thus rejects the hope, wide-spread after the First World War, that a new myth, a new religion would appear to replace Christianity. The images he uses for the irretrievably lost splendour and power of the gods are drawn from Babylon and taken from the Old Testament. The verse closes with an admonition to those who still live, who have descended from the 'Dämmerung' into the 'Nacht', to bring with them an offering to the dead gods and myths, as did Achilles the Myrmidon to his dead friend Patroclus. The *dunkler Wein*, which is to be poured out *ins Land*, does not here refer to love (as in No. 21, *Dir auch*), but to poetry, which preserves the memory of the dead gods and empty myths.

The final verse develops this image of the offering of wine to the dead and derives from it an affirmation of the whole of life, since *alles*, even the *Qual und Tränen des Seins*, is illuminated by and prospers in the flow of *dieser nächtige Wein*, the symbol of the remembrance, realization, and celebration of the past in poetry. The *Verfließen* of this wine corresponds to the silent flowing of epochal time, which Benn here calls *Äone*. The movement of the epochs leads to the infinite, back into the primeval ocean and the absolute, giving man who experiences it a feeling of rapture: *kaum noch von Ufern ein Stück*. The expression suited to this existential experience is no longer poetry, but silence, which became more and more important for Benn in the years that followed and a recurrent theme of his poetry. Thus the poem dies away with the challenge of the lyrical ego to itself, and gives back the symbols of fulfilment in life (*Krone*), of poetry (*Traum*), and of myth (*Götter*) to the *Bote der Nacht*, the kingdom from which they all derive and have originated since antiquity. In scarcely any other poem did Benn express quite so strongly and urgently his obligation to his poetic task which was so dependent on the final epoch of white mankind. Behind the images in this work is a clear reflection of Oswald Spengler's doctrine of resignation at the end of the heyday of a civilization.

l. 1. *Fänge*: 'fangs', cf. 'den Fang geben' = in hunting parlance 'to give the death blow'. The metaphor *Fänge des Lichts* in Benn's work evokes both the shining quality and also the coldness and animosity of the light that falls on man from the stars in the night sky, as well as man's sense of capture by the claws of unfathomable depths of light. This feature clearly distinguishes his night poems from those of the Romantics (Novalis).

l. 3. *Hirtengesänge*: cf. Theocritus' *Idylls*, Virgil's *Eclogues*, more recently Stefan George's *Buch der Hirten- und Preisgedichte* (1895), where the idyllic life of the shepherd, as in Greek antiquity, is praised. For Benn shepherds and huntsmen are the representatives of archaic forms of existence when man, nature, and the gods were united as one (cf. No. 31, *Am Brückenwehr* II). The songs of the shepherds are therefore, even for the modern poet, *Stimmen* which he must explore.

l. 5. *Stimmen*: cf. Benn's late conversation piece *Die Stimme hinter dem Vorhang* (1951): 'Wenn in allem das Heilige ist, müssen wir es suchen. Wenn es große Gebote gibt, mögen wir uns fragen, wie wir dazu stehen. Wenn es Rufe aus fernen Welten gibt, müssen wir uns bemühen, sie zu erlauschen' (*GW* II, p. 414).

l. 6. *deinen Kreis durchdacht*: in his autobiography *Doppelleben* (1950) Benn criticizes very often the modern concept of 'Geschichte' and says: 'ich habe mit dieser Geschichte nichts zu tun, den Vogel der Minerva locke ich nicht in meinen Bunker — mir nützt nichts der Ausblick und das Versprechen auf angebliche Geistzusammenhänge, ideelle Befruchtungen, Verzweigungen, Integrationen oder Auferstehungen, ich schreite meinen Kreis ab, Moira, ich schreite nicht die Geschichte ab, ich prüfe meine Aufgaben, meine Bindungen, zerre auch vielleicht an ihnen, aber der Kreis ist in mir beschlossen, ich blicke nicht über mich hinaus, ich versage mir diese Erleichterung, ich arbeite, ich suche Worte, ich zeichne meine Morphologie, ich drücke mich aus . . .' (*GW* IV, p. 166, partly quoted in 'Probleme der Lyrik', 1951, *GW* I, p. 520). In his *Vortrag in Knokke* (1952) Benn declared that the modern lyrical ego knows that there were 'immer Krise . . . immer Götterdämmerung'; that 'Kulturkreise gingen unter und Kulturkreise kamen . . . es war immer Apokalypse'. From this he concludes (referring to the lyrical ego): 'Darum hat es auch nicht die Angst, von der jetzt so viel geschrieben wird, die berühmte Lebensangst, es kennt die Periodizität des Kommens und Gehens, es macht seine Gedichte, es schreitet seinen Kreis ab, dann ist es zu Ende' (*GW* I, p. 546).

l. 11. *Götterkohorte*: neologism for 'Schar von Göttern' from the Latin word cohort, the sub-division of the legion.

l. 13. *Euphratthrone*: the tiered temple of the Babylonians, which was regarded as the throne of the gods.

l. 14. *Schrift und Wand*: Benn is thinking of the biblical story (Daniel 5) of the feast of King Belshazzar of Babylon, who in his drunkenness desecrated the holy vessels stolen from the Temple in Jerusalem. Then words of fire appeared on the wall of the royal banqueting hall which Daniel interpreted as a warning that the king would be overthrown and perish ('Mene tekel'): the king was killed that very night. Heinrich Heine (1797–1856) told this story in his famous ballad *Belsazar*. In contrast to the Old Testament version, Benn makes the divine warning refer (by using *ihre*) to the Babylonian gods.

l. 15. *Myrmidone*: in Homer's *Iliad* the Myrmidons, the followers of Achilles in the battle of Troy, are a race from the south of Thessaly and Aegina. Here Benn has in mind the offering of wine which Achilles brought by night to the burning funeral pyre of the dead Patroclus:

> . . . der schnelle Achilleus
> Schöpfte die ganze Nacht mit doppeltgehenkeltem Becher
> Wein aus goldenem Krug und goß ihn nieder zur Erde.
> Unablässig rief er die Seele des armen Patroklos.
> (*Iliad* xxiii. 218–21)

By addressing himself as *Myrmidone*, Benn regards himself as the warrior in a late and final epoch, and linked with the mythical antiquity of Greece.

l. 21. *die Äone*: Greek Aiōn = time, the epoch or the god of time, in Plato also eternity. Gnostic philosophy developed the doctrine of the succession of the aeons, which originate in and return to God. The New Testament contrasts the present-day aeon as the time of the world, with the future aeon as God's time (1 Timothy 1[17]). In *strömt die Äone* Benn combines two theories of Heraclitus in one image: that everything flows, and that the world is the plaything of the divine youth Aeon. In his essay *Zum Thema Geschichte* (1943) Benn says of Heraclitus: 'Er war nämlich einer, der das Sein überhaupt leugnete; die von ihm erblickte Welt zeigte nirgends ein Verharren, eine Unzerstörbarkeit, eine Dauer. Das war sein Grundgesicht: alles hat jederzeit das Entgegengesetzte an sich, in sich . . . Dieser Satz zielte nicht auf Anordnungen der Wirklichkeit, sondern auf das Nebeneinander vieler wahrer ungewordener, unzerstörbarer Realitäten im Wesen der Dinge. Es war eine logische Intuition, die sich hier aussprach, und es war ein Bild im Munde dessen, für den die Welt nur ein Spiel des schönen unschuldigen Äon war . . . Ein Spiel des Äon, ein Spiel der Parzen und der Träume' (*GW* I, p. 387; cf. also the poem *Melancholie*, *GW* III, p. 304).

l. 23. *Krone*: cf. Revelation 2[10]: 'Be thou faithful unto death, and I will give thee a crown of life.' In his autobiography *Lebensweg eines Intellektualisten* (1934), Benn promised himself this reward: 'allein und unverbittert in die Stunden des Dunkelwerdens sehen, dem will ich die Krone des Lebens geben' (*GW* IV, p. 63).

25. Regressiv

(Publ. 1927 in *Gesammelte Gedichte*.)

In order to remove everything romantic from his longing to return to the depths of the unconscious and to archaic forms of existence and give it a very cold, scientific name, Benn takes up here, as simultaneously in his essay *Lyrisches Ich* (1927), the biological term 'Regression'. On the origin of this Benn said: 'Robot in Frankreich schuf 1882 den später berühmt gewordenen Begriff der Regression und bildete ein Regressionsgesetz des Gedächtnisses, dessen Zerstörung er als einen Rückschritt vom Neuerem zu Älterem, vom Zusammengesetzten zum Primitiven, vom Willkürlichen zum Automatischen beschrieb' (*Der Aufbau der Persönlichkeit*, 1930, *GW* I, p. 100). In his poetry, however, Benn does not use this term in the sense of an actual regression of organs, but rather in the meaning of C. G. Jung, who spoke of a 'Neigung zur Regression auf tiefere und archaische Stufen' (*Psychologie und Alchemie*, 1944). On the basis of his thesis that 'Das Wasser ist das geläufigste Symbol für das *Unbewußte*', Jung continued: 'Der Weg der Seele . . . führt darum zum Wasser, zu jenem dunklen Spiegel, der in ihrem Grunde ruht. Wer immer den Stand der geistlichen Armut, das wahre Erbe eines konsequent zu Ende gelebten Protestantismus, für sich erkoren hat, gelangt auf den Weg der Seele, der zum Wasser führt. Dieses Wasser nun ist kein metaphorisches Gerede, sondern lebendiges Symbol für die dunkle Psyche' (*Über die Archetypen des kollektiven Unbewußten*, 1934). In similar fashion Benn formulated his concept of regression, which is the basis of this poem, as a liberation from the ego and an ascent into the unconscious: 'Ach immer wieder in diese Glut, in die Grade der plazentaren Räume, in die Vorstufe der Meere des Urgesichts: Regressionstendenzen, Zerlösung des Ich' (*Lyrisches Ich*, 1927, *GW* IV, p. 14; cf. No. 3, *Gesänge* I). At the same time poetry is at the service of this movement of the soul within itself: 'Regressionstendenzen mit Hilfe des Worts, heuristische Schwächezustände durch Substantive — das ist der Grundvorgang, der alles interpretiert . . .' (ibid.).

Benn's poem *Regressiv*, in which he sums up these ideas collected from and illuminated by Freud and Jung, begins as a lament: the first two verses are negative. They reject a series of things one after the other which can no longer offer to the ego, which is seeking to enter its own *Dunkel*, any point of departure on the path leading inwards (introversion). Here Benn goes further than usual in rejecting not only his own inner depths, but also the experience of love, the realm of biological life and sexual reproduction, even the *Wort*, and certainly the field of action as places where his own *Dunkel* could conceal itself.

In the second verse this restrained lament becomes an excited accusation in scornful and provocative tones. The *Götter und Tiere* in which mankind sought to find help and a resting-place at earlier stages of civilization are described as complete nonsense (*Faxen*), likewise belief in the God of creation, whom the poet places very contemptuously on the same level as a fraud (*Schieber*); once more the love relationship is cynically rejected. All this is not only worthless (*Bruch*), but threatening and fatal as well (*Katafalk*). This destruction of intellectual values and the human world is followed by paralysis of the ego, its separation from the outside world in the image of *Augen* which *von Muscheln zuwachsen*. The eye is the most highly developed human sense, which creates for the sake of its consciousness the opposition between the ego and the world and which causes the lyrical ego so much suffering. The closing of the eye by the shell, cipher image for an unconscious life enclosed within itself and concentrated around an inner darkness, does not only stand for the negation of the external world but also for the opening of the 'inneres Auge' and the illumination of an inner world of night, which is developed in the following verse. Thus the image that closes the second verse is ambivalent and marks the transition to the positive.

Verses 3 and 4, which are syntactically linked together, depict the process of *Regression* as the 'Auflösung des Ich' which is now beginning to flow; stimulated by feelings and visions it experiences the breakthrough to its subconscious and into the 'kollektives Unbewußte' (Jung). To describe these inner stations on the path into the darkness of the origins of life, Benn uses a series of images from the realm of ecstasy and dream, a vision of the south, of suffering and death: he describes this complete inner process in the last line by the pregnant expression *thalassale Regression* (see below).

l. 5. *Faxen*: Berlin slang: 'nonsense', 'stupidities'.

l. 6. *Schieber*: an expression from the twenties after the First World War for business men without a conscience who wanted to get rich quick and made illegal deals in black-market ('verschoben') goods or currency.

l. 7. *Bruch*: Berlin slang for 'something worthless, broken'. One of Benn's favourite words in his early work, standing e.g. in the poem *Chaos* (GW III, 82) for contemporary man and life which are threatened by destruction and downfall.

Katafalk: a structure on which coffins are carried. Here a synonym for corpses and death, and possibly to illustrate the contrast between external show and inner decay.

l. 10. *Korallenkolorit*: a metaphorical neologism for the red colour of the coral, which gives rise to the vision of South Sea islands as a place of archaic happiness in the vegetative unity of animal and sea.

l. 11. *Spaltungen*: the division of the ego into the ego which is controlled by the consciousness (cerebrum) and the ego which is controlled by the id, the unconscious (the brain stem), from which, according to Benn, the poetic vision springs. Cf. Ludwig Klages (1872–1956): 'Wer die Form des Personseins in der Ekstase zersprengt, für den geht im selben Augenblick die

Welt der Tatsachen unter, und es aufersteht ihm mit alles verdrängender Wirklichkeitsmacht die Welt der Bilder' (*Vom kosmogonischen Eros*, 1922, p. 108).
Niederbrüche: only through the weakening and collapse of the conscious ego can the lyrical ego return into its subconscious.

l. 13. *Schleierfähre*: metaphorical neologism from *Schleier*, the masking, blurring, and destruction of the consciousness in a state of intoxication and poetic ecstasy, and *Fähre*, the boat which rows across to the other bank of the unconscious. In addition to dream, ecstasy, and intoxication, death is also seen by Benn as a liberator from the world of consciousness; there is here too a reference to the image of Charon, the ferryman over the Styx.

l. 14. *stygische Blüten*: flowers of death and the underworld which blossom on the banks of the Styx in Hades. Benn frequently refers in his poems to asphodels, the flowers of death in classical Greece.
Schlaf und Mohn: in the poem *Betäubung* (*GW* III, p. 120) Benn names 'Schlafdorn und Mohnkelch' as means of producing intoxication and ecstasy and giving wing to poetic vision. Behind this too is the classical image of sleep and death as brothers, the one carrying a poppy, the other a lowered torch (*Das moderne Ich*, *GW* I, p. 21; cf. No. 26, *Du mußt dir alles geben*, verse 5).

l. 15. *Träne*: cipher image for individual suffering which leads back to the primeval depths of being; *wühlt* expresses a particular desire ('finale Lust'). Cf. *GW* V, p. 79.

l. 16. *thalassale Regression*: the adjective is a neologism, from the Greek *thalassa* = sea. By *Regression* Benn understood: 'Wasser *werden*— sich verändern, Veränderungen und Tiefe unter Wellen — ach, eine Stunde auf *einer* Ebene, auf *einem* Glück —' (*Roman des Phänotyp*, 1944, *GW* II, p. 176).

26. Du mußt dir alles geben

(Publ. 1929 in the periodical *Die literarische Welt* 5, No. 34, 23 Aug.)

On an autumn day which seemed a time of happiness, the poet senses that he is growing old and approaching death, and sums up his life in terms of absolute solipsism: in the age of nihilism there are no metaphysical powers, no gods through whose bounty life becomes rich and meaningful. In a state of utter solitude the individual must depend on itself; it is both giver and receiver of the meaning and value of life and of all human experiences, in this case the rich and joyful autumn hour, to which it gives itself up completely (verses 1 and 2). The third verse then looks back on the poetic achievement of the solitary ego, whose work has become detached from its creator and follows *seine eigene reine stille gelöschte Bahn*. In elegiac tones the poet contemplates his own predestined death, yet can call his time *leicht*, in the knowledge that his task and his life are completed. The fourth verse looks back on past love affairs and the poet describes himself as the *großer Verlasser*, who repeatedly gave up those he loved and thereby caused *Tränen und Zürnen*. But all softness and sentimentality are removed from these painful experiences by describing tears as *hartes Wasser* which falls upon his own hardness (*Steine*), so that even tragic experiences in love can be transcended in the light of the autumn day. The intermediary position between love and death is illustrated in the fifth verse in a mythical image, which the poet calls his *Wappen*: on classical gravestones Death and Eros were portrayed as youths with lowered torches, with the butterfly as the symbol of the soul. Between these two figures, which enhanced death as the brother of Sleep and Dream, Benn places the *Stier*, with which he often identifies himself (cf. No. 19, *Orphische Zellen*, verse 2). The evening moth (*Sphingide*), messenger of approaching death, ushers in the evening shadow of the South Sea, the realm of greatest happiness in life and of a harmonious affirmation of death.

The poem ends with a vision of the hour of death, when once more the symbols of perfection in life (*Olivenhaine*) and of art (*Säulen*) and its own beautiful death are drawn together. The *Boten* of this final vision, bathed *ganz in Rosen und Licht*, recall the appearance of the shining, rose-bearing angel in Stefan George's *Vorspiel* to the *Teppich des Lebens*, the messenger of the 'Schönes Leben', and the description of the death of the Duchess Violante von Assy in Heinrich Mann's trilogy *Die Göttinnen* (vol. iii, *Venus*, 1902/3), which Benn repeated in his essay *Heinrich Mann zum 60. Geburtstag* (1931): 'wenn die Farben verfallen, die Strahlen schräg stehen, wenn von den Decken und Wänden übereinanderstürzen die weiten Schatten, lehnt in der Dunkelheit einer gegen die Säule und hält die Hände hinter den Kopf gekreuzt, sein Fuß tritt lässig auf eine gelöschte Fackel, er ist nackt, er hat große, aufwärtsgebogene Locken, seine Augen blitzen blau, sein Mund mit kurzer, roter Lippe ist vor Kühnheit fast töricht, und siehe — es lächelt aus den Schatten' (*GW* I, p. 137). He also refers to this conclusion in his *Rede auf Heinrich Mann* (1931), in which he sees a vision of art in the future (*GW* I, p. 413).

l. 2. *Ahnen*: premonition, foreboding, which is linked to the *Traum* of poetry as a presentiment of death.

l. 3. *Werben*: the lyrical ego is enticed by the autumn day.

l. 4. *doldenverrauscht*: neologism, formed from *Dolde*, the inflorescence of flowers, and *verrauschen*, to pass, flow away; cf. the description of a vision in the short story *Querschnitt* (1918): 'Wie ist er einsam. Wie sieht er in die Ferne. Durch Gebüsch, feuchtrankig, kaum erspähbar ist die Stätte: da lehnt an Kelche sich der Tag, da rauscht die Dolde, im Park strömt über seinen Traum der Pan' (*GW* II, p. 76). The rustling of the flowers (cf. No. 16, *Schleierkraut*; No. 17, *Levkoienwelle*) gives rise to the panic experience of solitude, the *Traum*.

l. 5. *Sichel*: 'scythe': cf. No. 2, *D-Zug*, *l.* 6.
Sommermale: neologism: the signs of summer which now disappear in the autumn, the time of harvest.

l. 7. *Krüge und Wasserschale*: attributes of the harvester, as well as associations with mythical sacrificial offerings after the harvest.

l. 17. *der Eine*: in his 'Probleme der Lyrik' Benn contrasts the artist with the scholar: 'Er arbeitet allein, der Lyriker arbeitet besonders allein, da in jedem Jahrzehnt immer nur wenige große Lyriker leben, über die Nationen verteilt, in verschiedenen Sprachen dichtend, meistens einander unbekannt — jene „Phares", Leuchttürme, wie sie die Franzosen nennen, jene Gestalten, die das große schöpferische Meer für lange Zeit erhellen, selber aber im Dunkeln bleiben' (*GW* I, p. 517).

l. 18. *das Dumpfe*: the creative nucleus of the poem which arises from the irrational *dumpf* subconscious of the poet. Benn describes the 'Vorgang beim Entstehen eines Gedichts' in his 'Probleme der Lyrik' in these words: 'Der Autor besitzt: Erstens einen dumpfen schöpferischen Keim, eine psychische Materie. Zweitens Worte . . .' (*GW* I, p. 506). T. S. Eliot used Benn's idea with approval in his essay *The Three Voices of Poetry* (1953) and quoted Beddoes's verse: 'a bodiless childful of life in the gloom / crying with frog voice, "what shall I be?"'

l. 22. *Spindellicht*: neologism from *Spindel*, spindle, that part of the spinning-wheel on which the spun yarn is wound, and *Licht*. See *l.* 24 *Parze* below.

l. 23. *Rocken*: 'distaff', the upper part of the spinning-wheel on which the woollen or linen thread is placed before it is spun.
Lehne: *pars pro toto* = 'Lehnstuhl', the chair on which the spinning Fate sits.

l. 24. *die Parze*: the Fates or Parcae, who in classical mythology spin the fate of mankind, maintain it, and bring it to an end, often appear in Benn's poetry. He was particularly fond of Goethe's *Lied der Parzen* in *Iphigenie in Tauris* (cf. *Geliebte Gedichte*, 1953, *GW* IV, pp. 320–1). There is no discrepancy here with *l.* 10, *Götter geben dir nicht*, since in Benn's view man can and must determine his own life, though he has no say in its beginning or end.

l. 25. *Verlasser*: neologism: a person who has left many people he loved and by so doing has brought them suffering and tears.

l. 31. *wogengeblendet*: neologism: the ego is blinded, covered in the brightness of the light that is emitted by the *Wogen*, the full and flowing hours of life (cf. No. 22, *Trunkene Flut*).

l. 34. *Wappen*: symbol for the life of the poet, who sees himself placed as a *Stier* between Eros and death. Since he feels death to be close, he is able to abandon it, he has *Schon das Wappen verschenkt*.

l. 35. *Fackelhalter*: cf. Lessing (1729–81), *Wie die Alten den Tod gebildet* (1769).

l. 37. *Liden*: plural of the Italian *lido* = beach, shore.

l. 38. *Orangenmeer*: metaphorical neologism for the Mediterranean, on the shores of which are orange-groves. Cf. Goethe, *Mignons Lied*.

l. 39. *Sphingiden*: evening moths, seen here as messengers of death. In antiquity the butterfly was regarded as the symbol of the soul. It was in this form that the soul left the human body after death. Cf. Goethe's poem *Selige Sehnsucht*.

l. 43. *Olivenhaine*: from Benn's early poetry onwards the symbol of mythical happiness in the south. 'Die rotblauen Felsen von Delphi, die Glanzfelsen, ein Wald von grauen Ölbäumen schmilzt herauf aus der Tiefe des großen Tales' (*Roman des Phänotyp*, 1944, *GW* II, pp. 173–4).

l. 44. *Säulen*: often found together with olive-groves in Benn's visions of the south as symbols of the formal perfection of classical art. Cf. the short story *Querschnitt* (1918): 'Röte: ein Südlicht: Marmor und Hain, großes fernes, verlorenes Blut' (*GW* II, p. 76).

27. Immer schweigender

(Written 20 Nov. 1929, publ. Dec. 1930 in the periodical *Die Kolonne* 1, 9.)

In this poem the poet contemplates his own self in the face of death. He projects his gaze forwards into the realm of death, *die letzten Reiche*, from which seems to shine *das letzte Licht*, but since it is *kein Licht* it can afford man no comfort. Without illusion he awaits only the coming of death, the mythical saviour from the torments of life. The second verse turns back to *unnennbare Zeiten* which give rise to occasional *Rufe*, *Lieder*, unconnected images which appear to come from the fearful depths of the sea, the primeval source of all things (and the symbol for the 'kollektives Unbewußte' of man with his archetype). It is emphasized not only that these voices have a positive effect, but that one of these *unnennbare Zeiten* has wounded him in his innermost heart. It is part of this attitude of ever increasing silence, in praise of which this poem is written, that we do not learn which epoch has had this fatefully destructive effect. The final verse endows these emotions with archaic depths: they are as old as the sun and the night. But the dreams of an archaic past and the anxieties of modern man (*Bangen*) are criticized: they appear as misleading thoughts. Nevertheless, the poet sees himself on the way to perfection and transfiguration; the more he becomes solitary and approaches death, the more he is surrounded by absolute silence, the continual increase of which is emphasized by both the title of the poem and its close.

l. 6. *dir entblößt*: neologism: 'you have been for your own sake relieved of yourself or of your ego, you see yourself naked and free from illusion.'

l. 17. *Uralt war dein Verlangen*: cf. No. 33, *Die weißen Segel, ll.* 19–20, and Benn's essay *Der Aufbau der Persönlichkeit* (1930), where he speaks of the 'Erbgut des Stammhirns' and demonstrates that in 'psychotischem Zerfall' the 'archaische Trieb-Ich' 'emporgejagt von den Urtrieben' 'durch das zerfetzte psychologische Subjekt emporstößt' (*GW* I, p. 99).

l. 22. *in Fernen gestuft*: cf. No. 23, *Aus Fernen, aus Reichen*. In *gestuft* he expresses the idea of a climb up to higher levels of existence. Cf. Klopstock's ode *Die höheren Stufen* (1802).

28. Ein Land

(Written 16 Feb. 1933, publ. 1933 in the periodical *Die Literatur* 36, 1.)

The problem of death is treated in this poem in much the same way as in No. 23, *Aus Fernen, aus Reichen*, and in No. 27, *Immer schweigender*. Beyond the land of life, which is also the *Land der Untergänge* and the *dunkles Meer* of the absolute and the unconscious, there lies, distant and unapproachable, the kingdom of death which gives out no beam of light as a 'Zeichen' to those who are still alive. The transitory nature of this *Land der Untergänge* is made clearer in the second verse by the *zwitterndes Licht* which surrounds him, a twilight where life and death encounter each other as well as the deep feelings of *Urängste* and *Todesdränge* which affect the poet strongly. The symbols of man's unspoken knowledge of death are given in the third verse: the presumably Etruscan figures lying on their gravestones which *künden* of the world of death as they lie there in silence. Amongst them the fourth verse sees two kinds of people: the sufferers, who regard themselves as subject daily to a destructive fate (cf. No. 51, *Denk der Vergeblichen*), and those who determine their destiny themselves, *die Frein, die Lichten*. Both groups gaze and move in the same direction, but it is left open at the end of the poem whether they are going towards the world of human existence or to the kingdom of death. But their approach is identified with the approach of death.

l. 5. *zwitternd*: neologism from 'Zwitter', a hermaphrodite, standing here for twilight, dusk, which has an ambiguous character.

l. 6. *Urängste*: neologism. The fear of the individual human being rests, like all his basic emotions, on archaic experiences which have entered the 'kollektives Unbewußte' of his soul and which can rise from it at any time. Cf. No. 27, *Immer schweigender*, *ll.* 17–20.
Todesdränge: neologism for the longing for death. The plural expresses, like *Urängste*, the supra-individual quality of this urge.

l. 9. *Sänften*: 'stretchers', 'litters'.
Truhn: 'coffins'.

29. Dennoch die Schwerter halten

(Publ. 1933 in the periodical *Die Literatur* 36, 1.)

In this poem Benn strongly opposes the age of collectivism and the masses, and both Marxist and National Socialist ideology which preached that the individual was nothing, the collective everything. His view is that it is only the great individuals who count in history, individuals whom he sees as people who suffered greatly. They alone comprise the *soziologische Nenner*, from whom all phenomena of life and history derive. The influence of the life and philosophy of Friedrich Nietzsche behind the ideas of the first verse is clearly seen in the images which Benn uses in the following verse to depict human life as heroic suffering: he mentions *Sils-Maria* as the place where Nietzsche wrote his most important works in the solitude of the Swiss Alps, he refers to Nietzsche's *Ecce Homo* (1908), in which Nietzsche characterized his life, his suffering, and his work. Benn relates to this the classical image of the suffering Laocoon, just as the accusation of God in the third verse (*warum erschufst du das?*) is illustrated by the classical image of the dying Gaul. Behind the line *sie heute und morgen der Sieger* is Nietzsche's doctrine of the cyclic recurrence of human history, with which he connected his theory of *amor fati*. At the end of this poem Benn uses this idea to oppose Oswald Spengler's concept of the *Untergang des Abendlandes* and the decline of the white race. In place of the temptation to sink into the abyss and to give way to weakness, he puts forward the passion of his *heroischer Nihilismus*, the symbols of which are the swords of the spirit, with which, by his stubborn *dennoch*, he opposes the historical situation of his times, the *Stunde der Welt*. Later he embodied this attitude in the mythical figure of Pallas Athene, the armed goddess of the intellect, in his essay *Pallas* (1943, *GW* I, pp. 362–70).

l. 1. *soziologische Nenner*: Benn satirizes modern sociologists who are trying to achieve mathematical validity. In his essay *Zur Problematik des Dichterischen* (1930, *GW* I, pp. 67 ff.) he sharply rejects the application of their theories to the existence of the poet, and opposed it with his 'hyperämische Theorie des Dichterischen': 'Es gibt nur den Einsamen und seine Bilder . . .'

l. 6. *Sils-Maria-Wind*: Sils-Maria in Oberengadin, from 1881 to 1889 the home of Friedrich Nietzsche. This poem was first called *Sils-Maria*. Two other poems also published in 1933 have the same title (*GW* III, p. 153).

l. 9. *sterbende Krieger*: reference to the classical sculpture of the Dying Gaul (in Rome, Capitol Museum), the symbol of a heroic death after a hopeless battle against the conquerors.

l. 10. *schattenblaß*: neologism analogous with 'totenblaß', 'leichenblaß' = 'doomed'.

ll. 13–14. *Schlangen schlagen die Hauer, das Gift, den Biß, den Zahn*: the reference is to the later Hellenistic Laocoon group of figures from Rhodes (Rome, Vatican Museum). As early as the eighteenth century it was the object of conflicting interpretations in Germany made by Winckelmann, Lessing, and Goethe, above all in comparison with the description of the slaying of Laocoon and his sons by serpents in Virgil's *Aeneid.*

l. 15. *Ecce-homo-Schauer*: *Ecce homo* is the cry of Pontius Pilate at the sight of the scourged Christ in his cloak of purple and crown of thorns (John 19^5). Nietzsche chose it as the title of his autobiographical work *Ecce homo* (publ. 1908). Benn explains this line in his *Rede auf Heinrich Mann* (1931): 'Die Ecce-homo-Schauer: Nihilismus ist ein Glücksgefühl, und der Mensch hat in der Erkenntnis ein schönes Mittel zum Untergang' (*GW* I, p. 416).

l. 16. *Bahn*: 'blood vessel', 'artery' (*Blutbahn*) or 'life' (*Lebensbahn*).

l. 20. *dem nie Endenden zu*: the source of being, which gives rise to historical fate, which Benn praises and interprets in his oratorio for Paul Hindemith *Das Unaufhörliche* (1931, *GW* III, pp. 475–98). In his introduction to it he says: 'Wir wissen von der Schöpfung nichts, als daß sie sich verwandelt —, und das Unaufhörliche soll ein Ausdruck für diesen weitesten Hintergrund des Lebens sein, sein elementares Prinzip der Umgestaltung und der rastlosen Erschütterung seiner Formen . . . Auf das Individuum angewendet ist das Unaufhörliche allerdings ein tragisches, schmerzliches Gesetz, denn das Individuum ist so, daß es das „Stirb" mehr empfindet als das „Werde", daß es leidet, weil alles gleitet und vorüberrinnt . . .' (*GW* I, pp. 594–5).

l. 23. *die Schwerter*: a symbol of the world of the warlike mind, which Benn distinguished more and more radically at this time from the world of action, life, and history. In a letter published at the time this poem was published he referred to the concept of 'tragischer Heroismus' as the moving force behind his age: '. . . ich spreche von dem, was heute am Ende einer Epoche, nach so viel Abenteuern und Naturereignissen im Geschichtlichen und Geistigen *beim Ausgang der weißen Rasse, von dem ich fest überzeugt bin,* das Leben noch geistig tragen läßt und als schöpferischer Grund vorhanden sein könnte, geradezu als produktiver Trick, als darstellerische Methode, als halbwegs ansehnliches Sicheinredenkönnen, als Einbettungsmaterial übrigbleiben könnte: und da sehe und erlebe ich nichts, als diesen halb tragischen, halb dionysischen Untergrund des Wissens um das Ende und das Trotzdem des Weitermachens. *Amor fati.* Griechenland lebte davon. Die Parzen sangen *dies* Lied . . . Europa ist der Erdteil der Abgründe und der Schatten, denken Sie doch, daß im hellsten Griechenland Prometheus an den Felsen mußte und *wie* er litt!' (7 Sept. 1933 to Käthe von Porada, in *Gottfried Benn. Den Traum alleine tragen*, Wiesbaden, 1966, pp. 137–8).

30. Durch jede Stunde

(Dedicated to the authoress Käthe von Porada in a letter of 14 Aug. 1933, publ. 1933 in *Die Literatur* 36, 1.)

Tragic conflict as the underlying principle of the universe is the theme of this poem. It marks the beginning of a new shortened poetic form which was to become characteristic of Benn's work in the thirties, when the poet saw himself more and more condemned to silence. Benn, like Friedrich Hebbel (1813–63), whom he esteemed very highly, considered that this tragic flaw affected not only the individual, but the whole of creation, even the divinity itself ('Pantragismus'). The image of the *Wunde der Schöpfung*, from which Benn proceeds in the first verse, the blood of which permeates and colours every human experience and utterance, may well derive from *Dantons Tod* by Georg Büchner (1813–37). Danton, imprisoned in the Conciergerie prison, confesses before his execution that all he is looking for is peace: 'Im Nichts. Versenke dich in was Ruhigers als das Nichts, und wenn die höchste Ruhe Gott ist, ist nicht das Nichts Gott? Aber ich bin ein Atheist. Der verfluchte Satz: Etwas kann zu nichts werden! Und ich bin etwas, das ist der Jammer! — Die Schöpfung hat sich so breit gemacht, da ist nichts leer, alles voll Gewimmels. Das Nichts hat sich ermordet, die Schöpfung ist seine Wunde, wir sind seine Blutstropfen, die Welt ist das Grab, worin es fault.' For Benn, too, there is only the void behind the ever open *Wunde der Schöpfung*, but as the second and third verses show, it has a positive function: from it proceeds what Benn calls at this time the 'Verwandlung des Seins' (in *Die Schale*, 1933, *GW* III, p. 154), or the earth, thus taking up a theme from Rilke's latework: in his seventh *Duino Elegy* Rilke regards the 'Verwandlung der Erde' into the invisible as the highest task of poetry. Benn, who frequently referred to the 'formfordernde Gewalt des Nichts', is thus able to describe the blood that pours from the wound of creation as liquid honey (verse 2), indicating the transformation which can change absolute negativity into highest positivity. Thus the dynamic force of historical 'Werden', in the innermost centre of which (*Herz*) this *Seim* flows, can come to rest, and its place is taken by what Benn soon begins to call 'Statik' (see No. 48, *Statische Gedichte*). The real nature of the tragic universal law, which characterizes creation and the historical process, and which is represented in the third verse by the two famous tribes of horsemen of classical times and the early Middle Ages, remains unfathomable for man. The fourth verse describes the attitude of the poet as powerlessness in face of the baffling process of historical evolution. One must not ask about its meaning, since such questions cannot be answered, and one should not even try to comprehend it, but make the best of the given situation. All one can do is to bear, like Atlas, the *Himmel*, the symbol of change and the passing of time. As in his late poem *Nur zwei Dinge* (No. 54) the poet, doomed to suffer, is confronted by the 'Leere', the void, so here in the fifth verse the autumn day, bathed in mystic light, from which sprang the poetic vision which fills the poem and above all determines its conclusion, is contrasted in close juxtaposition with the *Wunde der Schöpfung*. The sight of the autumn fields after harvest and the voice of the shepherd are symbols for the poet which call upon him to turn towards his own depths (verse 6). This is then followed in the seventh verse by an upward flight into the *Bläue* of the absolute, described as a vision of higher space, superior to mankind, which is conscious of its own powerlessness in the face of the negative and the absolute (*Treue*) and accepts its position in quietness and silence. Benn does not mean here an ethical standpoint *vis-à-vis* his fellow men—which he longed for, but judged very dubious (see below)—but rather an aesthetic, metaphysical attitude of inner unity with the realms of the *Absolute* which he enumerates once more at the end of the poem, using cipher images.

ll. 3–4. *Wunde / der Schöpfung*: cf. also Benn's poem *Erst wenn* (1925, *GW* III, p. 99), in which he rejects the power to inspire of any mere 'Südlichkeiten' such as 'Olivenlandschaft', 'Tyrrhenisches

Meer', 'Weinzisterne', and even the Roman 'Villa d'Este' unless human suffering is added to nothingness: 'erst wenn die Schöpfungswunde / sich still eröffnet hat, / steigt die Verströmungsstunde / vom Saum der weißen Stadt.'

l. 11. *Skythen*: tribe of horsemen who settled from 100 B.C. onwards to the north of the Black Sea. They were described in detail by Herodotus and were famous for their art and ornamentation.

l. 12. *Hunnen*: a Tartar nomadic people, who came from Asia into Europe in the fourth century A.D., attacked and conquered the Alani and Ostrogoths, and under Attila built up a great empire to the north of the Black and Caspian Seas. In 451 they were defeated by the Romans and Visigoths in the battle of the Catalaunian Plains, and their empire broke up.

l. 18. *Sagenlicht*: neologism: the fruitful, creative *Stunde*, which the poet experiences here and now as the fulfilment of his existence, is filled with mythical light, and in it the old myths are brought to life.

l. 24. *tränke dich tief*: cf. No. 31, *Am Brückenwehr* II, *ll.* 3–4: 'du selbst bist Trank und Trinken, / der Denker, du.'

l. 26. *Ferngesicht*: neologism, the visionary gaze into the 'Fernen' and 'Reiche' beyond life—cf. No. 23, *Aus Fernen, aus Reichen.* Of this *Blick in Bläue* Benn says in his essay *Weinhaus Wolf* (1937): 'es zählen nur die höchsten Sphären, und das Menschliche zählt nicht dazu. Eine erbarmungslose Höhe, unablenkbar fliegen da die Pfeile, es ist kalt, tiefblau, da gelten nur Strahlen, da gilt nur eins: erkenne die Lage . . .' (*GW* II, p. 140).

l. 27. *Treue*: in the conversation piece *Die Stimme hinter dem Vorhang* (1951) it reads: 'Treue ist ein so ungeheuer innerer Prozeß, daß man ihn überhaupt nicht lehren oder verkünden kann' (*GW* II, p. 414).

l. 32. *es rinnt*: = 'verrinnt', 'passes away'. Behind this is Hofmannsthal's lament in the *Terzinen über Vergänglichkeit*: 'daß alles gleitet und vorüberrinnt', the awareness of the transience of all earthly things.

l. 33. *Reigen*: symbol of perfection and the unity of life and death, also of Nietzsche's doctrine of cyclic recurrence. Cf. No. 31, *Am Brückenwehr* IV, *l.* 23.

31. Am Brückenwehr I–IV

(Written in Oberstdorf in the Allgäu 4–6 Oct. 1934, publ. 1934 in *Die Literatur* 37, 2.)

This cycle of poems reflects Benn's self-criticism and self-reflection one year after Hitler had seized power. Until this time Benn had supported him in his writings and radio broadcasts but he was forced to admit, after the failure of the alleged 'Putsch' of the SA leader Röhm and the murder of many SA leaders (30 June–2 July 1934) on Hitler's orders, that the regime was run by gangsters. Benn's letters from this period, particularly to Ina Seidel, show his determination to have nothing to do with political powers and his contempt for those in power. These four poems, in which the 'I' and the 'You' of the poet speak alternately, are monologues: in the first edition Benn enclosed the 'I'-poems I and III in single inverted commas, the 'You'-poems II and IV in double inverted commas. In addition to his self-criticism they give an outline of his future work as a poet, now that the 'Träume der Vereinigung von Geist und Macht' were over and he had recognized that 'Es sind zwei Reiche' (*ABr.*, p. 60). It now seemed to him that only in the realm of art could the creative synthesis of opposites come about, which had failed in real life.

I

The poem begins with a concrete situation: the poet is standing on a bridge; he leans on the parapet over the rushing waters, over the exchange of elements that takes place in the water, which appears here as a symbol of life—a renewal of the river symbol of German classicism. The bridge as the place of meditation is found before Benn in Nietzsche's poem *Venedig* and in Hofmannsthal's lyrical drama *Das kleine Welttheater* (1897).

Benn is aware that he is facing a *neue Macht*, the true nature of which remains hidden. He has *weit gedacht*, i.e. 'seinen Kreis durchdacht' (No. 24, *Sieh die Sterne, die Fänge*, *l.* 6), has made his way in thought through the history of human civilizations and the development of modern man, without coming to a definite conclusion. Therefore he now turns away from *Dinge*, i.e. reality in the empirical sense, and releases its *Ringe*, i.e. its former causal and genetic relationships, and leaves them to the mysterious *neue Macht*. Meanwhile his gaze turns to the world of nature around him at the foot of the mountains, which has a primeval, idyllic character.

In verses 2–4 the sight of the *schiefergrau* water below him awakens in him a vision of the primeval word (Archaean period), in which there were only stones and rock strata but no life. This look back into the past in a state of inner 'Regression' is followed by a swing back to the present, the autumn season which, before it came to an end, could still offer dionysiac happiness, *Kelter- und Weingesänge*, ecstasy and 'finale Lust'. This double experience of nature gives rise to questions about the world, man, and God, which bring the first part of the poem to an end. The first question asks whether the world, past and present, should be thought of as belonging to God, the creator of all *Dinge*. Or does it belong to man, who, in contrast to God, the beginning of all things, regards everything in terms of transience and death, and realizes that, living in the quaternary age, he is facing the end of time? In the final verse the poet does not offer any answer to these questions, but asserts their intensity and at the same time admits the powerlessness of his thoughts. He does not make it clear whether they have lost their power in the face of the ancient might of the God of creation, who for Benn is a 'dunkler Gott' (*deus absconditus*), or in the face of the equally unknown *neue Macht*, of which he spoke at the beginning of the poem.

l. 5. *Brückenwehr*: a dam or barrage surmounted by a bridge. Benn repeatedly emphasized that to gaze at water calls for inner concentration and requires an effort of thought: 'Sich abfinden und gelegentlich auf Wasser sehen', it reads in the *Ptolemäer* (1947, *GW* II, p. 256).

l. 9. *Lauf*: 'watercourse', 'stream', 'river'.

l. 10. *Ton*: the colour *schiefergrau*, rather than *Ton* = 'a sound' or 'clay'.
Urgesteine: e.g. gneiss, mica, phyllite from the Archaean period. Granite is also included, to which Goethe devoted an essay, praising it as the most important primeval rock (see below, II, *ll.* 15–16).

l. 12. *Schichtenbau*: the structure of geological rock strata which become visible as the water in the river cuts more deeply into its bed.

l. 13. *Agonie*: the death-struggle of summer is linked with the dionysiac pleasure at the vintage.

l. 14. *Rebgehänge*: bunches of grapes hanging from the vines.

l. 15. *Kelter- und Weingesänge*: neologisms, metaphors for the people who harvest and press the grapes, singing as they work, and who *durchstreifen* the vineyards.

II

This attitude of resignation gives way in the second part to an imperative directed at the 'Du' of the poet; for him there is no renunciation of self, no final comfort, for the old powers (God, the *Geschichtsgewalten*, etc.) have no longer any obligation towards the ego. It must not let itself be overcome by creative *Rausch* and linger in such a mood, but be ever conscious that in its state of absolute solitude it must depend entirely on itself. Its dual character of *Trank und Trinken* recalls Rilke's *Sonette an Orpheus* (II, 29) with their doctrine of transformation: 'Ist dir Trinken bitter, werde Wein.' Benn simplifies this dialectic into a synthesis of opposites: *Trinken* or 'Sich-tränken' means for him to fill oneself with content through thought, to achieve inner fullness and depth (cf. No. 30, *Durch jede Stunde*, *l.* 24, 'tränke dich tief'). In his *Rede auf Stefan George* (1933) Benn had already declared that 'der heutige, der geschichtliche Mensch . . . nicht mehr im Zeitalter monotheistischer Beschwörungen lebt, sondern im Zeitalter nach Nietzsche' (*GW* I, p. 472), i.e. in the age of nihilism. In the first verse he sees as transient not only religious, metaphysical, and historico-political powers, but even his own poetic 'hyperämische Metaphysik', which reappears in part III (verses 5–6) as a temptation to relapse into *Rausch.*

In the second and third verses the poet who conceives of himself as and professes to be a man of intellect, a *Denker* is sharply distinguished from the *Hirt* and *Jäger* as representatives of earlier ages and epochs of human civilization. A similar opposition between the confusion of the present and the original unity of antiquity is found in Benn's oratorio *Das Unaufhörliche* (1931): 'Dunkle Stunde der Welt, / zerfallnes Heute: / frühe Stunde der Erde, / einst unzerklüftet, / Hirten und Jägern / ahnend geweiht —' (*GW* III, p. 487). In comparison with the shepherds playing their sweet *Schalmein*, who embody an idyllic form of life which knows no conflict, the poet regards himself as a tragic human being, who must make amends for his guilt and error, even if he may perhaps hope for forgiveness. Benn is not only moved here by thoughts of his own erroneous allegiance to National Socialism, but by the basic question: 'Ist Ausdruck Schuld? Er könnte es sein' ('Altern als Problem für Künstler', 1954, *GW* I, p. 578; cf. also No. 53, *Die Gitter*, *ll.* 3–4). Not long before, Benn had gone to great lengths in his apologia *Lebensweg eines Intellektualisten* (1934) to derive his name, which had been attacked as Jewish, from the Wendic 'Wenn' or 'Fenn' = fisherman, and therefore from 'Ur-Fischer', and claimed that his father, the strict Protestant pastor, bore 'Züge des Urjägers . . . der Megalithkultur' (*GW* IV, pp. 22, 23). Now, however, he firmly rejects this reactionary concept, influenced as it was by National Socialist interest in heredity and genealogy, that man of the present is the same as the *Jäger* of antiquity and the age of the great stone graves (*Megalith und Ur*). Now he is convinced that it is the artist's primary task to be a *Formalist*—a concept of the nature of art which the rulers of the totalitarian state in both Germany and the Soviet Union sharply rejected, as Benn well knew.

The fourth verse expresses once again, in the face of the transience of everything that is human, a longing for 'Regression' into an archaic age, and at the same time a longing to escape from the pressures of contemporary political powers into the non-historical. Yet this *Verlangen nach Urgestein* which Goethe knew (see below) now appears rather as a diverting temptation leading away from art and concentration on form, which he rejects. In the fifth verse, after he has become aware of his own fate, Benn withdraws even more decisively from the world of historical *Werden* which traces out an upwards-leading line of human development from the *Urgestein*, the megalithic culture, via the huntsmen and shepherds and now demands his entry into the world of action, into the reality of the present, which could only lead to error and guilt. He sees himself as bound, *gebannt*, to his task as artist, as a *Formalist*. In a letter of 30 April 1936 he likewise confessed: 'A bas — die Geschichte! Jenseits der Geschichte beginnt die Wirklichkeit, die anthropologische Wirklichkeit der geistigen Formen. Verraten wir die nie —' (*ABr.*, p. 70). He now regarded his task as the discovery of a perfected artistic form of the poetic 'Ausdruck' which would embrace the whole realm of earthly being and the total existence of man (*Himmel und Erde*).

The final verse is a variation of the first and emphasizes the solitude of the modern artist: there is no one to whom he can exhibit the results of his rigid formalist art—on the other hand he is at the mercy of persecution. The final lines affirm, however, the constructive power of the intellect: even as the world draws to its close, when there remains nothing but silence, the poet remains the bearer and proclaimer of creative thought.

l. 4. *der Denker*: in his radio talk 'Können Dichter die Welt ändern?' (1930) Benn speaks of the 'Notwendigkeit' which, according to Schiller's theory, limits the freedom of the poet, and says of it: 'Die ist das Geheimnis des Denkens und des Geistes überhaupt. Sie trifft nur wenige, und Dichter und Denker sind in ihrer letzten Form vor ihr identisch. Wie jene Skulptur von Rodin: der Denker, der über dem Eingang zur Unterwelt steht, ursprünglich der Dichter hieß, ihnen beiden gilt der Spruch am Sockel des Steins: der Titan versunken in einen schmerzlichen Traum' (*GW* IV, p. 222). The rhetorical celebration of the 'Denker' in the oratorio *Das Unaufhörliche* (1931) also relates to the poet: 'Der Mann, / der Denker, / das Hirn der Höhe, / der große Gräber: / in ahnenalten Reihen / umzieht er Welten ordnend: / Gesetz' (*GW* III, pp. 481–2).

l. 6. *Schalmein*: 'shawm', shepherd's pipes (up to 1933 also the name of wind instruments used in communist workers' bands), an instrument of temptation.

l. 10. *Megalith*: Benn is referring to the age of the great stone constructions (such as megaliths, e.g. Stonehenge) which were erected in the neolithic age. In his autobiography *Lebensweg eines Intellektualisten* (1934, *GW* IV, p. 25) he places them erroneously in the palaeolithic ice age.
Ur: Ur of the Chaldees from which Abraham set out for Canaan (Genesis 11^{31}).

l. 11. *Formenpräger*: neologism for the artist and poet as a *Formalist*. Cf. *Rede auf Stefan George* (1933): 'Der abendländische Mensch unseres Zeitalters besiegt das Dämonische durch die Form, seine Dämonie ist die Form, seine Magie ist das Technisch-Konstruktive' (*GW* I, p. 473).

l. 12. *weiße Spur*: metaphor for the white race, the European population of Western civilization, from which Benn, unlike the National Socialists, did not see himself as separate.

l. 14. *Bach- und Brückenschein*: neologism: the light which proceeds from the *Bach*, the symbol of life which flows and passes away, and tries to enter into the 'Meer' of the absolute; and the light from the *Brücke*, the place of existential realization and the union of opposites (cf. Goethe's *Märchen*, 1795).

l. 16. *Urgestein*: cf. Goethe's essay *Über Granit* (1784): 'Ich fürchte den Vorwurf nicht, daß es ein Geist des Widerspruches sein müsse, der mich von Betrachtung und Schilderung des jüngsten, mannigfaltigsten, beweglichsten, veränderlichsten, erschütterlichsten Teiles der Schöpfung (sc. des menschlichen Herzens) zu der Betrachtung des ältesten, festesten, tiefsten, unerschütterlichsten Sohnes der Natur geführt hat.'

l. 20. *Formalist*: Formalism originated in Russia and was used there from 1915 onwards by Viktor Shklovsky and other literary critics to describe modern poetry corresponding to Italian Futurism and German Expressionism. Form became absolute, language and content were subordinate. From 1927 onwards 'Formalismus' and 'Formalist' became terms of abuse in the vocabulary of communist aesthetics for all 'bourgeois' poets who did not follow the official party line of socialist realism. Benn's repeated emphasis of this concept in this cycle of poems is a conscious affront to the National Socialist theory of art and to socialist realism.

l. 23. *Schweigen*: This need for silence, which Benn assumed from this time onwards after turning away from current events, was later described by him as follows: 'Die Lage war nicht so, daß man noch für andere sprechen konnte, zu anderen sprach, kaum durch ein Zimmer drangen die Sentenzen, für sich allein trieb man die Gebilde vor' (*Der Ptolemäer*, 1947, *GW* II, p. 241).

III

Behind this poem is an awareness of the rhythm of poetic creation, in which hallucinatory states of ecstasy, vision, and intoxication alternate with a creative urge controlled by sober consciousness. Once more the poet passionately opposes the imperative demand for artistic creation with a plea for *Tiefe* and intoxication, for he feels that the obligation to mould forms is a burden and a curse. The contrast with part II is energetically intensified in order to make the synthesis of opposites in part IV more credible.

The poet looks at *Stunden* of inner absorption, when all differences between old and new are removed and the antitheses (*Wasser und Welle*—depth and surface, darkness and light) flow together into a single song. He thinks here of the hours of mystic participation which led him to a state of ecstasy away from the burdensome historical world into the depths of the soul, back to the archetypal collective unconscious: 'Die Seele aber trachtet nach Tieferem als der Erkenntnis, nach etwas Tieferem, das ihr Ganzheit und Vollendung gibt' (*Zur Problematik des Dichterischen*, 1930, *GW* I, p. 77). Once more Benn refers here to his idea of 'hyperämische Metaphysik', characteristic of his middle period, according to which the poet is a magician who can evoke anew the myths of antiquity: 'immer und zu allen Zeiten wird er wiederkommen, für den alles Leben nur ein Rufen aus der Tiefe ist, einer alten und frühen Tiefe, und alles Vergängliche nur ein Gleichnis eines unbekannten Urerlebnisses, das sich in ihm Erinnerungen sucht' (ibid., *GW* I, pp. 82–3). At the period when this poem was written Benn frequently contrasted oriental knowledge of the soul and techniques of meditation with the world of history and European glorification of action, which were exaggerated to extremes by the National Socialists: 'Nur nicht handeln! Wisse das und schweige. Asien ist tiefer, aber verbirg es!' he wrote in *Weinhaus Wolf* (1937, *GW* II, p. 151). Looking back Benn stated in the *Ptolemäer*: 'Asiatisches durchkreuzte sehr häufig meine individuelle Penetranz, als deren Echtestes ich immer das Amorphe empfand, das Ambivalente ...' (1947, *GW* II, p. 245). He emphasizes here, however, that introversion is not a sinking down into the formless and shapeless, but a different type of form, which is opposed here to that of the artist.

In the middle of the third poem a notable rhythmical change takes place: the short and snappy 2–3-beat iambic lines give way to dactyls, which make the rhythm softer and more resonant. This more lively and singing rhythm is maintained until the middle of the fourth poem, when the short rhythm of poems I–III returns. The final verses 5–6 are an urgent plea, almost a prayer, to an unknown higher power to be given fullness of life and be wafted away into the ecstasy of dream and intoxication. The critical artistic effort which went into the *Hülle*, the superficial aspects of the piece of work, now appears as a *Hölle*, a curse the artist has laid upon himself, from which the poet would like to be free. The plea for inner riches is answered in the fifth verse by rich rhymes (*reich sein—weich sein*).

IV

The fourth poem antithetically opposes this wish for inner depth with the view of a mountain region and then proceeds to synthesize the opposites. Mountains and eagles are images of silent clarity, strength, and perfection, standing for the realms of absolute intellect which Benn describes as in opposition to productive life and therefore *unfruchtbar*. Rilke has a similar picture of an (inner) mountain landscape with eagles in the late poem *Ausgesetzt auf den Bergen des Herzens* which ends with the lines: 'Und der große geborgene Vogel / kreist um der Gipfel reine Verweigerung. — Aber / ungeborgen hier auf den Bergen des Herzens . . .' The transience of everything earthly is partially true of the realm of purely biological life with its vegetative joy in existence, symbolized here in *Früchte*, whilst the realm of constructive intellect is identified with eternity. Few, however, can achieve this. *Nahe am Schöpfer züchten / wenige Arten sich* is true both of the eagles, which symbolize the creative mind, and of man as the possessor of the constructive mind which strives upwards to the sphere of the absolute and transcendental—intended here as a challenge to higher development. *Das Blaue*, as Benn calls this sphere, has the same symbolic value as 'l'azur' for the French symbolists Baudelaire, Mallarmé, and Valéry: it is identical with the absolute silence of empty space. With great decisiveness the poet now opposes the *Gestalten* to the *Stimmen* which call upon him to retreat within himself and free himself, to the *asiatisch tief* song of part II, to the longing for *Tiefe* (verse 3). In giving them form, the poet serves these *Gestalten*: they stand not only above man who reflects on the world and himself (*Brückenwehr*), but also above those realms of history (*Völker*) which have become *stumpfe Gewalten*, and above nature (*Schnee und Meer*). It is characteristic of empty transcendence, as the realm of absolute intellect and nothingness appear to Benn, that he does not name these *Gestalten*, but in the fifth verse formulates the *Gesetz der Form* which these *Gestalten* have imposed upon him. He emphasizes strongly that this law affects not only him but the whole of humanity (*Rasse*). The concept of inner *Fülle*, which referred at the end of part III only to *Tiefe* and *Schöpfung*, now stands for the artistic task of giving form and shape, the essence of which is unity, both externally (*Hülle*) and internally (*Tiefe*), in the completed work of art. 'Die scheinbare Antithetik der Schlußstrophe des dritten Teils wird nunmehr aufgehoben. *Form* und *Tiefe*, *Hülle* und *Fülle* sind keine Gegensätze, die sich ausschließen, sondern sie können als Elemente dichterischen Schaffens nur zusammen wirksam werden. Traum und Rausch können für sich selbst nicht bestehen, und eben deshalb ist der Künstler aufgerufen, die endogenen Bilder der mystischen Partizipation in die Statik und Abgeschlossenheit der Form zu überführen, bis sie *die ganze Tiefe trägt*. *Form* und *Tiefe* sind ein *Reigen*; aber die Tiefe erhält ihre Gültigkeit und Dauer erst in der Bindung durch die Form. Denn „Keiner . . . wird den Schluß jener Mythe anders wünschen als daß Dionysos endet und ruht zu Füßen des klaren delphischen Gottes" (Expressionismus). Damit wird nun auch deutlich, was sich hinter der *neuen Macht* verbirgt, von der zu Beginn des Gedichts die Rede war: die Kunst als die „Antithese aus Rausch und

Zucht", die zur Synthese im geschaffenen Kunstwerk führt' (H.-D. Balser, op. cit., p. 139).

ll. 1–2. *Grate, Gipfel*: the *Grate* (mountain ridges) and *Gipfel* of poetry. Cf. the Goethe quotation in the note to *ll.* 19–20.

l. 3. *Adler, die wirklichen*: Benn emphasizes that he means the actual birds; he wrote in his autobiography *Lebensweg eines Intellektualisten* (1934): 'Der Mensch hat einen getrübten Blick rückwärts, vorwärts keinen. Er ist ja nur ein halbgelungenes Wesen, ein Entwurf, das Werfen nach einem Adler, schon riß man die Federn, die Flügel nieder, aber die ganze Gestalt schlug noch nicht um — wird sie einmal ganz umschlagen, so, daß ihr Herz unmittelbar am Herzen der Dinge ruht?' (*GW* IV, p. 67, and see p. 262). The eagle as the symbol of the constructive mind is found in Hölderlin's late hymn *Patmos* and in Nietzsche.

l. 4. *schweigend und unfruchtbar*: positive, not negative attributes of the intellect. Cf. Benn's comments on poetry: 'Im Gedicht ist die Sprache zur Ruhe gebracht, und der Mensch lebt, gestillt, für einen Augenblick im Schweigen' (*GW* IV, p. 263). And he says of the artist: 'Ist der Künstler nicht vielleicht a priori geschichtlich unwirksam, rein seelisch phänomenal . . .?' (*GW* I, p. 73).

ll. 7–8. Cf. *Weinhaus Wolf* (1937): 'Das Wesen des Menschen ist die Gestaltungssphäre. Nur in der Gestaltungssphäre wird der Mensch erkenntlich, nur in ihr werden die Gründe und Hintergründe seiner Erschaffung klar, nur aus ihr seine Tierreihenstellung deutlich, Fläche in Tiefe überführen, Worte durch Beziehung und anordnendes Verwenden zu einer geistigen Welt eröffnen, Laute aneinanderketten, bis sie sich halten und Unzerstörbares besingen, dies ist ihre Tat . . . Völker die ihn (sc. den konstruktiven Geist) ertragen als angreifende, spaltende, lebenzersetzende Sondermacht, stehen rassisch hoch . . . Völker, die ihn in alle Formen zur Gestaltungssphäre dringen lassen, sind züchterisch groß' (*GW* II, pp. 132–3).

l. 9. *das Blaue*: cf. Benn's essay *Weinhaus Wolf* (1937): 'es zählen nur die höchsten Sphären, und das Menschliche zählt nicht dazu, Eine erbarmunglose Höhe, unablenkbar fliegen da dic Pfeile, es ist kalt, tiefblau, da gelten nur Strahlen, da gilt nur eins: erkenne die Lage, bediene dich deiner Mittel, du bist verpflichtet zu deiner Methode, wo du erschufst, kannst du nicht weichen —: Du stehst für Reiche, nicht zu deuten und in denen es keine Siege gibt' (*GW* II, p. 140).

l. 16. *Schnee und Meer*: cf. No. 54, *Nur zwei Dinge, l.* 10.

l. 17. *formen*: Benn's assertion that form is the highest task of the modern artist is expressed in 1932 in his essay *Nach dem Nihilismus*: 'Ja, die gezüchtete Absolutheit der Form, deren Grade an linearer Reinheit und stilistischer Makellosigkeit allerdings nicht geringer sein dürften als die inhaltlichen früheren Kulturepochen, selbst bis zu den Graden vor dem Schierlingsbecher [sc. of Socrates] und vor dem Kreuz [of Christ] — ja, nur aus den letzten Spannungen des Formalen, nur aus der äußersten, bis an die Grenze der Immaterialität vordringenden Steigerung des Konstruktiven könnte sich eine neue *ethische* Realität bilden — *nach* dem Nihilismus!' (*GW* I, p. 161).

ll. 19–20. In his essay 'Altern als Problem für Künstler' (1954) Benn indicated that this formulation derives from one of Goethe's maxims: 'Wie viele Stunden meines Lebens habe ich vor dem Satz des Balkongotts [sc. Goethe] verbracht, ihn gedreht und gewendet . . .: „Auf ihrem höchsten Gipfel scheint die Poesie ganz äußerlich. Je mehr sie sich ins Innere zurückzieht, ist sie auf dem Wege zu sinken." — Was soll das heißen? Ich muß also mein Inneres verleugnen, Farcen mit ihm treiben, dies ist die Voraussetzung für Poesie, was ist diese dann eigentlich noch? Zaubern, Seiltrick, Nichts und darüber Glasur?' (*GW* I, p. 577). Back in 1931 Benn had already praised the combination of 'Oberfläche' and 'Tiefe' in Heinrich Mann's writing; this combination derives from Nietzsche's *Epilog* to his *Nietzsche contra Wagner*: 'O diese Griechen! sie verstanden sich darauf, zu *leben*! Dazu tut not, tapfer bei der Oberfläche, der Falte, der Haut stehenzubleiben, den Schein anzubeten, an Formen, an Töne, an Worte, an den ganzen *Olymp des Scheins* zu glauben! Diese Griechen waren oberflächlich — *aus Tiefe*.' Hofmannsthal has a similar challenge to the modern artist in his *Buch der Freunde* (1922): 'Die Tiefe muß man verstecken. Wo? An der Oberfläche' (*Aufzeichnungen*, ed. H. Steiner, 1959, p. 47).

ll. 23–4. *Reigen*: a symbol of completion, like Rilke's circle. In his short story *Querschnitt* (1918) Benn expressed the quintessence of his poetry: 'Wenn wir aber lehrten den Reigen sehen und das Leben formend überwinden, würde da der Tod nicht sein der Schatten blau, in dem die Glücke stehen?' (*GW* II, p. 77). The concept derives from the Persian mystic Jalal-ud-Din Rumi

(1207–73): 'He who knows the power of the ring dance does not fear death. For he knows that love is fatal.' In *Psyche. Seelenkult und Unsterblichkeitsglaube der Griechen* (Heidelberg, 1893, vol. ii, p. 27), which had a great influence on Benn's concept of antiquity, the classical scholar Erwin Rohde interpreted this Persian saying and linked it with the cult of Dionysus. This is also the source of Hofmannsthal's concept of the 'Reigen': in his lyrical drama *Der Tor und der Tod* which Benn knew well, this is stated by Death when he introduces himself to Claudio: 'Aus des Dionysos, der Venus Sippe, / Ein großer Gott der Seele steht vor dir. / . . . / Und du, hingebend dich im großen Reigen, / die Welt empfingest als dein eigen: / In jeder wahrhaft großen Stunde, / Die schauern deine Erdenform gemacht, / Hab ich dich angerührt im Seelen-grunde / Mit heiliger, geheimnisvoller Macht.' Cf. also his praise of Jalal-ud-Din Rumi's words in his essay *Sebastian Melmoth* (1905, *Prosa II*, 1951, p. 138). On the combination of 'Form-Tiefe-Reigen-Adler' cf. Benn's interpretation of this concept of the 'Reigen', written in the same year as the cycle of poems (*GW* II, p. 77): 'die wäre das Prinzip, das nie den Stoff verläßt (Stein, Ton, Wort) und doch nur der Schöpfung folgt und ihrem transzendenten Ruf, ein Prinzip, das die allein den höchsten Völkern der menschlichen Art eingeborene Macht zum Kanon erhöbe, konstruierte und formal erarbeitete Dinge aus sich herauszustellen, sich in ihnen zu lösen, Qual und Dränge in ihnen zu erlösen, sie dann persönlich zu verlassen, sie dann sich selber zu überlassen, aber so geladen mit arthafter Spannung und so weittragendem und unzerstörbarem Sinn, daß andere Geschlechter dieser Menschenart noch nach Jahrtausenden an ihnen die Epochen messen und in ihnen sich, ihre Rätsel, ihr ewig verschleiertes Wesen, ihr ganzes katastrophenunterlagertes Sein bindend erkennen' (*Lebensweg eines Intellektualisten*, 1934, *GW* IV, pp. 66–7).

32. Einsamer nie

(Written at the end of Aug. 1936, publ. 1936 in *Ausgewählte Gedichte*, 2nd ed.)

This is one of the first of Benn's 'statisch' poems, of which the central theme is his loneliness as a poet in a time of darkness (cf. No. 36, *Wer allein ist*, and No. 55, *Worte*). This is affirmed here without any lamentation. For him the late summer and the autumn are more than mere seasons which arouse moods of melancholy in man. Benn's poetry springs from the totality of existence, not from an isolated emotion. For this reason he not only rejected the word 'Stimmung' in its traditional meaning of a particular lyrical mood which leads to the writing of a poem, but frequently ridiculed it as an expression of inadmissible weakness: 'Die Existenz ist die Stimmung, die ihn bewegt und die er fordert, hart und unaufhörlich', he writes in his *Roman des Phänotyp* (1944, *GW* II, p. 153). The *Erfüllungsstunde*, the end of the summer and the autumn, when mature nature reaches its climax, is therefore a lyrical cipher image. Particularly in the late 'statisch' poems it conjures up associations, rather than simply maturity in the biological sense which is seen as something positive. It indicates in a general anthropological sense the turning-point from maturity into decline (autumn and winter) which immediately follows.

At the sight of maturing nature, the brilliance and joy of summer, which burns for the last time in *rote und goldene Brände*, the poet asks himself the bitter question of the meaning of his own life and the poetry which he has achieved with so much pain and difficulty. For the *Reich* of poetry he turns to the image of the *Garten* as used by the Symbolists and also by Stefan George, Hofmannsthal, and Rilke to describe the self-contained and enclosed realm of absolute art. Benn regards himself excluded as a poet from the simple, unproblematic happiness of nature and the average man. But he does not prove to be a sentimental nature poet, longing for the return of the lost unity between man and world. Unlike Thomas Mann's *Tonio Kröger*, he does not praise, half ironically, half longingly, the 'Wonne der Gewöhnlichkeit', but rather decisively affirms his destiny, his absolute, inevitable solitude. He does not need any *Sieg* or *Siegsbeweise*, for poetry is now for him the artist's lonely monologue and can no longer fulfil the task of providing the interpretation and solution of the mystery of existence for all mankind. He therefore quotes Rilke's words from his *Requiem für Wolf Graf Kalckreuth* (1908): 'Wer spricht von Siegen? Überstehn ist alles'—words which inspired all his generation (*GW* IV, p. 29). At the time when this poem was written he himself wrote in his critical essay *Weinhaus Wolf*: 'Du stehst für Reiche, nicht zu deuten und in denen es keine Siege gibt' (*GW* II, p. 140). In place of a union between absolute total art and the totalitarian state ('Drittes Reich'), or between art and power, which he had attempted to find since 1933, he now seeks a union between art and solitude. As he is totally committed to the realm of the intellect, he knows that he has thus had to renounce all claims to happiness in the normal sense. He describes the task of the poet by the memorable antithetical concept of *Gegenglück*, an ambiguous term. Commitment to the intellect demands an attitude to life which opposes the demand for mere happiness, but contains within itself a higher happiness which can be achieved through suffering and solitude. Dionysiac intoxication is now replaced by apolline clarity of form in art.

l. 2. *Erfüllungsstunde*: neologism.
l. 3. *Brände*: flowers.
l. 4. *Gärten*: cf. Stefan George, *Das Jahr der Seele* (1897), Hugo von Hofmannsthal, *Der Tod des Tizian* (1892), R. M. Rilke, fourth *Duino Elegy*, *l.* 21.
l. 12. *Gegenglück*: neologism, found already in 1916 in the short story *Die Insel* (*GW* II, p. 42), where it refers to dionysiac ecstasy in intoxication and dream.
Geist: a concept central to Benn's work from the thirties onwards, which for him is superior to nature and life, in the sense of Hegel's (1770–1831) *Phänomenologie des Geistes*, which Benn often quoted. In modern times it is no longer manifested in religion but in philosophy and above all in art: 'Geist oder Leben! Verwirklichung von Geist im Leben ist nicht mehr' was the bitter conclusion that he drew in 1937 in *Weinhaus Wolf* (*GW* II, p. 145).

33. Die weißen Segel

(Publ. Jan. 1936 in the poetry series *Das Gedicht* and later dedicated to his Bremen friend F. W. Oelze.)

The poem shows the confrontation of two worlds: the world of history and the world of art. Benn frequently used the image of the *weiße Segel* for history, as for example in 1931 in his *Akademie-Rede*: 'auch die Geschichte [ist] heute nur noch vorhanden als kongestive Synthese, als Impression von großen Massen, von Dreadnoughts heute und von weißen Segeln einst' (*GW* I, p. 433). To the historical perspectives from early times up to the present day he allotted differently coloured 'Segel': 'Wenn ich plötzlich über allen Meeren und Fluten die Segel sehe, weiße, braune, vielfarbige, die von Salamis, die der Mayflower und womöglich einige vom Titicacasee, von den Urzeiten bis zu den Meetings von Cowes: war das nichts?' (*GW* II, p. 241; cf. also p. 232). At the same time as this poem was written he angrily addressed his contemporaries: 'Leben wollt ihr, euer weißes, erfülltes, sich verwirklichendes Leben im Prunk der Derbys und im Schnee der Regatten — jetzt kommt keine Gnade mehr, jetzt kommt die Nacht' (*Weinhaus Wolf*, 1937, *GW* II, p. 146).

Benn begins by furnishing the world of history with positive colours, in that he speaks of a *leuchtende Fahrt* and recognizes its justification as *eine Segel-Art*. In the second verse he turns to antiquity, when man was nearer to creation, as the undivided *der Eine* in whom animal and human were united like the centaurs of antiquity. He lived in a world of myth, sacrifice (*Rauch*), and the ritual sacrificial feasts (*Widdermahl*). His relationship with the external world was still intact. Then began the development of the historical world (verse 3), which only knows an uninterrupted evolution and advance (*Kiel im Elemente*), and which in its desire for power approves of war (*Bug in Wurf und Wehr*), but does not question itself and holds the questioner at bay. Even where it appears to have come to rest (verse 4: *Spill und Tau am Lager*), it remains essentially unstable (*der Topp sich dreht im Nu*); it can change suddenly, and has no room for the thinker and poet.

The poet now turns his glance from the *weiße Segel* to himself. In face of the signs of victory of the historical world of power (*Flagg' und Fahnen*), he calls upon himself (verse 5) to consider in silence (*gedämpft*) his own being and true worth, which are questioned by this world. Just as the historical process derives from primeval antiquity, so his own consciousness (*Gefühl*) has similar origins and can recall a long series of ancestors (*Ahnen*). But the poet is not only a passive descendant of the past; through struggle and suffering he has enriched himself. It is characteristic of his consciousness that he is his own ultimate judge (verse 6), that there are no longer any divine powers that can of their mercy grant him something, such as the bread and wine in the Eucharist, which in classical antiquity were also gifts from the gods to men (cf. No. 26, *Du mußt dir alles geben*). They have been replaced by his own *Leiden und Denken*, and only through them and no longer through a religious cult can he achieve a relationship with the whole *Sein* of the world. 'Es gibt nur den betrachtenden und den leidenden Geist. Heute und hier. Denken ist Leiden' (*GW* IV, p. 259).

The two final verses define the poet's task in the present; the seventh verse is a synthesis of Orient and Occident, as in Goethe's

West-östlicher Divan, a synthesis which also unites nature and intellect. The symbol of Asia, which stands for nature, is the *Ströme . . . uralte, zaubergebleicht*, in which man seeks purification and in which his ashes are submerged after death. To swim through these streams, *östliche Ströme durchschwimmen*, therefore means to turn towards the void that stands behind all being. The essential task of Western man, on the other hand, who personifies intellect, is to determine his own position in the world ('Erkenne die Lage' is the first maxim of life in *Der Ptolemäer*, 1947, *GW* II, p. 232), in this instance by gazing upwards (cf. No. 31, *Am Brückenwehr* IV, his contemplation of the mountain peaks and ridges). Implied here too is what Benn calls 'Wertfolge und Perspektive in die Zukunft' (*GW* II, p. 139). The eighth verse is pure gnomic poetry. In it Benn takes up Rilke's doctrine that it is the task of the poet to transform the earth into inwardness and intellect, which is thus formulated in the seventh *Duino Elegy*:

> . . . Sichtbar
> wollen wirs haben, wo doch das sichtbarste Glück uns
> erst zu erkennen sich gibt, wenn wir es innen verwandeln.
> Nirgends, Geliebte, wird Welt sein, als innen. Unser
> Leben geht hin mit Verwandlung.

At this time, when he had finally retired from the world of politics and developed a harsh dualism of life and intellect, history and art, action and contemplation (cf. *Weinhaus Wolf*, *GW* II, p. 139), Benn included himself amongst those 'die schweigend die Verwandlung erwarteten' (*Der Ptolemäer*, 1947, *GW* II, p. 223). His concept of *Verwandlung* is more embracing than Rilke's, in that for him not only does it mean the artistic transformation of the external world, first into the inwardness of the poet, and then into the work of art of the poem, but also, biologically and historically speaking, it refers to the physical and spiritual mutations of mankind. In addition his work has frequent associations with the mythical stories of antiquity told in Ovid's *Metamorphoses*, and with Goethe's concept of metamorphosis and development.

l. 1. *Bogen*: ambiguous: the weapons of the warriors on the ships, or the curves described by the sailing-boats. Behind this is the image of the 'Lebensbogen', cf. the poem *Wir ziehn einen großen Bogen* (1951, *GW* III, pp. 266–7), which gives a much gloomier picture of the journey of life.

l. 3. *Wogen*: as early as 1931 Benn referred very contemptuously in the poem *Was sagt ihr zu dem Wogen der Geschichte* (publ. 1933, *GW* III, pp. 148–9) to the 'Wogen' or 'Wellen' of European history as it hastened towards its downfall.

l. 5. *Des hohen Tiers*: in his essay *Sein und Werden* (1935), written about the same time as this poem and a useful aid to its interpretation, Benn speaks, inspired by Julius Evola's book *Erhebung wider die moderne Welt* (1935), of the 'Bild des frühen, hohen, des transzendenten, des Traditionsmenschen . . . , des Menschen, der die Überlieferung trägt. Die Lehre nun dieses frühen Menschen ist so, daß sie dem heutigen Europäer, soweit er überhaupt die Mittel besitzt, sich ihr geistig zu nähern, als völlig katastrophal, abnorm und destruktiv erscheinen muß; denn sie lautet: es gibt zwei Ordnungen, eine physische und eine metaphysische; zwei Naturen: eine niedere und eine hohe; die niedere ist das Werden, die hohe ist das Sein. Die Bewegungsformen der niederen sind Strömung, Unruhe, Bedürftigkeit, begierdehaftes Einswerden, Ohnmacht sich zu vollenden; die des Seins: Zucht, Reinigung, Fasten, in sich selbst Sein, Weihen. Mit anderen Worten, sie gibt das Bild des ursprünglichen, des Traditionsmenschen, prinzipiell des Menschen so: der Mensch ist Geist, einsamer unentrinnbarer Geist' (*GW* IV, pp. 255–6).
des Einen: cf. No. 26, *Du mußt dir alles geben*, where the poet refers to himself as 'der Eine', characterizing his absolute uniqueness and solitude in a godless world.

l. 6. *zentaurisch*: an adjective formed from 'Zentaur', centaur, in Greek mythology a creature consisting of the body of a horse and the upper part of a man. Benn describes early man as a unity of opposites, who does not yet suffer from the division between nature and intellect, body and consciousness, as does modern man. Cf. the poem *Sommers* (1948, *GW* III, p. 232).

l. 7. *frühe Welt*: the mythical epochs of human existence before the beginning of historically recorded time, which Evola called 'Traditionswelt' (*GW* IV, p. 254).

l. 8. *Rauch und Widdermahl*: Benn says of early man: 'Das Maß aller Dinge: verwahrt im Ritus, anerkannt im Opfer . . .' (*GW* IV, p. 256).

l. 13. *Spill*: 'capstan', 'winch'.

l. 14. *Topp*: the topmast. Benn is referring to the pennant fixed to the top of the mast, showing the direction of the wind, and therefore affecting the course of the ship. An image for the sudden change of direction of historical evolution.

l. 25. *Ströme*: an image often used by Benn from the philosophy of Heraclitus, whom he regarded as an Asian since he came from Ephesus. In *Sein und Werden* there is an analogous statement: 'Die Tradition, die die Schöpfung dem Menschen zu tragen übergab, heißt: Geist. Unwandelbarer, unreduzierbarer Geist. Geist ohne Werden. *Panta rhei* ['everything is in a state of flux'—Heraclitus] — das ist Natur; der Mensch das Maß aller Dinge, das ist Geist' (*GW* IV, p. 256). Here Benn is attempting to synthesize East and West, nature and intellect.

l. 26. *zaubergebleicht*: neologism: the East as the world of magic.

ll. 27–8. 'Hohes und wertes Leben, das ist immer Leben mit Bezug auf Universalität, Leben mit Sicherheit im Sein, Unbeirrbarkeit des inneren Besitzes bei tiefem Verwandlungswissen; autonomes Leben, gleichgültig gegenüber dem Menschlichen; altes Leben, rückgewendetes Leben' (*Sein und Werden, GW* IV, p. 259; cf. also p. 257, *ll.* 1–4).

ll. 29–30. Of intellectual people as guardians of tradition in the modern age Benn says in *Sein und Werden*: 'Sie sind die Wachenden, und wenn die Zeiten gekommen sind, lenken sie die Kräfte der Auferstehung' (*GW* IV, p. 261).

34. Das Ganze

(Written probably 1934, publ. Jan. 1936 in *Das Gedicht.*)

An autobiographical poem, written at a time when Benn felt misunderstood and in self-defence wrote his *Lebensweg eines Intellektualisten* (1934). Looking back his life appeared to him cleft into harshly opposing experiences, which he presents in verses 1 and 2 in a series of antitheses, and the question as to what was the driving-force behind these *Stürme* of life remained open for the time being.

The second verse emphasizes his loneliness and unhappiness, his characteristic way of experiencing everything deeply, which gave the outside world no insight into his inner life. The image of the *Ströme* hints that his life was moving in a meaningful direction towards a goal and that his artistic intentions would be fulfilled.

The third verse is directed against one-sided views of his personality and his work, and opposes both those who considered him constructive and those who considered him destructive: these were only partial reflections of his total personality. Only the poct can realize the totality and unity of his life and work.

In the fourth and fifth verses the poet's youth, when he still possessed some undefined faith, is confronted by the moment when he saw himself face to face with his own destiny. The dark power which hangs over human existence and determines it appears as a *nacktes Haupt, in Blut, ein Ungeheuer,* like the Medusa or the Sphinx. The inhumanity of this power, in which all the cruelty and harshness of life are revealed to the poet, appears to be softened by the tears which hang from the eyelashes of this monster. These are less a sign of sympathy with man than a symbol of the suffering which characterizes human existence. Similar thoughts are expressed in Benn's essay *Sein und Werden* (1935): '. . . dem Blick rückwärts, was antwortet ihm, was sieht herauf? Ein unheimlich dunkles Gesicht sieht herauf aus der Traditionswelt, über den Rand der Dinge, über das Brachfeld, über die katalaunischen Gefilde: etwas Menschlich-Warmes, Göttlich-Gütiges —? nein: Sphinx!' (*GW* IV, p. 260).

35. Leben — niederer Wahn

(Publ. 1936 in *Ausgewählte Gedichte,* 2nd ed.)

Here Benn polemicizes against the concept of life which dominated a great deal of philosophy from the beginning of the twentieth century onwards and especially that of Friedrich Nietzsche, as well as Wilhelm Dilthey, Georg Simmel, Henri Bergson, and Hermann Keyserling. This so-called 'Lebensphilosophie' assigned an absolute value to life, and in its biological and psychological aspects put it higher than the intellect. This is expressed particularly aggressively by the philosopher Ludwig Klages, whom Benn detested, in whose main work, *Der Geist als Widersacher der Seele,* which appeared 1929–33 in four volumes, Life and Intellect appear as irreconcilable opposites.

Benn now turned against this anti-intellectual irrationalism, which he had worshipped in his youth. Having been forced to recognize the fatal results of these ideas in the abstruse ideology of National Socialism, he now professed firm belief in the constructive powers of the intellect and its expression in artistic form. Yet he still found life and intellect in opposition: 'Nicht das Leben durch Erkenntnisreize biologisch steigern und züchterisch vollenden, sondern gegen das Leben ansetzen den formenden and formelhaften Geist. Es ist demnach nicht die faustisch-physiologische, sondern die anti-naturalistische Funktion des Geistes, seine Expressive, die wir heute über der Erde sehen' (*Weinhaus Wolf,* 1937, *GW* II, p. 148). He said repeatedly:

'Das, was lebt, ist etwas anderes als das, was denkt, das ist eine fundamentale Tatsache unserer Existenz und wir müssen uns mit ihr abfinden' (*Doppelleben*, 1943/4, *GW* IV, p. 128). 'Wer Leben sagt, ist schon gerichtet' (*Der Ptolemäer*, 1947, *GW* II, p. 214 ff.).

Leben, as the first verse declares, is not the highest value, but a base illusion of immature or unfree people. Behind the antithesis *Knaben und Knechte — du von altem Geschlechte* is Benn's polemic against the idea propagated by National Socialist propaganda that the Germans were a 'junges Volk' and therefore destined to conquer the old and decadent peoples of Europe. Benn opposes this optimism about the future by the conviction that the white race had come to the *Ende der Bahn*, was facing downfall, and could expect no new future. This was also true for the persona which is speaking here (verse 2), with its longing for ecstasy and the experience of cosmic union. In the third verse this disillusion with love and religion is increased, but in the final verse this conclusion, that life always ends in destruction, is opposed by Benn's 'Artistenevangelium', which demands 'im Geschaffenen das Ewige zu bewahren' (*Rede auf Heinrich Mann*, *GW* I, p. 413). The work of art, the perfected form, is sharply separated from its creator, the artist. He must withdraw from the thing he has finished, which is taken out of his hands. Benn's thesis that artistic form is *Glaube* rests on Nietzsche's statement that art is the ultimate metaphysical activity of mankind in an age of nihilism. In describing art as *Tat* Benn is opposing the historical world with its glorification of action. The poem *Die Form* extends and varies this final verse:

Die Form —

Die Form, die Formgebärde,
die sich ergab, die wir uns gaben —
du bist zwar Erde,
doch du mußt sie graben.

Du wirst nicht ernten,
wenn jene Saat ersteht
in den Entfernten,
dein Bild ist längst verweht.

Riefst den Verlorenen,
Tschandalas, Parias, du,
den Ungeborenen
ein Wort des Glaubens zu.

(1944, *GW* III, p. 235)

l. 7. *Stundenvertauschung*: neologism: in the creative moment, which Benn, like Hofmannsthal and Rilke, called a 'Stunde' and made subject to imaginary 'Stundengötter' (cf. No. 42, *Gedichte*), the world and the poet are at one, the division between object and subject disappears; this Benn experiences as *Vertauschung*.

l. 11. *wie es entgleitet*: cf. Hofmannsthal's *Terzinen über Vergänglichkeit* I (1894): 'Dies ist ein Ding, das keiner voll aussinnt, / Und viel zu grauenvoll, als daß man klage: / Daß alles gleitet und vorüberrinnt.'

l. 12. *Zerstörung*: in the poem *Zerstörungen* (1951, *GW* III, p. 335) Benn lists all the associations that this word aroused in him.

l. 16. *Statuen*: following the example of Rilke's *Neue Gedichte*, written when he greatly admired Rodin, Benn used *Statuen* as an image of formal perfection in art as expressed in poetry and prose. Thus he writes in his early poem *Der junge Hebbel* (1913, *GW* III, p. 21): 'Ich schlage mit der Stirn am Marmorblock / die Form heraus . . .', and in his *Rede auf Heinrich Mann* (1931): 'eine Handbreit Prosa in tagelanger Arbeit wie eine Statue zu meißeln, lückenlos die Seite, kühl der Satz' (*GW* I, p. 415). The ideas expressed in the closing lines were supported by words from André Malraux's *Psychology of Art* which Benn frequently quoted in his old age: 'Mögen die Götter am Tage des Gerichts den einstigen Formen des Lebens das Volk der Statuen gegenüberstellen! Dann wird von der Gegenwart der Götter nicht die von ihnen geschaffene Welt der Menschen Zeugnis ablegen, die Welt der Künstler wird es tun' (*GW* I, pp. 549, 400).

36. Wer allein ist —

(Publ. Dec. 1936 in the periodical *Die Literatur* 39.)

The loneliness of the poet is regarded here as the prerequisite for the inspiration and vision which give rise to the poem. As in No. 19, *Orphische Zellen*, the poet appears here as one who has been initiated into a mystery, not of life, but of art. The first verse then presents the creative process which begins with the *Zeugung* and *Keimnis* of poetic images which fill the poet like a *Flut* (cf. No. 22, *Trunkene Flut*). Their glowing light reanimates even the shadowy myths and gods of the past.

This creative solitude is absolute; it results not only from an unbridgeable gulf between the poet and mankind, but from man's existence as such. This is seen in the second verse in which the poet appears as a thinker, who has cut himself off from the outside world, only to recreate it within himself. By *Schichtung* Benn understands here the total intellectual heritage of mankind which has been gathered from the beginning of time and which, according to the teaching of C. G. Jung, dwells in the depths of the unconscious (cf. No. 19, *Orphische Zellen*). But it is a prerequisite of the rebirth of these images and archetypes that they should be raised from the unconscious into the sphere of the intellect and consciousness. When the poetic process is conceived as analogous with the biological processes of procreation and birth, then the sphere of normal human life, which mainly consists of *Nähren und Paaren*, the materialistic enjoyment of life and reproduction, merits the poet's contempt. He denies that it has any value, since mere living does not represent for him the highest goal but rather what he calls *niederer Wahn* (cf. No. 35, *Leben — niederer Wahn*).

The final verse stresses the emotional coldness with which he observes from afar and without sympathy all the changes that take place on the *Erde*, by which he means above all historical changes and those political developments resulting from war which the poet himself has experienced in his own lifetime. It is this world of action, not the poet with his commitment to the life of the intellect, that is subject to the law of *Stirb und Werde* which Goethe expressed in his *Selige Sehnsucht* (*West-östlicher Divan*, 1819):

> Und so lang du das nicht hast,
> Dieses: Stirb und Werde,
> Bist du nur ein trüber Gast
> Auf der dunklen Erde.

To this praise of an eternal life force Benn opposes the static nature of formal perfection in art. This sphere, which he called 'Ausdruckswelt', is dominated by silence and perfection. Benn's late *Statische Gedichte* correspond to the ideal expressed in the last line: *formstill sieht ihn die Vollendung an.*

l. 3. *Keimnis*: neologism: the birth and unfolding of poetic images by analogy with the germination and flowering of plants. In the lecture 'Probleme der Lyrik' (1951) Benn declares that the birth of a poem begins with the 'dumpfer schöpferischer Keim', which the author carries within himself, and calls it 'eine psychische Materie' (*GW* I, p. 506). Cf. No. 26, *Du mußt dir alles geben, l.* 18.

l. 5. *Schichtung*: geological concept (= stratification), here a metaphor for the intellectual and spiritual stages of development of humanity and the individual. Benn developed this theory of psychological and intellectual stratification in 1930 in his essay *Der Aufbau der Persönlichkeit*. There he explained that the great idea of modern psychology is 'der Schichtungsgedanke des Psychischen, das geologische Prinzip. Die Seele ist in Schichten entstanden und gebaut . . .' (*GW* I, p. 98).

l. 11. *Stirb und Werde*: this was also the title of the German translation of André Gide's autobiography *Si le grain ne meurt* (1924). Benn, who greatly respected Gide, curtly rejected the book (28 Aug. 1931 to Thea Sternheim, *ABr.*, p. 49).

l. 12. *formstill*: neologism: the repose of perfect form in a poem or work of art which links it to the surrounding silence. There is a striking analogy with Winckelmann's famous description of Greek statues, 'edle Einfalt und stille Größe', which became the accepted ideal of German classicism.

37. Auf deine Lider senk ich Schlummer

(Publ. Dec. 1936 in the periodical *Die Literatur* 39.)

This occupies a special place in Benn's love poetry, since it is not dedicated to one but to two women, as revealed by his publisher Max Niedermayer (*Gottfried Benn. Den Traum alleine tragen*, Wiesbaden, 1966, p. 162). The first is Ellinor Büller-Klinckowström, the other probably Tilly Wedekind, the widow of the writer Frank Wedekind and a friend of Benn's since 1930. Here too the real theme is the unbridgeable loneliness of the poet even in love, an 'Eros der Ferne', as he wrote in the poem *Liebe* (*GW* III, p. 175) in words which recall Rilke's 'besitzlose Liebe'. Only the poet is the 'tief Gebender', whilst the two women who try to understand him are too weak to give him anything or to understand his true nature. The lover, as with Plato and Rilke, stands higher than those he loves; he is the tragic sufferer who must bear alone the burden and the dark side of existence.

38. Anemone

(Written Good Friday 1936 in Nenndorf, near Hanover, publ. Dec. 1936 in the periodical *Die Literatur* 39.)

The antithesis of life and intellect, characteristic of Benn's late period, also encompasses the realm of nature: he contrasts modern life, with its brutal use of force and which is *ohne Güte*, with the flower which in the early spring forces its way through the cold, unfriendly earth. The anemone gently addresses to the poet, who has been deeply moved by what he sees, *ein Wort des Glaubens, des Lichts*, which signifies for him the promise of a new, more beautiful future. An aesthetic belief in the perfection of artistic form is expressed through the image of the crown of flowers and the summer which will weave it as a *Krone aus großen Blüten*. Benn did not believe in the possibility of a religious or humanitarian revival.

In a similar way Elisabeth Langgässer, in her poem *Frühling 1946*, and Wilhelm Lehmann, in *Deutsche Zeit 1947*, use the anemone as a symbol of the resurrection and renewal of man after a period of night, chaos, and downfall.

39. Astern

(Publ. 28 Apr. 1936 in the *Deutsche Allgemeine Zeitung*.)

Astern is one of the most completely 'statisch' late summer poems of Benn's Hanover period. The evocation of the asters, the poet's favourite flower from his early period onwards, gives rise to images in which the late summer is celebrated as the highest moment of fulfilment immediately before the end which is approaching. The keyword *Astern* conjures up the many-coloured autumn flowers, which in their abundance and riot of colour give the illusion of summer despite the approach of autumn with its 'schwälende Tage', and give the countryside a misty appearance, as if it were covered by smoke. This evokes a feeling of timelessness: *alte Beschwörung*, *Bann*; the 'alte Dinge' appear and grant a moment of mystic participation. This existential feeling is immediately raised by Benn to the mythical level through a description in classical terms of the gods as the givers of this *zögernde Stunde*, when time seems to stand still, and summer and autumn, life and death are held in equilibrium.

The contents of this *alte Beschwörung* evoked by the asters are given in the next verses, all three of which begin with *Noch einmal* and have a charm-like quality induced by repetition. First of all it is the summery sunlight which shines *noch einmal*. Benn personifies it, but immediately contrasts this dreamlike vision with the sceptical, disillusioning question: *was brütet das alte Werden / unter den sterbenden Flügeln vor?* and expresses the feeling that the end of life is nevertheless close at hand. The power that has determined the fate of man since primeval times is personified as a big bird, which brings forth new life shortly before its death, but is nevertheless doomed to die itself. The poet, who will still experience *noch einmal das Ersehnte, den Rausch, der Rosen Du,* also personifies the summer and portrays it as a mythical figure like light and *Werden.* Thus this moment which hovers between summer and autumn, happiness and gloom, acquires mythical depth. Though the poem is written in the present tense, the poet refers to the summer in the preterite, as if he has risen from his recollections. The summer is symbolized by the swallows which announce and end it. Through their downward motion they transform the *Vermuten,* the feeling of a dreamlike fulfilment of life, into the *Gewißheit* of the end. They *streifen die Fluten und trinken Fahrt und Nacht,* i.e. they become messengers of death, they lead the way into the darkness of death.

l. 1. *schwälend*: because it is more expressive, Benn uses the archaic spelling for *schwelend,* 'smouldering, smoking', recalling potatoes cooking on open fires in the autumn.

l. 3. *die Waage*: Benn owes this image to Eduard Mörike's (1804–75) *Um Mitternacht*:

> Gelassen stieg die Nacht ans Land,
> lehnt träumend an der Berge Wand,
> ihr Auge sieht die goldene Waage nun
> der Zeit in gleichen Schalen stille ruhn . . .

For him too the summer takes up the same attitude of *Lehnen* and watching. The image of the balance is also found in Benn's poem *Wenn dir am Ende*—(No. 41, 1939).

l. 6. *der Flor*: flowers, blossom, from the Latin *flora.*

l. 10. *der Rosen Du*: roses, as summer flowers, are particularly close to the poet; they are a *Du* for him, since their beauty makes suffering and the void disappear for a moment. Cf. *Gärten und Nächte* (1943): 'Ach, hinter Rosenblättern / versinken die Wüsten, die Welt' (*GW* III, p. 209). The fading of their petals announces the end of the summer and of the illusion that 'Stunden' and 'Träume' will last for ever: 'Wenn erst die Rosen verrinnen / aus Vasen oder vom Strauch / und ihr Entblättern beginnen, / fallen die Tränen auch' (*Rosen, GW* III, p. 237).

l. 12. *Schwalben*: the beginning and end of summer are marked by the swallows' arrival and departure. Benn speaks of the longing for swallows that will come and stay for ever; cf. *September* (1944): 'goldene Wärme und Purpurbeeren, / benagt von Schwalben, ewigen, / die nie von dannen ziehn —' (*GW* III, p. 205).

40. Tag, der den Sommer endet

(Publ. Jan. 1936 in the series *Das Gedicht.*)

In this poem the ageing poet looks back objectively on his life and artistic achievements. His work is done; as he grows older he is surrounded by a feeling of timelessness (cf. No. 39, *Astern*), in which even the images which comprised his poetic world are drawing further away from him. Both his own life and art are subject to the transience and uniqueness of nature, which speaks to the poet through signs like the ancient gods. Thus the final *Tag* of summer means more to him than the mere date of a natural event; it is a symbol, primarily for the end of creative ecstasy, which Benn represents in the first verse by images from Heraclitus: *Flammen, Fluten,* and *Spiel.* The distance between the poet's ego and the images created by him increases (verse 2), they grow pale and become timeless (*entrücken sich der Zeit*); they are still reflected in the water, the sphere of the unconscious and the absolute, and thus become permanent in contrast to the transient existence of the poet, who becomes more and more estranged from the 'trunkene Fluten' of his inner being.

In the third verse the poet turns to his own life, from whose struggles and battles he finally escaped by taking refuge in poetry. But still he has to bear these burdens, whilst the battle of life goes on outside this sphere of the intellect, represented by the image of the marching *Schwärme, Scharen,* and *Heere.* The poet now sees the younger generation continuing the old battle (cf. the poem *Den jungen Leuten* in *Destillationen,* 1953, *GW* III, p. 455).

The final verse links chiastically the images for art (*Rosen, Flammen, Zeichen*) with images for the heroic life, as found in Nietzsche (*Waffenspanner, Pfeile, Banner*). The adverb *weit* places these symbols out of the poet's reach in the distance expressed in the first verse between the poet and his inner self. The image of the falling *Zeichen* is taken up again, the banners are furled, and the two realms of art and life are made subject to the law of transience.

The word *Unwiederbringlichkeit,* which takes up the whole of the last line, and is the key-note to the whole poem, stresses its uniqueness. The poet's feeling of resignation, in a period of confusion and withdrawal into self, contradicts Nietzsche's teaching of eternal recurrence, and apparently Benn's own theory of the 'Auferstehung' of the earth in the eternity of the absolute work of art, which outlasts its own creator. Benn's position thus becomes more radical.

l. 2. *Zeichen*: cf. Heraclitus: 'The lord, whose is the oracle at Delphi, neither utters nor hides his meaning but shows it by a sign' (*Fragment* 93).

l. 3. *Flammen*: according to Heraclitus, fire is the beginning of all things. The image of the flame for the poet and thinker comes from Nietzsche's *Ecce homo* with its final line: 'Flamme bin ich sicherlich.' It is also found in Stefan George's famous poem from the *Stern des Bundes* (1914): 'Wer je die flamme umschritt, / Bleibe der flamme trabant . . .' To Benn it means poetic ecstasy.

l. 4. *Fluten*: cf. No. 22, *Trunkene Flut*, an image for the creative ecstasy of the poet.
Spiel: the metaphysical concept of the world as the plaything of the Aion, taken from Heraclitus (*Fragment* 52). The idea of art as an aesthetic game, in which man first comes to consciousness of self, is found in Schiller's *Briefe über die ästhetische Erziehung des Menschen* (letter 15). Cf. No. 47, *V. Jahrhundert* III.

l. 7. *Wasser*: according to Thales of Miletus (*c.* 624–545 B.C.), water is the basis of all things, into which they, reflected here as poetic images, finally return. On the teaching of Jung that water is the symbol of the unconscious and the mirror of the soul, cf. No. 25, *Regressiv*.

l. 13. *Rosen*: as in Rilke's late work ('on se décide pour la rose ou pour la médaille', *Poèmes français*), an image for poetic life, which is evoked by the roses and forms an antithesis to the heroic life.
Waffenspanner: archer, crossbowman, or rifleman who must brace his weapon before he fires. In the Middle Ages the knights were served by *Waffenspanner*, who handed them the bent crossbow.

l. 14. *Pfeile*: cf. No. 31, *Am Brückenwehr* IV, *l.* 9, the quotation from *Weinhaus Wolf* (*GW* II, p. 140). Stefan George wrote of the poetic word as a 'Pfeil' in the preface to the *Teppich des Lebens* XVI: 'Da steigt das mächtige wort — ein grosses heil — / Ein stern der auf verborgenen furchen glimmert / Das wort von neuer lust und pein: ein pfeil / Der in die seele bricht und zuckt und flimmert.'

l. 16. *Unwiederbringlichkeit*: neologism from the adjective 'unwiederbringlich', by analogy with 'Unendlichkeit', etc. The poet is referring to a metaphysical power, such as the void, which stands behind everything. Cf. Benn's oratorio *Das Unaufhörliche* (1931) and his own interpretation of it (*GW* III, pp. 594–9).

41. Wenn dir am Ende—

(Written on 4 Mar. 1939, publ. posthumously in *Primäre Tage*, 1958.)

Benn contrasts the experience of the transience of the world and the awareness that he is living in a final period of human civilization with his faith in the timelessness and permanence of poetic images and art. Nature no longer shows herself to the ageing poet in the harsh contrast of earth and heaven, but rather in tender transitions, nuances, and colours. Everything is in harmony and equilibrium, an existential situation, which allows neither bitterness nor complete reconciliation of opposites. But even this harmony is counterbalanced in the third verse by the experience of pain, which has positive force (*gelobt*). The experience of the burden of existence is necessary for poetic vision (the *Sich-Schliessen* of the *Gesichte*); these arise from this inner equilibrium, for which Benn, as in the poem *Astern* (No. 39, *ll.* 3–4), uses the image of the *Waage*, which is laden with *viele Gewichte*.

42. Gedichte

(Written 1941, publ. Aug. 1943 in the private edition *Zweiundzwanzig Gedichte*.)

In his late poems Benn strikes the solemn note characteristic of the late work of Goethe, whose poems he had taken with him to Landsberg. Here he follows Goethe's *Prooemion* (1817): 'Im Namen dessen, der Sich Selbst erschuf!', in which the poet interprets nature in the name of God, who always remains unknown, even though he influences the whole world. The poet enthusiastically experiences the *Unermeßlichkeit* of the world, in which everything becomes for him an image of the godhead.

In contrast to Goethe's religious fervour, Benn's poem is full of resignation and gloom. In three long verses, the form of which resembles a *Stanze* (five-stress iambic eight-line verse with alternating feminine and masculine rhymes), but without the rhyming couplet at the end, Benn discusses the relationship of art to reality, faith, power, and history. A climax similar to that of the *Stanze* form is reached in the final verse by the repetition of the motif *Gedichte* and the gnomic conclusion of the last line.

Even the modern poet, who has no religious or metaphysical message, speaks in the name of a supra-personal power, which determines the fate of man. It grants *Stunden*—the fruitful moments of art and life—in the name of the 'Stundengott', who can only be experienced in such moments. But his message remains obscure—*doch unausdeutbar bleibt das Stundenlied,* he writes in the final verse—like this mysterious God himself, whom Benn often describes as 'dunkel'. He cannot be seen, but only felt from the shadow that he throws over the *Jahr* of life and history, which he brings to an end. Art, which today speaks in the name of the *deus absconditus,* receives metaphysical dignity and a task to fulfil in the present historical situation in which the poet finds himself (*im Schicksal des Geschlechts, dem du gehört*). As so often in Benn's work, it is the final era of the white race. But he does not feel himself called to be its interpreter, and asks the meaning of this age. He turns away from its *fragloses Auge* to the sphere of art and poetry, in which a new creative process is taking place, contrasting with the chaos which reigns in the sphere of history. The destruction, dissolution, and break-up of the accepted view of the world (*die den Blick zerstört*), which Benn also calls 'Wirklichkeitszertrümmerung' or 'Zusammenhangdurchstoßung', is necessary for the moment of creative synthesis. As so often, Benn here reverses the relationship between subject and object: the *Dinge* appear here as the active elements; they free themselves from their usual relationship with reality and intrude coldly into poetic visions. To this the poet reacts by producing a new *Bindung*, which for Benn has the secret character of poetic magic. As early as 1927 he says of the *mystische Bannung* of objects through poetry: 'Schwer erklärbare Macht des Wortes, das löst und fügt. Fremdartige Macht der Stunde, aus der Gebilde drängen unter der formfordernden Gewalt des Nichts. Transzendente Realität der Strophe voll von Untergang und voll von Wiederkehr: die Hinfälligkeit des Individuellen und das kosmologische Sein, in ihr verklärt sich die Antithese . . .' (*Lyrisches Ich*, *GW* IV, p. 14). At the end of this verse Benn takes a look into the realm he calls the *Gestaltungssphäre*: 'Das Wesen des Menschen ist die Gestaltungssphäre . . . Fläche in Tiefe überführen, Worte durch Beziehung und anordnendes Verwenden zu einer geistigen Welt eröffnen, Laute aneinanderketten, bis sie sich halten und Unzerstörbares besingen, dies ist ihre Tat' (*Weinhaus Wolf*, 1937, *GW* II, p. 132).

The second verse leads from the relationship between art and reality to the opposition between art and history. The historical world seems doomed to collapse in ruins (cf. No. 11, *Schädelstätten*); there is nothing permanent about it, only destruction and death. The poet, on his way to determine his own position in the present, passes significant historical stations of suffering, which reiterate his thesis (cf. No. 29, *Dennoch die Schwerter halten*) that what counts in history is not masses and nations, victory and triumph, but only the suffering of great individuals. Christ, from whom Benn had earlier estranged himself, is given a very positive value during the anti-Christian period of National Socialism; here he is referred to as *tiefste Seele* and his struggle and inner suffering on the Mount of Olives are evoked. With him Benn includes the ruling families of the Angevins and Hohenstaufen in their struggle for the possession of southern Italy in the thirteenth century. But the stations of suffering in history are, as the colon indicates, prefigurations of the situation of the modern poet, whose position is *ein neues Kreuz, ein neues Hochgerichte.* This image is consciously ambiguous: the poet too appears as the sufferer and the one who has been crucified. Benn said of the poets in his lecture 'Probleme der Lyrik' (1951): 'Eigentlich sind sie nur Erscheinungen, und sind diese Erscheinungen dann tot, und man nimmt sie vom Kreuz, muß man ehrlicherweise zugeben, daß sie sich selbst an dieses Kreuz geschlagen haben — was zwang sie dazu? Etwas muß sie doch gezwungen haben' (*GW* I, p. 516). Behind these words is a quotation from Henrik Ibsen that Benn knew: 'Dichten heißt, sich selber richten' ('Soll die Dichtung das Leben bessern?', 1955, *GW* I, p. 589).

The position of the poet in the modern world is *eine Stätte ohne Blut und Strang*, since it is a place of intellectual suffering. Yet he is not only the sufferer and crucified, but also the judge and critic of his times, who *schwört in Strophen, urteilt im Gedichte.* Therefore his intellectual place in life can be regarded as identical with that of the Fates, who silently determine the fate of men as they spin their web of destiny and sing the *Stundenlied* (cf. No. 26, *Du mußt dir alles geben, ll.* 21–4).

The final verse takes up again the solemn invocation of the first verse, and stresses the darkness of God and the inability of man to grasp the meaning of his message, the *Stundenlied.* As in his sketch *Erkenne die Lage* (1944), Benn conveys here in general terms that God is indeed alive and 'lebendiger dann je', but that he does not interfere 'unmittelbar in den Daseinskreislauf' (*GW* II, p. 281). But should even a shadow of God fall on the *Jahr am Steingeröll der Weltgeschichte*, by which Benn means the final epoch when all forms of religion have been destroyed (*Geröll der Himmel*), and when even the world of politics has led to destruction (*Geröll der Macht*), then it is only that shadow of the divine *der das Jahr vollendet* that gives this epoch its form and conclusion and even a lasting meaning, however obscure. At the end of the poem the *Stunde* of the poet is once more brought face to face with this epochal *Jahr* in the night-time of the present: he too is a lonely sufferer, like Christ on the Mount of Olives. The poet's situation becomes more poignant, since he can no longer pray to God (cf. *GW* II, p. 281). The place of a dialogue between God and man has been taken by the monologue, *das Selbstgespräch des Leides und der Nacht*. This monologue is supra-personal, in so far as it is not a conversation between the lyrical 'I' and the lyrical 'Thou', but a monologue within the supra-personal powers controlling the lives of men. The poet, who has lost his world and roots, can only exist in the poem itself, which, as Benn frequently emphasizes, no longer directs its message towards other men, but as an 'absolutes Gedicht' silently revolves within itself, shut off from the outside world.

l. 2. *gehört*: abbreviated form of 'angehört hast'.

l. 9. *Weltruine*: neologism: the *Weltgeschichte* (*l.* 21) is seen as a great building which has fallen into ruin and is surrounded by *Steingeröll* (cf. No. 11, *Schädelstätten*).

l. 10. Cf. Mark 14^{26} ff. and Rilke's poem *Der Ölbaum-Garten* (1906), which in turn is influenced by Gérard de Nerval's *Le Christ aux oliviers*. A model for this was Jean Paul's *Rede des toten Christus vom Weltgebäude herab, daß kein Gott sei* (from *Siebenkäs*, 1795). Early in his life Benn recognized the tragedy of the suffering of Christ and stressed its futility: 'O ewiges Überall, o ewiges Nirgendwo, o ewiges Umsonst; des Juden, der sich selbst sich übergab, das Weltall schweigt zu tief' (*Das letzte Ich*, 1921, *GW* II, p. 96). In the decade when the *Gedichte* were written, Christ became an ideal in the age of nihilism: 'Dies ist das Gesetz: Nichts ist, wenn je etwas war, nichts wird sein. Der schönste und der tiefste Gott geht vorüber, der einzige, der das Geheimnis des Menschen trug: je größer der Erkenntnis, um so unendlicher das Leid' (*Weinhaus Wolf*, 1937, *GW* II, p. 150). Here he draws close to Socrates (p. 151) as the embodiment of the intellectual man who conquers through suffering and death.

l. 11. *Posilipp*: a hill south-west of Naples, which separates the Gulf of Naples from the Gulf of Pozzuoli. It is called after the villa 'Pausilypon' = 'ease the pain', which belonged to a Roman nobleman. It is not certain whether Benn knew what the name meant.

Anjouine: In 1266 Charles of Anjou conquered Sicily in the battle of Benevento. The House of Anjou then ruled Naples.

l. 12. *Stauferblut*: neologism: the family of the Hohenstaufen, which ruled Germany and Italy from 1138 to 1268.

Racheschritt: neologism: in 1267 the last Staufer, Konradin, a grandson of Frederick II, tried to reconquer southern Italy and Sicily, but was defeated by Charles of Anjou and beheaded in his presence on 29 October 1268 in a public square in Naples. In 1328 the House of Anjou also died out.

l. 19. *Schatten*: cf. the introductory chapter 'Der Stundengott' in the *Roman des Phänotyp* (1944, *GW* II, pp. 152–5), in which the poet as the 'Phänotyp', i.e. 'die Summe aller in einem einzelnen Individuum tatsächlich erscheinenden Wesenszüge' (*GW* I, p. 90), and as an existentialist sees himself as a 'Schattenspiel', as 'die Silhouette des Stundengotts'. It is also possible that here the *Schatten* means the great poet, whose *Stundenlied* alone can bring the epoch, the *Jahr* to its close. Edgar Lohner (*Passion und Intellekt*, pp. 194–5) interprets this image as referring to Christ, whose public life only lasted a year, and sees the *Stundenlied* in what he preached—but this interpretation is too narrow. That Benn understood God to be the highest transcendental power can be seen from the prayer which he quoted from the sayings on the black stone of the Kaʿba, from which he takes this image: 'Nimm uns im Schatten Deines Thrones auf an dem Tag, an dem kein anderer Schatten mehr sein wird als Dein Schatten' (*Roman des Phänotyp*, 1944, *GW* II, p. 163).

l. 20. *Stundenlied*: neologism for the song sung by the Fates or the *Stundengott* which enters into the poem. In his *Akademie-Rede* Benn says that the poet in a state of 'schöpferische Lust', which he calls 'Stunde', catches sight of the 'Stundengötter, die auflösen und gestalten' (*GW* I, p. 437), but behind them stand blind nature and the void.

43. Bilder

(Written 1941, publ. Aug. 1943 in the private edition *Zweiundzwanzig Gedichte*.)

In this poem Benn gathers together all the negative aspects of suffering, need, and depravity which painters such as Rembrandt or the Expressionists displayed in their portraits. He was not only seeking to recognize *Züge derer, die es malten*, i.e. of the great artists as individuals, those who lived outside bourgeois society and therefore 'paid' for the life they led; he also built up from them the image of the artist as such, whom he calls *den großen Genius — Ihn.* The poem sums up the conclusions Benn had come to in his essays *Genie und Gesundheit* (1930, *GW* I, pp. 84–9) and *Das Genieproblem* (1930, *GW* I, pp. 107–22) on the relationship between genius and decadence, abnormal sexuality, and criminality. Later he came back to and reiterated the images of this poem in his lecture 'Altern als Problem für Künstler' (1954, *GW* I, pp. 552–82).

l. 3. *gedunsen*: in his essay *Das Genieproblem* Benn explains the process of 'Genieerklärung und Geniebildung' by the fascination which the life of depraved and fallen artists arouses: 'man geht seinem Leben nach, man stößt auf Abstieg von der Höhe, elendes verkommenes Alter, sehr suggestiv ist Armenhaus, aufgedunsenes Gesicht, trübe Augen, nun setzt die Mythe ein . . .' (*GW* I, p. 117).

l. 5. *Felle*: derogatory, for skin that has grown old.
Stoppeln: stubbly beard, sign of physical neglect.

l. 6. *Fuselräusche*: drunkenness produced by cheap, badly purified alcohol (*Fusel*). In *Genie und Gesundheit* Benn lists forty-seven great artists and statesmen who were drunkards or who died as the result of drink and narcotics.

l. 7. *Korn*: spirits distilled from corn.
prellen und täuschen: cf. the relationship between genius and criminality which Benn repeatedly stressed. In 'Altern als Problem für Künstler' he writes: 'Es ist noch nicht lange her, daß der dreiundachtzigjährige Degas sagte: „Ein Bild ist etwas, das ebensoviel Geriebenheit und Lasterhaftigkeit verlangt wie ein Verbrechen . . ."' (*GW* I, p. 571).

l. 8. *Stummel*: cigarette or cigar stub. The syntactical combination of the present participle *fischend* and the past participle *verwahrt* is characteristic of Benn's wilfully severe and yet nonchalant attitude to language.

l. 9. *Lebensabend*: cf. 'Altern als Problem für Künstler' (1954): 'Lebensabend, diese Lebensabende! Die meisten mit Armut, Husten, krummen Rücken, Süchtige, Trinker, auch einige Kriminelle, fast alle ehelos, fast alle kinderlos, diese ganze bionegative Olympiade, eine europäische Olympiade, eine zisatlantische, die den Glanz und die Trauer des nachantiken Menschen durch vier Jahrhunderte trug' (*GW* I, p. 570).

l. 11. *Hochhinauf*: neologism for the artists' workshops which were mostly found in cheap attics.

l. 12. *Leihhaus*: Benn said of Rembrandt in *Das Genieproblem*: 'Er war zu Lebzeiten zunächst ein angesehener Maler, aber gar nichts Einzigartiges, in der zweiten Lebenshälfte galt er als manieriert und bekam keine Aufträge mehr und verkam schließlich bekanntlich trunksüchtig und gepfändet im Armenhaus' (*GW* I, p. 117; cf. the poems *Gewisse Lebensabende* I–II, *GW* III, pp. 239–42, in which the aged Rembrandt and Shakespeare speak).

Abflußrohr: from a statement by the painter Max Beckmann, which Benn quotes: 'Ich würde in Abzugskanälen wohnen und durch alle Gullys kriechen, wenn ich mir nur dadurch die Möglichkeit rettete, zu malen' — Benn adds: 'Nattern, Gullys, Abzugskanäle — das ist das Vorspiel zu den Lebensabenden' ('Altern als Problem für Künstler', *GW* I, p. 570).

44. Ein Wort

(Publ. Aug. 1943 in the private edition *Zweiundzwanzig Gedichte*.)

In this poem Benn praises the power of the poetic word and clearly alludes to the account of the creation in Genesis (1 ff.) and the beginning of St. John's Gospel, 'In the beginning was the Word'. He wrote to Dieter Wellershoff: 'Das Wort ist die Selbstbegegnung der Schöpfung und ihre Selbstbewegung. Im Anfang war das Wort und es wird am Ende sein . . .' (22 Nov. 1950, *ABr.*, p. 205). An earlier version of this poem written in 1929 bears the title *Schöpfung* (*GW* III, p. 415); it begins with the picture of the creation of the world in six days, but then refers it to the poet and his creative word, which Benn calls here *Chiffre*. By this Benn understood a 'stilistische Figur' composed of words, a 'gedrucktes Bild' or 'schwarze Letter' (*Lyrisches Ich*, 1927, *GW* IV, p. 12), which is 'ein Kunstprodukt' ('Probleme der Lyrik', 1951, *GW* I, p. 511). It contains a coded message, which he describes here as the perception of life and the revelation of its meaning, which can suddenly emerge through the poetic word. That the power of the word can cause the sun to stand still recalls Joshua, who during the battle of Gibeon commanded the sun and the moon to stand still (Joshua 10^{12-13}), whilst the image of the silent spheres goes back to Pythagoras' teaching of the harmony and music of the spheres. This word of creation becomes the centre-point to which everything refers, the essence and source of new poetic worlds.

The second verse continues this song of praise but restricts it even further: the poetic word illuminates the emptiness of the world like a flash of lightning, not like the eternal stars, suns, planets, and fixed stars, but like the comets and meteors which shine for a moment and then quickly disappear—an image for the lyrical poem which is also found in the late work of Rilke (*Spanische Trilogie*, 1913). Benn's belief in the magical power of the poetic word which gives life and meaning is no longer so absolute and complete as for the French and German Symbolists, but made relative and limited by deep scepsis. This is seen at the end of the poem when he describes eternal darkness as the space in which the world and the individual find themselves and which can only be illuminated from time to time by poetry.

l. 6. *Flammenwurf, Sternenstrich*: neologisms for the sudden flaring up and fading of the poetic word.

45. Abschied

(Publ. Aug. 1943 in the private edition *Zweiundzwanzig Gedichte.*)

The theme of this elegy written during Benn's late period in classical blank verse is *Abschied* in an all-embracing sense, as Rilke used the term in his late poetry (*Sonette an Orpheus* II, 13, 'Sei allem Abschied voran . . .'). In this monologue the poet faces death and says farewell to the world and the art of poetry itself.

The 'Du' addressed in the first verse is the solitude of the ageing poet, not a feeling but an existential situation, which is also the theme of many other poems written at this time. In three similes (a rare feature in Benn's style) the nature of *Einsamkeit* and *Überleben* is described in the first few lines as pain (in the image of the bleeding wound and the blood which flows from it), as the clouding of the mind (in the image of the night, as it spreads over the countryside in the evening), and—positively—as the fulfilment of existence despite all difficulties (in the image of roses which flower in every garden). The absolute loneliness of the modern poet arises both from his old age (*Alter*) and from the loss of contact with man and reality (see the second verse), from the survival of his own dreams, poetic images which *entrücken* themselves from him (cf. No. 40, *Tag, der den Sommer endet*), and finally from an excess of suffering and conviction.

The second verse takes up the theme of the loss of reality and develops it into the thesis which is repeatedly found in Benn's poetry: that reality is only *Wahn*. Even Dr. Rönne in Benn's early story was filled with 'die Trance . . ., daß es diese Wirklichkeit nicht gäbe' (*GW* IV, p. 30). The 'Trennung von Ich und Welt', which began in classical antiquity and led to the concept of an objective reality as distinct from individual consciousness, Benn called, at the time this poem was written, 'die schizoide Katastrophe, die abendländische Schicksalsneurose' and called reality 'Ein quälender Begriff . . . der als Verhängnis über dem Abendland lastete' (*Provoziertes Leben*, 1943, *GW* I, p. 337). He had always been interested in the Indian teaching of the veil of the Maya, according to which the world is only illusion (*Trug der Einzelheiten*): 'nein, die Erscheinungen genügten *nicht*, es mußte etwas geben, dahinter, in den Schleiern, wo der Demiurg die Welten mischte: eine Seele, ein Letztes, eine Ordnung, einen Sinn' (*Diesterweg*, 1918, *GW* II, p. 457). There is no longer any connection between the *tiefes Ich*, the creative basis of the lyrical ego, which appears here as the real norm, and reality in the traditional sense. But behind this challenge to turn inwards into one's own creative depths there is what Benn called 'das uralte Menschheitsverlangen nach Überwindung unerträglich gewordener Spannungen, solcher zwischen Außen und Innen . . . zwischen Ich und Wirklichkeit' (*Provoziertes Leben*, *GW* I, p. 340). On the path of introversion the poet no longer receives from within *Wort und Zeichen* but only silence, concealing the knowledge of the transience of all earthly things. This attitude of resignation, renunciation of direct expression, and emphasis of the silence which dwells behind all poetic utterances is conceived as an *Abwärtsführen / zu Nacht und Trauer und den Rosen spät*. Thus the elegiac images of the first verse appear once more: this tripartite structure is characteristic of the poem as a whole, as seen at the beginning of the second verse in the three participles.

The third verse asks about the real nature of his earlier poetic self, which has become so estranged that it itself has become its own legend and forgotten its earlier existence. It becomes clear from the three juxtaposed questions that this earlier *tiefes Ich* had a direct relationship with itself, its own thoughts and questionings, and above all its own poetic *Wort*, which Benn describes here in the metaphor *Himmelslicht* from Goethe's dramatic fragment *Prometheus* (1773). For Goethe and for Benn it signifies the union which can be experienced in the poetic expression of the human and absolute intellect, which endows the word with a power which Benn considers lost in modern times.

This is followed in the second half of the third verse by a terrible self-accusation that he himself has destroyed (*vertan*) his *Wort*, his *Himmelslicht*. How this destruction of the word came about is not stated. But part of the explanation lies in his consciousness of individual guilt that he lent his voice as a poet to the barbaric powers of the age, the National Socialists. There is, too, a more general, objective feeling of guilt, which Kierkegaard formulated in his famous saying that the aesthetic existence of the poet, seen from a religious standpoint, is sinful. This appears in Benn's late work where he opposes the idea of Martin Heidegger that art is the 'Sich-ins-Werk-Setzen der Wahrheit': 'in der Kunst geht es ja nicht um Wahrheit, sondern um Expression' and adds self-critically: 'als letzte Frage — ist Ausdruck Schuld? Er könnte es sein' ('Altern als Problem für Künstler', 1954, *GW* I, p. 578).

But the poetic work of art as such still remains an unchallenged achievement, even if it has not brought victory or fame, and the poet must content himself with having achieved his own satisfaction. This leads to the picture of autumn which takes up the whole of the fourth verse, for everything that is said here of this *letzter Tag* can be directly referred to the existence and artistic work of the poet. The negative statements of the third verse are answered here by a positive picture, despite all limitations, of a full creative moment filled with 'finale Lust' (*spätglühend*), in which the world opens itself up once more to the poet in *weite Räume*, but yet accompanies the falling motion of existence, the *Abwärtsführen* (verse 2) to its end and death: *ein Wasser führt dich zu entrücktem Ziel*. It is characteristic of this existential farewell situation that the creative state of the poet is liberated and given over to nature, which—reversing the realistic idea of mimesis—is a reflection of both art and its creator. The movement of the *hohes Licht* in nature, which produces *im Schatten sich ein Widerspiel*, corresponds to the celebration of the poetic word as *Himmelslicht* (verse 3), and can therefore be referred back to the poet, who is like the *letzter Tag*: *er spielt sein Spiel, und fühlt sein Licht*, but who in contrast to unfeeling nature is conscious of his own being and actions. The attitude of *Abschied* from nature, life, and art, which expects neither visible profit nor reward, is finally able to renounce even recollection: the closing words *ohne Erinnern nieder* can only be understood if one remembers that Benn derived all his poetic thoughts and images from memory, referring both to Plato's idea of anamnesis and to modern psycho-analytic theories of the 'kollektives Unbewußte'. Now that the poetic work is completed, that everything has been said, even the sphere of his own inner depths can be included in the *Abschied* and renounced.

l. 4. *Matte*: poetic term for meadow, grass.
Schattenflur: neologism; through death the living become shadows.

l. 20. *Himmelslicht*: in Goethe's dramatic fragment *Prometheus* (1773) Prometheus says enthusiastically to Minerva (*ll.* 100–16): 'Und du bist meinem Geist, / Was er sich selbst ist; / Sind von Anbeginn / Mir deine Worte Himmelslicht gewesen! / Immer als wenn meine Seele spräche zu sich selbst, / Sie sich eröffnete / Und mitgeborne Harmonieen / In ihr erklängen aus sich selbst: / Das waren deine Worte. / So war ich selbst nicht selbst, / Und eine Gottheit sprach, / Wenn ich zu reden wähnte, / Und wähnt ich, eine Gottheit spreche, / Sprach ich selbst. / Und so mit dir und mir / So ein, so innig / Ewig meine Liebe dir!' The importance for Benn of Pallas Athene as the goddess of the intellect is seen in his essay *Pallas* (1943, *GW* I, pp. 362–70).

46. Wenn etwas leicht

(Publ. Aug. 1943 in the private edition *Zweiundzwanzig Gedichte*.)

This poem, which consists of a single sentence, contrasts nature and art, unity of being and the duality of human existence. In the face of riches, the beauty and inexhaustibility of natural phenomena, above all of flowers and light, the poet, reflecting on himself, laments that the potentialities of man are so limited. Consciousness of his own weight and restrictedness (verse 1) disappears at the sight of the *Glyzinienpracht*, their lightness and ecstasy (*Rauschen*). The light (verse 2) brings about everything that is denied to the poet: it comes in *Strahlen*, it is capable of transforming itself and creates contact between individual objects, whilst the poet in his solitude must remain enclosed within himself. The *Rausch* given out by the flowers and streaming light creates the dialectical unity of the dynamic and static, flowing and resting, which is portrayed in the third verse. From the praise of this ecstatic intoxication derived from existence itself, which seems now unattainable to the poet, springs the demand for renunciation and restriction in face of the abundance of nature and its manifestations. The poet must limit himself; his task is to preserve these *Stunden*, which open his eyes to his own inner depths and limited potentialities, but not to express himself in elegiac laments.

Stephen Spender has quoted this poem (translated by Christopher Middleton) in his book *The Struggle of the Modern* (1964) because it is a prototype for the situation of the modern artist.

l. 2. *Glyzinienpracht*: neologism analogous to 'Blütenpracht'. *Glyzinien* = *Wisteria sinensis*, blue flowering creeper.

47. V. Jahrhundert

(Publ. 1948 in *Statische Gedichte.*)

The heyday of Greek antiquity, which Benn discussed in great detail in his essays *Dorische Welt* (1934) and *Pallas* (1943), is seen in this trilogy, written towards the end of the Second World War and inspired by mass murder and genocide, from the point of view of death. Above all Benn portrays the way in which classical art overcame death through the belief in resurrection found in the Eleusinian mysteries and the myth of Achilles and Helen on the island of Leuke, with which he closes the trilogy. His source is Erwin Rohde's *Psyche. Seelenkult und Unsterblichkeitsglaube der Griechen* (Heidelberg, 1892), which Benn read in 1920.

I

The introduction consists of the lament of a man of ancient Athens who has a vision of his own burial ceremony and his journey into the underworld, filled with the ultimate loneliness inevitably linked with death. This poem is self-explanatory and does not have to be deduced from part II. Benn follows Erwin Rohde's chapter 'Pflege und Verehrung der Todten' (vol. i, pp. 216–58) in every detail. For him the dead Athenian, through his burial ceremony and particularly his crowning with the myrtle wreath, is a worshipper of Demeter (Ceres), who after death entered the underworld, the kingdom of Pluto (*Plutonien*), whose entrance lay in Eleusis.

l. 1. *attische Lekythe*: slim white clay vessels, painted with black mythological figures. 'Unter das Lager wurden Salbgefäße jener schlanken Bildung gestellt, wie sie Gräber so zahlreich zurückgegeben haben' (Rohde, vol. i, p. 219).

l. 2. *Überfahrt*: of the souls of the dead in Charon's boat. Rohde describes the 'Hadesfahrt des Odysseus' (vol. i, pp. 302–6) and refers to 'die Bilder in attischen, den Todten in's Grab beigebenden Gefäßen . . ., auf denen die Seele dargestellt ist, wie sie am schilfigen Ufer auf den Fährmann wartet, der sie hinüberfahren soll, von wo niemand wiederkehrt' (ibid., p. 306).
Schlaf: the classical concept of death as the brother of sleep. Cf. Homer, *Iliad*, xiv. 231 and No. 26, *Du mußt dir alles geben*, *ll.* 35–6.
Staub: the Jewish–Christian view of mankind; cf. Genesis 3^{19}: 'Dust thou art, and unto dust shalt thou return'.

l. 3. *Hadesmythe*: neologism.

l. 4. *Myrte*: 'Das Haupt des Todten pflegte man nach einer, dem Homer noch unbekannten Sitte mit Kränzen und Binden zu schmücken, wie es scheint, zu Zeichen der Ehrfurcht vor der höheren Weihe des nun Geschiedenen' (Rohde, vol. i, p. 220). 'Auf der Archemorosvase ist es ein Myrthenkranz, den eine Frau dem Archemoros auf das Haupt zu setzen im Begriff ist. Die Myrthe ist den *Χθόνιοι* heilig und daher sowohl den Mysten der Demeter als den Todten der Myrthenkranz eigenthümlich . . . Auch Grabmale bekränzte, bepflanzte man vorzugsweise mit Myrthen . . . Die Bekränzung bedeutete stets eine Art Heiligung irgendeinem Gotte' (ibid., p. 220, n. 2).
Pappellaub: perhaps an image for the loneliness of the dead added by Benn; cf. No. 9, *Pappel*.

l. 5. *Zypresse*: cf. *V. Jahrhundert* III, *l.* 8: 'weiße Zypresse ist der Hadesbaum'.

l. 6. *Rosen*: symbol of the previous festivals of the living in contrast to the cypress, the symbol of death. For Benn always a sign of abundance of life.

l. 7. *weißer Thymian, Tarant und Dosten*: 'In Athen breitete man, aus einem superstitiösen Grunde, der Leiche Origanon unter' (Rohde, vol. i, p. 219). 'Origanon (Doste, weißer Thymian) hat apotropäische Kraft; es verscheucht böse Geister . . . Legt man Doste und Tarant den Wöchnerinnen bei, so können ihnen die Volande und Gespenster nichts thun' (ibid., p. 219, n. 1).
Tarant: marsh gentian with blue or white flowers.
Doste: wild marjoram, origanum.

l. 9. *Mahl*: 'Von der Bestattungsfeier zurückgekehrt, begehen die Familienangehörigen . . . das Leichenmahl. Auch dies war ein Theil des Seelencultes. Die Seele des Verstorbenen galt als anwesend, ja als Gastgeber' (Rohde, vol. i, p. 231). *Weiheguß*: 'Man brachte Weihegüsse den Todten dar, am letzten Tage des Festes' (Rohde, vol. i, p. 238).

Räucherschwaden: 'Weihrauch bei der Darbringung' (Rohde, vol. i, p. 241, n. 3).

l. 10. *Hain*: 'Baumpflanzungen, bisweilen ganze Haine, die das Grab . . . umgaben, sollten den Seelchen als Lustort dienen' (Rohde, vol. i, p. 230).

l. 11. *Flöte, Zykladen*: 'Karisch-phrygische Trauerflöten' are mentioned by Rohde (vol. i, p. 225, n. 1) as accompaniment to burials in Athens. The Cyclades, islands in the Aegean Sea, almost encircle the island of Delos, the sacred island of Apollo, on which no dying man was allowed to remain. Here they stand for the immortality of the gods which appears beyond the reach of men, the theme of parts II and III.

l. 12. *Plutonien*: the plural of 'Plutonion', the place of worship of Pluto, a sacred place in Eleusis where a grotto in the rocks was regarded as the entrance to the underworld, into which Demeter's daughter Persephone was abducted. Rohde discusses the 'Plutonien' in vol. i, pp. 212–15, in connection with the 'Cultus der chthonischen Götter' and gives a detailed description of the Eleusinian mysteries (see below, part II).

II

After this lament on death and the final solitude of the dead follows the Greek version of belief in resurrection, the myth of Demeter and Persephone, which was represented and relived in the Eleusinian mysteries. With death (in part I) corresponds the description of a Greek landscape in the valley of Eleusis before the coming of spring, characterized by frost, numbness, and barrenness. According to the Greek myth, Demeter, after Pluto had abducted her daughter into the underworld, was forced to wander around looking for her, causing the earth to remain barren out of anger and grief. According to the Homeric hymn to Demeter, she was granted admission to the underworld at Eleusis and received her daughter back, after Zeus had decreed that Persephone should spend only a third of the year in Hades, the rest of the time with her mother. When the two goddesses met on the black rocks of Eleusis, the curse put on the earth was lifted. Their reunion was celebrated by the Athenians every year in the spring and in September in the Eleusinian mysteries, in which the initiates were promised a higher existence after death. Benn describes not only the conquest of death through the mysteries, but the heightening of life: the procession of the mystery in the third verse becomes something directly experienced in the present and the poet participates as an initiate in the procession (cf. No. 19, *Orphische Zellen, ll.* 9–16). Behind the images in this verse is the experience of the creative process, out of which springs the work of art, the poem: ecstasy, freedom from the power of fate, unsparing self-analysis. Resulting from this is the renewal of *alte Dinge*, the myths and archetypes of the past, which slumber in the very *Blut*, the subconscious of man, and are reawakened, experiencing their resurrection in the poem. The place of a religious belief in resurrection is taken by a radically aesthetic belief.

l. 3. *Schicksalsschweigen*: neologism. Through the curse of barrenness put on the earth by Demeter, the development of nature and man has come to a stand-still; destiny no longer exists, only deathly silence and immobility. This negative outlook gives way in the final verse to a more positive interpretation: whilst taking part in the mystery, man is freed from the power of fate which threatens him with destruction and death: *jedes Schicksal ruht.*

III

The third poem depicts another classical myth in the survival of the spirits of Achilles and Helen on the island of Leuke, whose white cliffs lie in the estuary of the Danube. By day Achilles sings the *Päan*, the song of praise to the god of light, Phoebus Apollo, who is also the god of death. Otherwise the island is a realm of silence and dreams. Achilles, who has already drunk of the waters of Lethe, the river of the underworld, and has therefore *viel vergessen*, appears to people who land on the island only in their dreams, giving them the mute signs of an oracle. They are allowed to land on the island by day, whilst Helen, accompanied by doves, the birds of the goddess of love Aphrodite, may also spend the night there. Together they overcome the shades and death through their *Spiel*. They revive the memory of the happy and tragic past that lies behind them—the judgement of Paris that began the Trojan war, after Paris had given Aphrodite the apple, because she promised him Helen as the most beautiful of all women, and the death of Achilles by Paris' arrow.

In lines 1–10 Benn follows in every detail the story of the classical myth as retold by Erwin Rohde (*Psyche*, vol. ii, p. 371, particularly n. 2). But in the closing lines 11–12, for which he alone is responsible, he gives the myth a unique meaning by introducing the idea that Achilles and Helen, as blessed spirits, bring about the repetition of the past in their *Spiel*, and therefore remove the weight of destiny and death in aesthetic contemplation. Thus the artistic concept of *Spiel*, which Benn took over from Schiller and Nietzsche, gains metaphysical depths.

48. Statische Gedichte

(Written in 1944, publ. 1948 in *Statische Gedichte*.)

When Benn sent his Swiss publisher Peter Schifferli of the Zürich Arche-Verlag a manuscript with about fifty poems from his late period, for which he suggested the title *Statische Gedichte*, he wrote in explanation (on 23 November 1947): 'statisch ist ein Begriff, der nicht nur meiner inneren ästhetischen und moralischen Lage, sondern auch der formalen Methode der Gedichte entspricht und in die Richtung des durch Konstruktion beherrschten, in sich ruhenden Materials, besser noch: in die Richtung des Anti-Dynamischen verweisen soll. Gelänge es mir, diesen Eindruck zu verwirklichen, würde es zeigen, daß aus meiner chaotischen expressionistischen Generation, deren einzigen Überlebender ich wohl bin (Trakl, Heym, Werfel, Hasenclever, van Hoddis, Else Lasker-Schüler sind tot, allein Joh. R. Becher lebt, aber er ist andere Wege gegangen) — doch eine innere Klärung hervorgehen konnte, die nicht abfallende Ermüdung der produktiven Kräfte bedeutet, sondern schöpferische Bändigung der schweren existentiellen Zerwürfnisse und Krisen, mit denen meine Generation aus konstitutioneller Anlage und durch die exorbitanten äußeren Verwicklungen von Anfang an zu kämpfen hatte. Statik heißt also Rückzug auf Maß und Form, es heißt natürlich auch ein gewisser Zweifel an Entwicklung und es heißt auch Resignation, es ist antifaustisch . . .' (*Briefe*, Zürich, 1960, pp. 7–8).

Statische Gedichte is therefore to be regarded as a programmatical poem which poignantly summarizes the most important themes of Benn's late poetry. The *Tiefe des Weisen*, i.e. of the poet himself, is shown in his turning away from the concept of *Entwicklung*, which had been dominant in Western ideology since the eighteenth century. It was a basic concept for Goethe; in the nineteenth century it became the all-embracing principle of biology, anthropology, and psychology, above all because of Darwin and Spencer. With its help the German scientist Ernst Haeckel (1834–1919) hoped to solve the secret of the universe. In his youth Benn believed in evolution in the Darwinian sense, and in his earliest prose piece *Gespräch* (1910) said of Darwin: 'Er bedeutet doch nur, daß alles, was ist, dem Gesetz der Entwicklung unterstellt ist; daß unser Leben verknüpft ist mit vielen anderen Leben, ja daß wir verwandt sind mit allem, was überhaupt Leben heißt' (*GW* IV, p. 183). But once Benn had become convinced that there was a basic antagonism between life and intellect, through which the spheres of action (life and history) had become radically separate from art, he began to reject this belief in evolution (cf. No. 36, *Wer allein ist*, verse 3, where as early as 1936 he formulated his law of 'Statik'). Here he clearly conceives it in biological terms (*Kinder und Kindeskinder*) in the sense of belief in the advancement and the higher evolution of mankind, which he was unable to differentiate.

In the second verse his own inner peace and isolation, which nothing could disturb or penetrate from the outside, and which is identical with inner clarity, is contrasted with the unrest of the modern world, which for lack of clarity had put itself into the hands of an aimless dynamism. His polemics are directed against all ideologies (*Richtungen*), against *Handeln* and travel: 'Es gab innerhalb der weißen Völker zwei Klassen von Menschen, die handelnden und die tiefen, und Kunst war nichts anderes, als sich eine Methode zu schaffen, um die Erfahrungen des tiefen Menschen zur Sprache zu bringen . . . einmal der Geschichtliche und einmal der Zentrale, einmal der Handelnde und einmal der Tiefe, einmal das Leben und einmal der Geist' (*Weinhaus Wolf*, 1937, *GW* II, p. 139). Against the senselessness of historical action and the aimlessness of modern desire for travel Benn sets the picture of the sage, who remains in his room and looks at the world out of his window (cf. the essay *Der Radardenker*, 1949: 'Der Mann am Fenster! Die Gedankengänge im Heim! Der Radardenker auf seinem Sessel!' (*GW* II, p. 262)). He gazes out on an evening scene, a valley in which the *Schatten* collect, and a path bordered by two poplar trees which leads to death. That the words *du weißt — wohin* are a cipher image for death is shown by the final verse of the poem *Epilog 1949* IV: 'Es ist ein Spruch, dem oftmals ich gesonnen, / der alles sagt, da er dir nichts verheißt — / ich habe ihn auch in dies Buch versponnen, / er stand auf einem Grab: „tu sais" — du weißt' (*GW* III, p. 345).

The third verse begins with the new concept of *Perspektivismus*, which Benn describes as a synonym for *Statik*. It comes from Nietzsche, who opposed the traditional concept of the absolute truth of Christian, idealistic philosophy with his strongly subjective ideology, which demands of every intellectual human being that he set his own perspectives. The unequivocal traditional picture of the world is replaced by the multiplicity and ambiguity of continually changing perspectives. Benn's concept of *Perspektivismus* is closely linked with the aphorism No. 481 from the *Wille zur Macht*, in which Nietzsche no longer recognizes any 'Tatsachen' in the sense of scientific positivism, but only subjective 'Interpretationen' of the world, which no longer has a single metaphysical meaning: 'Soweit überhaupt das Wort „Erkenntnis" Sinn hat, ist die Welt erkennbar: aber sie ist anders *deutbar*, sie hat keinen Sinn hinter sich, sondern unzählige Sinne. — „Perspektivismus".' In 1930 Benn entitled an essay *Fazit der Perspektiven* and in 1932 described Goethe's 'gegenständliches Denken' as a 'weittragendes perspektivisches Erfühlen von Zusammenhängen und Ursprüngen' (*Goethe und die Naturwissenschaften*, *GW* I, p. 186). In the following year he wrote to his friend F. W. Oelze: 'An Stelle des Begriffs der Wahrheit und Realität, einst theologisches, dann wissenschaftliches Requisit, tritt ja jetzt der Begriff der Perspektive' (27 Jan. 1933). The identification of the concept *Perspektivismus* with *Statik* rests on Benn's theory that the poet who limited himself to 'Maß und Form' and remained quietly within his inner being was continually drawing new perspectives from within himself, an activity that is demonstrated in the second part of the third verse: *Linien anlegen, / sie weiterführen / nach Rankengesetz — / Ranken sprühen* —. Linear art takes the place of the artistic combination and interweaving of themes and motifs into an organic whole, as in traditional poetry. It now juxtaposes different aspects and perspectives, the modern 'Montagekunst', which Benn defined thus: 'Jetzt werden Gedankengänge gruppiert, Geographie herangeholt, Träumereien eingesponnen und wieder fallengelassen. Nichts wird stofflich-psychologisch mehr verflochten, alles angeschlagen, nicht durchführt. Alles bleibt offen. Antisynthetik. Verharren vor dem Unvereinbaren' (*Doppelleben*, 1950, *GW* IV, p. 164). This 'Stil der Zukunft' is not mere caprice but obeys an aesthetic law which Benn here calls *Rankengesetz*. From 1900 ornamental plant motifs had been raised to the artistic principle of the 'Jugendstil' (art nouveau). Very early on Benn had become aware of the free linear line as an artistic principle in Cretan and Mycenean art (cf. *Der Garten von Arles*, 1920, *GW* II, p. 86). For him it possessed a fascination which bridged the millennia. The linear tendencies in his own style are not only seen in the image of *Ranken sprühen*, printed with double spacing and thus indicating the climax of the poem, but are also emphasized in a second image taken over from Nietzsche's poem *Vereinsamt.* It begins: 'Die Krähen schrein / Und ziehen schwirren Flugs zur Stadt: / Bald wird es schnein — / Wohl dem, der jetzt noch — Heimat hat!' Benn was preoccupied all his life with the despairing lament which is the climax to this poem: 'Wer das verlor, / Was du verlorst, macht nirgends Halt.' In contrast to Nietzsche, however, he does not note the flight of the crows in an impressionistic manner, in order then to turn it into a symbol of solitude and despair, but uses the flight itself to express his own inner feelings. *Winterrot* hints at finality and death, *Frühhimmel* on the other hand at a new beginning.

For Benn artistic activity had always been 'ein Wurf von Formen, ein Spiel in Fiebern, sinnlos und das Ende um allen Saum' (*Die Reise*, 1916, *GW* II, p. 36; cf. *GW* IV, p. 37). This *Sprühen* and *Auswerfen*, images for the eternally-orientated poetic expression, is always followed by a swing to *sinken lassen*—the withdrawal of the poetic word, transition into silence. The end of the poem accentuates this by the cryptic *du weißt — für wen*, which leaves the interpretation open.

Statische Gedichte: this concept was first coined by Richard Huelsenbeck (born 1892), one of the founders of Dadaism, who differentiated in his programmatical piece *En avant dada* (1920) between 'bruitistic', 'simultanistic', and 'static' poems. Whilst the first two have as their subject noise and movement, the static poem works with isolated individual words, which evoke an unlimited number of associations: 'Das statische Gedicht macht die Worte zu Individuen, aus den vier Buchstaben Wald tritt der Wald mit seinen Baumkronen, Försterlivreen und Wildsauen, vielleicht auch eine Pension heraus, vielleicht Bellevue oder Bella-Vista.'

l. 1. *Entwicklungsfremdheit*: neologism, expressing Benn's rejection of belief in evolution and progress.

l. 6. *Richtungen vertreten*: D. Wellershoff, *G. Benn*, p. 30, quotes Laotse: 'Was gruppiert sich nicht alles um diese Konfession der Individualität: Mönchische *vita contemplativa* und Pascals Bemerkung, alles Leiden komme daher, daß die Menschen nicht ruhig in ihrem Zimmer bleiben können, Schopenhauers Willensverneinung und dahinter der Erlösungsweg der indischen Religionen, Nichtsmachen und Versenkung, auf dem sich die Seele dem Strudel des Sansara entzieht und schließlich

Sinnsprüche aus dem Taote-King wie dieser: „Wenn ich wirklich weiß, was es heißt, im großen Sinn zu leben, so ist es vor allem die Geschäftigkeit, die ich fürchte.“ So Laotse. Und so, modern formuliert, der gleiche Gedanke bei Benn: *Richtungen vertreten . . .*'

l. 15. *zwei Pappeln*: cf. No. 9, *Pappel.*

l. 16. *du weißt*: cf. No. 13, *Entwurzelungen* (1925): 'dunkler als Kreuz ein Pfosten / trägt die Worte: „Du weißt“' (*GW* III, p. 118).

l. 19. *Linien anlegen*: in 'Altern als Problem für Künstler' (1954) Benn declares the identity of form and content to be a 'kunstphilosophische Illusion', and says: 'aus dem Osten höre ich dieselbe Melodie, Meister Kung Dsi sagt über die Maler: „Bei wem die Bedeutung die Linien überwiegt, der ist roh“ — also auch für ihn ist das Höhere, das Manipulierte, das Angefertigte der Stil' (*GW* I, pp. 577–8).

l. 21. *Rankengesetz*: neologism for the rules that govern linear art.

l. 23. *Krähen*: cf. No. 49, *Nasse Zäune, l.* 4.

l. 24. *Winterrot von Frühhimmeln*: neologisms.

49. Nasse Zäune

(Written 1944, publ. posthumously 1958 in *Primäre Tage.*)

A winter poem, in which the poet's gaze falls upon the fences which are wet from the rain and snow as they stand enclosing cottage gardens. Benn contrasts with them the baroque ornamental garden, with its expensive tulips and costly hyacinths, which is not found in the poor countryside of the east German plain. In his identification of the modest cottage flowers behind the wet fences and palings with the *alte bewährte Ranunkeln* of the Dutch flower painter van Ostade, it becomes clear that these fenced cottage gardens are a symbol of his own art. As a result, this apparently only impressionistic 'statisches Gedicht' describing reality turns out to be absolute poetry. Even these *über Land geweht* fences are 'ein Wurf von Formen'; as *Gartenabgrenzung* and *kleine Ordnungszeile* they have a static quality, but are surrounded by unrest and decay; *Krähenunruhe und Pappelentblätterung*, both major symbols in Benn's poetry, are seen here negatively, as signs of loneliness and approaching death. Even the *nasse Zäune* themselves are threatened by decay through *Holzfäulnis und Moosansatz*, caused by snow and salt. Out of the silence that surrounds these villages and gardens resound as individual voices *die alten Laute*, which predict *Verfall*. The poem expresses the resignation and sadness that filled the poet shortly before the end of the Second World War in face of the approaching collapse with its unforeseeable consequences for the poet in Landsberg.

l. 4. *Krähenunruhe*: neologism. That for Benn crows are the birds allotted to the modern poet is shown in No. 48, *Statische Gedichte*, *ll.* 23–4. In his essay *Zur Problematik des Dichterischen* (1930) he says of the poet: 'immer und zu allen Zeiten wird er wiederkommen, für den alles Leben nur ein Rufen aus der Tiefe ist, einer alten und frühen Tiefe, und alles Vergängliche nur ein Gleichnis eines unbekannten Urerlebnisses, das sich in ihm Erinnerungen sucht. Eine dunkle, eine unverbrüchliche Gestalt. Sein großes Tier die Krähen: „sie schrein und ziehen schwirren Flugs zur Stadt, bald wird es schnein, weh' dem, der keine Heimat hat"' (*GW* I, *ll.* 82–3—quotation from Nietzsche's poem *Vereinsamt*).

Pappelentblätterung: neologism. Cf. No. 9, *Pappel*, and No. 48, *Statische Gedichte*, *l.* 15. The leaves falling from the poplar are a cipher image for the poet who is threatened by decay and death.

l. 13. *fl.*: florin.

l. 17. *Ranunkeln*: 'buttercup'.

Ostade: the Dutch painters of peasants and flowers Adriaen van Ostade (1610–85) and Isaac van Ostade (1621–49).

ll. 18–25. That Benn is thinking of the poetic 'Ordnung' and 'Eingrenzung' of the world in the poem is shown by the third verse of *Gedicht* (publ. 1955):

> Du weißt, du kannst nicht alles fassen,
> umgrenze es, den grünen Zaun
> um dies und das, du bleibst gelassen,
> doch auch gebannt in Mißvertraun.
>
> (*GW* III, p. 298.)

Cf. also No. 8, *Kretische Vase*, described as a 'Ton-Zaun' around the 'Zug mykenischen Lichts'.

50. Orpheus' Tod

(Written 26 Aug. 1946, publ. 1948 in *Statische Gedichte*.)

This poem, which in the form of a monologue revives the classical myth of the death of Orpheus, arose from Benn's deep grief at the suicide of his second wife Herta. She poisoned herself out of fear of the approaching Red Army on 2 July 1945 in a village on the Elbe where Benn had sent her three months earlier to save her from the dangers of the fighting in Berlin. Orpheus is here the mythical symbol for the modern poet and his tragic fate, as in Rilke's *Sonette an Orpheus*, Elisabeth Langgässer, and others. In this elegy Benn follows in almost every detail Ovid's *Metamorphoses* (10. 64–146), the description of the death of Orpheus, in the translation by Johann Heinrich Voss (Berlin, 1798), which he adapts to his characteristic 'Montagetechnik', re-arranges, and modifies with his own ideas.

The three-part poem (verses 1–2, 3–5, 6–7), in which Orpheus is the lonely failure who did not succeed in bringing back Eurydice from Hades alive, begins with the praise of the power of song, which is able to transform nature. By playing his lute Orpheus covers the bare *unwirtlich* rocks of the Rhodope mountains, where he lives alone, with forest and fruit-bearing bushes and trees. His life, which is threatened by the raging north wind and the unfriendly forces of nature, is dedicated solely to the memory of his dead wife, whose form and being is transfigured by the distance which death places between the living and the dead. The fate of Eurydice is as tragic as that of the poet, since she has found no peace with the shades in Hades, but wanders around searching.

This introduction is followed in the next three verses (3–5) by the temptation of sensuality as embodied in the water and mountain nymphs who both praise the singer and tempt him to give up his singing, since they fear the power which he exerts over the forces of nature. Orpheus answers their temptation to give himself up to ecstatic, sensual *Vergessen*, and their threats, with a decisive *Nein*. He vows his constancy to his dead wife and rejects the maenads in advance, to whom Benn gives the names of mythological figures from Ovid's *Metamorphoses*.

This profession of loyalty brings about the death of Orpheus (verses 6–7), whom the angry maenads assail with stones, branches, and axes and finally tear apart. The final image—Orpheus' lute which is carried downstream and fills the banks with music—suggests that the suffering and torn Orpheus has been absorbed into nature where his song continues to resound.

In this great poem which sprang from Benn's own painful experience, he declares the superiority of the poetic spirit over the daemonic forces of sensual, natural life, the victory of loyalty over all erotic, sexual temptations, and above all the power of art that conquers death: the song (the lute) remains, even when the poet dies.

l. 2. *Erebos*: Greek for the darkness of the underworld, Tartarus. In the Greek myth Erebos was the son of Chaos and the brother of Nyx (night).

l. 3. *Rhodope*: mountains in the south-west of Bulgaria with great pine forests. Cf. Ovid, *Metamorphoses*, 10. 64–97, 11. 1–66.

ll. 17 ff. Cf. Ovid, 10. 74–5.

l. 19. *anwinken*: neologism analogous with 'anstürmen', 'to wave on or past'.

Felsenschönen: neologism for the rock and mountain nymphs.

l. 21. *Faune*: classical Latin goat-like spirits of nature, corresponding to the Greek Pan and the satyrs.

Schratte: spirits of the woods and nature.

ll. 22–3. *Sänger, Aufwölber von Bronzelicht, Schwalbenhimmeln*: neologisms. The singer, who praises the light, conjures up in his song the imaginary expanses of a bronze-coloured, autumnal light, the heavens, in which swallows fly. Cf. No. 39, *Astern*, where this image is also found.

l. 36. *Iole, Dryope*: daughters of King Eurytus. Cf. Ovid, *Metamorphoses*, 9. 325–96. Here Iole tells of the fate of her sister Dryope, who was turned into a tree.

Prokne: Procne, the daughter of King Pandion of Athens, the wife of Tereus, who was turned into a maenad, and then by the gods into a swallow (Ovid, *Metamorphoses*, 6. 423–674).

l. 37. *Atalanta*: famous Arcadian huntress. Ovid, 10. 560 ff., tells of her race with Hippomenes.

l. 39. *Lais*: the name of the famous Corinthian courtesan in the fourth century B.C.

l. 45. *laubbeschwichtigt*: neologism, abbreviated version of Ovid, 11. 7 ff.: 'der Thyrsus / Flog zu dem tönenden Munde des apollonischen Sehers. / Aber mit Laub umsponnen, bezeichnet' er, ohne Verwundung.' Cf. also 11. 27–8: 'Sie bestürmen den göttlichen Sänger, und schleudern / Laubumwundene Stäbe, zu anderem Dienste geweihet.'

l. 46. *ährenbesänftigt*: neologism, analogous with *laubbeschwichtigt* with no precedent in Ovid.

l. 47. *nackte Haune*: cf. Benn's letter to Edgar Lohner on 19 Feb. 1952: '„Haune" ist ein Wort, das ich in meinem Leben nie gehört hatte, bis ich es in Ovids *Verwandlungen* in seinem Gedicht *Orpheus* in der Übersetzung von Johann Heinrich Voß fand. Es erschien mir ein gutes Wort, ich forschte ihm nach, jedoch ohne Erfolg. Da ja aber Johann Heinrich Voß ein sehr starkes und originelles Übersetzungsgenie war, muß er das Wort gekannt haben, und es muß sich damals, zumindest in Norddeutschland, gebraucht worden sein. Ich nehme an, daß es mit Huhn garnichts zu tun hat, sondern man muß nach der Stelle annehmen, daß es sich um eine Art Waffe gehandelt oder um einen Gegenstand der Feldbearbeitung, also auch eine Art Hacke oder vielleicht ein Eisen vom Pflug. In Berlin ist der Ausdruck ganz unbekannt.

Hacke ist Feldhacke. Vielleicht haben Sie die Möglichkeit, sich Ovids Verwandlungen, die ja ein wunderbares Buch sind, aus einer Bibliothek zu leihen. Sie werden dann an dieser Stelle sehen, daß es sich um Waffen gehandelt haben muß, mit denen die rasenden Weiber Orpheus töteten' (*ABr.*, p. 227).

51. Denk der Vergeblichen

(Written 13 Apr. 1950, publ. 16 Jan. 1951 in the *Neue Zeitung*, Frankfurt, and in the collection of poems, *Fragmente*, 1951.)

Despite his contempt for humble human existence, Benn shows interest and sympathy in his later period for those who lead quiet, unnoticed lives, such as the old waiter in the pub on the corner where he drank his beer every evening (cf. *Das sind doch Menschen*, *GW* II, pp. 336–7). He is also moved by those who are shy (*Menschen getroffen*, *GW* III, p. 321), who are 'innerlich sanft und fleißig', pure as angels, and arouse in him the question as to the source of 'das Sanfte und das Gute', which however remains unanswered. With the moods of despair by which he is often threatened (verse 1) he contrasts these futile human lives, in order to cheer himself up with the thought that he himself was allowed to live a well-ordered existence and feel secure throughout his life. Benn never knew the modern feeling of existential fear, as is seen above all in his ironical and alienating introduction to W. H. Auden's *The Age of Fear* (1951). In this poem he draws conclusions about his own life and includes among the *große Stunden* particularly those of creative excitement: *viele Beschenkungen / aus Rausch und Morgenröten*, as well as those resulting from unexpected turns which his life had taken in consequence of the battles of two world wars and revolutions. He sees all the moments of his own life and his own intellectual attitude of introversion, recollection, etc., his poetic striving for expression exemplified on a lesser scale in the lives of these insignificant, unnoticed people (verse 2), with the result that his life as a poet appears meaningful and complete despite the tragedy and the menace of the void.

l. 6. *pflegen*: 'sich etwas pflegen' is a neologism analogous with 'sich etwas leisten', and stresses the extraordinary aspects and the 'Luxuriöse' of the aesthetic life of the poet.

l. 8. *Endverglimmen*: neologism for the obliteration of man at the end of his life.

l. 9. *aus dem Unergründlichen*: fate or God. Cf. the oratorio *Das Unaufhörliche* (1931).

l. 12. *inngewendeten Gesichts*: neologism for 'nach innen gewendet', 'turned inwards away from the unfriendly outside world'.

52. Satzbau

(Publ. 1951 in *Fragmente*.)

Since his early days Benn had been concerned with the problem of a new syntax, a modern means of expression, and as early as 1916 this was made the main theme of his story *Die Insel*: 'Rönne lebte einsam seiner Entwicklung hingeben und arbeitete viel. Seine Studien galten der Schaffung einer neuen Syntax... Den Du-Charakter des Grammatischen auszuschalten, schien ihm ehrlicherweise notwendig, denn die Anrede war mythisch geworden' (*GW* II, p. 40). He was thus striving for a purely monologic art of expression, independent of the world, mankind, and everyday speech, which would deal primarily with problems of form rather than content.

Since there is in the present, as Benn once explained in a letter, 'keine tragfähige Substanz mehr im Inneren und kein psychologisches Gefüge mehr' (18 Sept. 1948 to Max Niedermayer, *ABr.*, p. 127), he is able in the first verse of this poem to cast aside, with a sweeping movement of the hand, such concepts as *Himmel*, *Liebe*, and *Grab* as the main themes of traditional poetry. They have become uninteresting and irrelevant for the modern poet, since there are no new aspects to be treated, and they have in addition lost their general applicability. He suggests as a completely new and urgent problem, which has not been treated by every poet and become hackneyed, the *Frage nach dem Satzbau*, which centres here on the question of the *Warum*, the inner *Antrieb*, which is behind the artistic striving for expression and brings it to fruition.

In the second verse, before trying to give an answer to this difficult question, Benn characterizes this striving for expression with examples from the field of drawing and graphic art, whilst poetry is also mentioned briefly as *reimen*. The third verse begins with the cry *Überwältigend unbeantwortbar!*, since in Benn's opinion artistic expression is not evoked for external reasons and purposes, but by what he calls *Ausdruckszwang*, i.e. an inner driving-force from the unconscious. The nature of this can only be surmised, and the poet can only try to explain it by analogies from psycho-analysis and ethnology. The inner driving-force, which is *ferngesteuert* by an unknown power, derives from a *Gehirnlage*, which is identical with the collective unconscious (C. G. Jung). In primeval times the mythical concepts of the *Heilbringer* and the *Totemtier* gave man hope of salvation and an increase in his powers. Since religions have lost their unifying force, art 'als die eigentlich metaphysische Tätigkeit des Menschen' (Nietzsche) has taken over their function, and is behind the attempt to find purely formal expression. As an analogy for the irresistible power of this *Ausdruckszwang*, which ignores content in favour of form, Benn uses here a crude medical image: sexual excitement and the artistic urge come from the same root. He is also aware that there are changes and historical stages in the development of art, so that he regards exclusive concentration on form at the expense of content as something transitory that will be replaced by new artistic possibilities. But for the present the idea that he presents in this poem is valid: *aber heute ist der Satzbau / das Primäre*. The aim is the absolute word and the absolute sentence: 'In jedem Satz muß alles stehn, er kann sich auf nichts außerhalb seiner selbst mehr beziehn, es gibt ja keinen Anfang und es gibt ja kein Ende, das wären ja Raum-Zeitvorstellungen aus einer anderen chaotischen Welt, er also muß sich selber ordnen, selber tragen, alles umschlingen, für alles stehn — er muß — um seinem Inneren zu genügen — absolut sein in jeder Chiffre, in jedem Wort. Das ist die Krise!' (18 Nov. 1948 to M. Niedermayer, *ABr.*, p. 127).

The fourth verse concludes with a quotation from Goethe, which is purposely meaningless, perhaps as an example of the new artistic form of expression which is cleansed of all content. Like the poetry of Klopstock or of Goethe, it is directed at the few, not at the masses. Benn thus reveals his belief in a strictly aristocratic concept of art, which links him with Stefan George. But it must be emphasized that he was not concerned with 'Lebensentzifferung und Lebensdeutung', as B. von Wiese maintains in his interpretation of this poem, but rather with an absolute art that was completely emptied of all the meaning and content of traditional art, that was completely autonomous and concerned only with the problem of form. His ideal exponents of this were André Gide in *Paludes* (1895) and the German Expressionist Carl Einstein with his novel *Bebuquin* (1912).

l. 3. *Kulturkreis*: a concept in Oswald Spengler's (1880–1936) philosophy of history. Here Benn is referring to modern Western civilization as the last of the eight civilizations discussed by Spengler.

l. 19. *Heilbringer*: 'Saviour'. Behind this is the romantic idea of the mediation of art between God and man, which Benn however regarded as *verspätet*, i.e. out of date.

Totemtier: in anthropology this term refers to animals which are treated as emblems of a clan or an individual. They can bestow particular magical powers, a belief which is based on mystical, prelogical identity between man and beast. Cf. J. G. Frazer, *Totemism and Exogamy*, 1910, Lucien Lévy, *La Mentalité primitive*, 1922, and Sigmund Freud, *Totem und Tabu*, 1913. For Benn the body is the bearer of these primeval ideas: 'Von weither liegt in ihm ein Traum, ein Tier, von weither ist er mit Mysterien beladen, von jenen frühen Völkern her, die noch die Urzeit, den Ursprung in sich trugen, mit ihrem uns so völlig fremden Weltgefühl, ihren rätselhaften Erfahrungen aus vorbewußten Sphären, in deren Körpern das Innenbewußtsein noch labil, die Konstruktionskräfte des Organismus noch frei, das heißt dem Bewußtsein als dem Zentrum der Organisation zugängig waren, noch beweglich war, was heute längst der Willkür entzogen ist, biologisch von uns differenter Typ, archaische Masse, Frühschicht, die im Totem noch das Tier begriff mit warmer Wunde' (*Zur Problematik des Dichterischen*, 1930, *GW* I, pp. 81–2). In an important 'Marginalie', in which Benn calls the poet an experimenter in the 'Laboratorium für Worte', he says of him: 'Für ihn ist das Wort real und magisch, ein moderner Totem' (*GW* I, p. 390).

l. 20. *Priapismus*: persistent erection of the penis after disease or spinal injury; cf. the lecture 'Probleme der Lyrik' (1951): 'Das Wort ist der Phallus des Geistes, zentral verwurzelt' (*GW* I, p. 510). In a letter of November 1950 to Dieter Wellershoff, Benn describes the process of poetic *Satzbau* thus: 'Natürlich hatte man Vorbilder, die einem vorschwebten, natürlich bewegten einen innere Strebungen, natürlich hatte man Notizen von Dingen und Sätzen, die einen aus irgendeinem Anlaß einmal erregten, aber der Ablauf beim Schreiben dann war völlig unter Zwang. Man fühlte, das nächste Wort *muß* so viel Silben haben, es muß beladen sein mit Glanz oder Abstieg oder Trauer. Vergessen wir auch nicht den Reiz und die Rettung, die aus gebrochenen Worten, angedeuteten Silbenwurzeln kommt, aus Anklängen, gemischt aus Inhaltlichem und Diphthongen. Kurz primär ist ein inneres Bild des zu formenden Satzes, an dem modelliert man instinktiv so herum bis er so klingt, wie man ihn wollen mußte, damit in einem gelöst wird, was als Last und Zwang, als Fremdkörper, einen bedrangte. Es ist ein Vorgang von ausgesprochen katarrthischem [*sic*, kathartischem] Charakter, es ist ein Eliminationsprozeß, ein Durchgang von panischen Insulten und Bedrängungen, ein phallischer Prozeß mit dem Ziel, Spannungen zu beseitigen und produktive Füllungen zu applanieren' (*ABr.*, p. 202).

53. Die Gitter

(Publ. 1951 in *Fragmente.*)

Benn's favourite Bible quotation was the lament of Jeremiah (Lamentations 3[7]): 'God has walled me in, so that I cannot escape, and has laid heavy chains about me.' In this he found a confirmation of the loneliness and isolation of his existence as a man and a poet, and of the tragic experiences of his long life.

In this poem the *verkettet* railings and walls, which have enclosed the poet, appear both as salvation from the oppressive environment and as destiny. With the same feelings about existence Benn wrote in a discussion of the novel *Sackgassen* by Thea Sternheim: 'Du willst ein Ich sein, gut, aber das heißt, du bist ummauert, eingemauert, die Gitter zu' (1952, *GW* IV, p. 305). This is linked with the reproachful question about the relationship of the 'Ich' to the 'Du', the fellow human being: *doch wen rettetest du?*, the answer to which is negative, in the sense of a reproach to oneself for having failed ethically (cf. No. 45, *Abschied*, verse 3).

The second and third verses describe the life of the poet in brief images: his place of origin was the north German plain, his life was conditioned by many changes and dependent on a vague *anderer*, a relationship that is described as *bitter* (verse 4), and from which the poet had finally and eternally taken refuge in the *Gitter* of his own isolation. It can only be presumed that here Benn is referring to God as the creator and preserver of mankind. Benn was forced to recognize his existence, only to escape from him by withdrawing into himself: 'niemand ist ohne Gott, das ist menschenunmöglich, nur Narren halten sich für autochthon und selbstbestimmend. Jeder andere weiß, wir sind geschaffen, allerdings alles andere liegt völlig im Dunklen' (*Erwiderung an Lernet-Holenia*, October 1952, *GW* IV, p. 312). In *Eine Leiche singt* (*Morgue II*, No. III (GW III, 360), written on 8 January 1913) he sees death as his only salvation from the 'Gitter' of existence:

> Erlöst aus meinem tränenüberströmten
> Gitter. Erlöst aus Hunger und aus Schreck.
> (*l.* 6–7)

54. Nur zwei Dinge

(Written on 2 Jan. 1953, publ. 26 Mar. 1953 in the *Neue Zeitung*.)

This poem too, like so many of Benn's late poems, results from a survey of his life and his evaluation of his existence. As he looks back on his experiences, he extends the concept of form from the aesthetic to the existential: *Ich, Wir und Du* appear as forms of life in the sense of relationships and community with other human beings, love and friendship, which are regarded in a tone of resigned renunciation, since they are all linked with pain. It arose not from external unhappiness, but from the unanswerable question of the meaning of life and art (verse 1). This question, which preoccupied Benn particularly in his early days, is rejected in the second verse as a naïve *Kinderfrage*, and he contrasts with this the realization of the mature man, the 'spätes Ich', and his insight into the laws that govern life. In face of the *fernbestimmt* categorical imperative *Du mußt* issued by an unknown force, one can only obey in all spheres of life, of which three are named here: *Sinn* as the sphere of thought and research into the meaning of life, *Sucht* as the sphere of suffering, disease, from which the realm of genius cannot be separated, as Benn showed in his essay *Genie und Gesundheit* (1930, *GW* I, pp. 84–9), and finally *Sage* as the sphere of poetry, which revives myths or creates new ones. With these three spheres of the poet's life correspond at the beginning of the third verse the three ever-recurring poetic images in Benn's poetry: roses, symbols of the beauty and the brightness of fulfilled creative moments in life; snow, which stands for the coldness and sublime solitude of the sphere of the artist; and finally the sea, as the realm of the infinite, the absolute and depth of consciousness. But they are all subject to the law of eternal change and transience. The end of the poem declares that what finally remains is emptiness, to whose 'formfordernde Gewalt' Benn frequently referred, and the *Ich*, which is *gezeichnet* by suffering and bitter experiences, and which opposes the challenge of the void and its artistic form with its *Dennoch*.

l. 9. *fernbestimmt*: neologism. Cf. No. 52, *Satzbau*, *l.* 18: 'ferngesteuert'. The technical image of 'Fernsteuerung' is used by Benn in the metaphysical sense of the question of the invisible controller of human fate.

55. Worte

(Publ. 1955 in *Aprèslude*.)

The solitude, unhappiness, and obscurity of the poet, which are treated in many of Benn's late 'statische Gedichte', are seen here in the light of his relationship with language. From early on Benn emphasized the fascination which *Worte* had for him: 'Worte, Worte — Substantive! Sie brauchen nur die Schwingen zu öffnen und Jahrtausende entfallen ihrem Flug' (*Lyrisches Ich*, 1927, *GW* IV, p. 13). Here Benn's chief concern is with the poet's lifelong struggle to discover and explore the nature of words, which is a never-ending process, since the very essence of words is unfathomable depth. Benn, like Stéphane Mallarmé, Stefan George, the young Hofmannsthal, and Rilke before him, distinguishes poetic language from everyday speech. He sees a contrast between the reflecting, uncertain attitude of the poet towards language, who considers the word, struggles to know its *Seele* and to explore the experiences of mankind which have been stored up in it since the primeval beginning of time (*Vor- und Urgesicht*), and the *unbedenklich* naïve attitude of the man in the street, from whose lips speech flows unhindered (*perlt*), whilst the poet speaks hesitatingly, only to end finally in silence. The fourth verse makes the existential comparison between the bright, happy life and the passing and *Vergilben* of the poet's years, the meaning of which lies not in fulfilment of life, but in artistic achievement, the prerequisite of which is a struggle with language which pursues him into his very dreams (*Silben* as *pars pro toto*).

l. 3. *Clairons*: French for bugles, here a symbol for fame.

l. 6. *Vor- und Urgesicht*: neologism for the poetic vision of the inaccessible primeval depths of the past, which are revealed to him in the word. Cf. *Lyrisches Ich* (1927): 'Ach immer wieder in diese Glut, in die Grade der plazentaren Räume, in die Vorstufe der Meere des Urgesichts: Regressionstendenzen, Zerlösung des Ich! Regressionstendenzen mit Hilfe des Worts, heuristische Schwächezustände durch Substantive — das ist der Grundvorgang, der alles interpretiert . . .' (*GW* IV, p. 14). 'Jahrtausende entfallen ihrem Flug. Botanisches und Geographisches, Völker und Länder, alle die historisch und systematisch so verlorenen Welten hier ihre Blüte, hier ihr Traum — aller Leichtsinn, alle Wehmut, alle Hoffnungslosigkeit des Geistes werden fühlbar aus den Schichten eines Querschnitts von Begriff' (*GW* IV, pp. 13–14). Cf. also his essay *Urgesicht* (1929, *GW* II, pp. 107–18).

l. 10. *Menschenhort*: neologism for the realm of biological human life that is contained in the circle of procreation, birth, and death. Cf. No. 32, *Einsamer nie*, *ll.* 9–12 and No. 36, *Wer allein ist*, *ll.* 7–8.

56. Nike

(Written 14 June 1955, publ. 1955 in *Aprèslude*.)

Benn was inspired to write this poem by a Greek vase, with a representation of Nike offering a sacrifice to the gods with bowed head. Once more the question is asked whether life and art are connected with victory and happiness. The classical goddess of victory, Nike, was the daughter of Styx, the nymph of the underworld, and the Titan Pallas, and therefore originally belonged to the gods of the primeval age of Chronos (Latin: Saturn). But as the third verse of the poem emphasizes, she helped Zeus in his battle against his father Chronos and the Titans, which marked the beginning of a new epoch. Benn places this myth at the end of the poem, and together with Zeus as the ruler of the new age, he names Apollo as the god of song and Persephone as the goddess of the underworld, who spends part of her life every year on earth, and thus embodies the alternation of death and resurrection (cf. No. 47, *V. Jahrhundert* II). Though on such classical vases Nike is usually seen making an offering to Zeus (or standing on the hand of statues of Zeus and Athene), Benn does not reveal what or to whom she is sacrificing. In the first verse he begins with the somewhat strange question of whether she is offering up blood or wine. This can only be understood from the idea of sacrifice and the symbolism of blood and wine in Benn's work as a whole, where the life of the artist appears as a continual self-sacrifice in the service of art (cf. No. 19, *Orphische Zellen*). Blood is the symbol for the realm of the sensual, vital, primeval, and unconscious, out of which arise poetic images (cf. No. 25, *Regressiv*); the wine stands either for poetic intoxication and intellectual ecstasy, or for love (cf. No. 21, *Dir auch —*). If the nature of the sacrifice must remain open, then we must not question its meaning after the victory of the forces of the intellect over the powers of the formless, limitless, and chaotic. The poem hints that even the goddess of victory is subject to the power of a higher fate, which forces her to perform such a mysterious sacrifice.

The second verse, which emphasizes the grief and the defencelessness of the goddess, suggests in the form of a question, an answer to the final question of the third verse (what Nike might see in the night): it is hinted that in a vision she sees the Christian legend of Saint Sebastian, who died a martyr's death after being shot with arrows. Benn uses this reference, not for religious reasons, but in the same symbolic way as Thomas Mann in his story *Der Tod in Venedig* (1911), where it is said of the art of Gustav von Aschenbach that it is born of 'Heroismus der Schwäche': 'einer intellektuellen und jünglinghaften Männlichkeit . . ., die in stolzer Scham die Zähne aufeinanderbeißt und ruhig dasteht, während ihr die Schwerter und Speere durch den Leib gehen . . . Denn Haltung in Schicksal, Anmut in der Qual bedeutet nicht nur ein Dulden; sie ist eine aktive Leistung, ein positiver Triumph, und die Sebastian-Gestalt ist das schönste Sinnbild, wenn nicht der Kunst überhaupt, so doch gewiß der in Rede stehenden Kunst' (*GW* 8, 1960, p. 453). Benn is using classical myth and Christian legend as equally valid symbols for human suffering and struggle. Both refer to a purely aesthetic question: 'doch wo sind Sieg und Siegsbeweise / aus dem von dir vertretenen Reich?', which he posed in the poem *Einsamer nie* (No. 32, 1936), and answered that he served 'dem Gegenglück, der Geist'. Such a 'Gegenglück' he sees embodied in the sacrificing Nike, lamenting after her victory.

The recapitulation of the classical myth in the third verse and the figure of Sebastian in the second together point to the fact that Benn, like J. J. Bachofen (1815–87) in his book on *Mutterrecht* (1861), distinguished three stages of the mythical, historical evolution of mankind: the domination of the Titanic and chthonic forces of sensuality; the battle and victory of the Olympian gods of the intellect, form, and art, who restrain the chthonic, Orphic, and dionysiac forces and accept them into their midst; and the final stage of Christianity as the 'religion of absolute inwardness' (Hegel) and the transfiguration of suffering and death. Benn, like Hölderlin, clearly regards the post-classical period as an age of darkness.

l. 3. *Liebesmahl*: originally the feast of charity of the early Christians (Jude 12, from the Greek *agape*). Feasts associated with Greek cults (Eranos, Thiasoi), and Plato's *Symposium* as the celebration of divine Eros, caused Benn to relate the concept, which he also knew as the name given to the banquets of Prussian officers, to the victory banquet of the gods after the battle with the Titans.

. 5. *attische Lekythe*: there is no known picture of Nike on an Attic lekythos; presumably Benn has freely transferred the picture on a vase to a funeral vessel, a symbol important in Benn's work (cf. No. 47, *V. Jahrhundert* I, *ll.* 1 ff.).

57. Kann keine Trauer sein

(Written on 6 Jan. 1956, publ. in *Merkur* 10, 5, May 1956, p. 401.)

Benn's last poem, written two months before he died, when he was suffering from the illness which was to kill him. The poem is an attempt to portray his death as a meaningful end to his life and to prevent others from mourning. The theme of the death of the poet, which Rilke also treated with great understanding in one of his *Neue Gedichte*: *Der Tod des Dichters*, and in the late poem *Zu der Zeichnung, John Keats im Tode darstellend*, is exemplified by Benn in the death of Annette von Droste-Hülshoff (1797–1848), who died in Meersburg on Lake Constance, where the room in which she died is still preserved; in Friedrich Hölderlin (1770–1843), who lived and died in mental derangement in the house of the master-joiner Zimmer in Tübingen, now called the Hölderlin-Turm, which stands by the banks of the Neckar. These two poets of the eighteenth and nineteenth centuries, whom Benn greatly admired, are followed by poets of his own age: Rilke, George, and Nietzsche. Rainer Maria Rilke (1875–1926) died of leukaemia in the Swiss clinic Valmont near Montreux, Stefan George (1868–1933) in the Clinica Sant'Agnese in Locarno in Switzerland (Benn's *wohl* is therefore unnecessary), Friedrich Nietzsche (1884–1900) in the house of his sister Elisabeth Förster-Nietzsche in Weimar after a long illness in a state of mental derangement. Benn's attention is focused not so much on the dying poets themselves, but on the beds and objects which surrounded them in death, which are also subject to the law of transience, the *schmerzlos-ewiger Zerfall*.

The second verse contrasts death and life, the external and the inwardness of men, where divine potentiality is to be found: *Keime aller Götter*, as well as the inherited predisposition to a happy life and death. This inner union of the opposites of divine and earthly, human and animal appears divided and destroyed in the outside world, and Benn asks who separated the words from the objects to which they refer, who created the division between concept and reality—a problem which he had followed up since his essay *Das moderne Ich* (1920)—and who on the other hand had brought about the mingling of the agonies of the dying and the places where they suffer, of which the first verse spoke. The fact that there is no question-mark shows that Benn has no answer.

The poem ends in the third verse with the expression of inner distance from dying and of resignation, a state which admits neither denial nor affirmation, not even mourning, much less regret or lament for life and death. The whole of life seems like a dream, the dream of an unknown god, a supernatural being which moves in its sleep. In death the individual becomes united with it—thus the poem ends with the imperative: *schlafe ein!*

ll. 11–12. Cf. 'Soll die Dichtung das Leben bessern?' (1955): 'Die Dichtung bessert nicht, aber sie tut etwas viel Entscheidenderes: sie verändert. Sie hat keine geschichtlichen Ansatzkräfte, wenn sie reine Kunst ist, keine therapeutischen und pädagogischen Ansatzkräfte, sie wirkt anders: sie hebt die Zeit und die Geschichte auf, ihre Wirkung geht auf die *Gene*, die Erbmasse, die Substanz — ein langer innerer Weg. Das Wesen der Dichtung ist unendliche Zurückhaltung, zertrümmernd ihr Kern, aber schmal ihre Peripherie, sie berührt nicht viel, das aber glühend. Alle Dinge wenden sich um, alle Begriffe und Kategorien verändern ihren Charakter in dem Augenblick, wo sie unter Kunst betrachtet werden, wo sie sie stellt, wo sie sich ihr stellen. Sie bringt ins Strömen, wo es verhärtet und stumpf und müde war, in ein Strömen, das verwirrt und nicht zu verstehen ist, das aber an Wüste gewordene Ufer *Keime* streut, *Keime des Glücks und Keime der Trauer*, das Wesen der Dichtung ist Vollendung und Faszination' (*GW* I, p. 593).

l. 12. *Gen*: gene, Greek for predisposition, inherited characteristic. Genes are arranged in the chromosomes of the cell nucleus in an ordered pattern. The totality of all genes is called a genotype, the constant picture of inheritance. The opposite of this is called the phenotype, the changing manifestation. Benn writes of both concepts, cf. his *Roman des Phänotyp* (1944).

ll. 20 ff. On 24 Aug. 1949 Benn wrote to Nele Soerensen of his relationship with God: 'Aber ich bin ja gar nichts, durch mich läuft nur etwas hindurch, dessen Herkunft und Sinn mir immer schleierhaft war und mit jedem Tag schleierhafter wird' (see Nele Soerensen, *Mein Vater Gottfried Benn*, Wiesbaden, 1960, p. 81). Cf. *Querschnitt* (1918): 'Das Leben ist nicht unseres, sondern das Laster eines Gottes, der verborgen bleibt' (*GW* II, p. 78).

. 24. Ernst Nef makes the end of the poem refer to Shakespeare's Hamlet, for whom dying is sleeping and who dies with the words 'The rest is silence', and to Schiller's Wallenstein, who leaves Gordon with the words: 'Gut' Nacht, Gordon! / Ich denke einen langen Schlaf zu tun, / denn dieser letzten Tage Qual war groß . . .'; cf. also Shakespeare's *Tempest*, where Prospero says: 'We are such stuff / as dreams are made on, and our little life / is rounded with a sleep.' In Büchner's *Dantons Tod* Act IV Julie poisons herself and dies with the words: 'Schlafe, schlafe!'

INDEX OF FIRST LINES